THE VISIBLE POOR

THE VISIBLE POOR

Homelessness in the United States

JOEL BLAU

New York   Oxford • OXFORD UNIVERSITY PRESS • 1992

Oxford University Press

Oxford   New York   Toronto
Delhi   Bombay   Calcutta   Madras   Karachi
Petaling Jaya   Singapore   Hong Kong   Tokyo
Nairobi   Dar es Salaam   Cape Town
Melbourne   Auckland
and associated companies in
Berlin   Ibadan

Copyright © 1992 by Oxford University Press, Inc.

Published by Oxford University Press, Inc.,
200 Madison Avenue, New York, New York 10016

Oxford is a registered trademark of Oxford University Press

Library of Congress Cataloging-in-Publication Data
BLau, Joel.
The visible poor : homelessness in the United States / Joel Blau.
p. cm. Includes bibliographical references and index.
ISBN 0-19-505743-0
1. Homelessness—United States.
2. Homeless persons—United States.   I. Title.
HV4505.B52   1992   362.5′0973—dc20   91-29828

9 8 7 6 5 4 3 2

Printed in the United States of America
on acid-free paper

Acknowledgments

For help in the writing of this book, I am indebted to many people.

Alfred J. Kahn of the Columbia University School of Social Work deserves special mention. He not only stewarded the dissertation that is, by now, this book's somewhat distant ancestor, but also made many useful suggestions about the book itself. Above all, his principled disagreement with the perspective of this study has strengthened it appreciably.

Likewise, I want to thank Christopher Dykema, who read and edited the manuscript with painstaking care. Christopher and I have been commenting on each other's writing for about twenty-five years. I hope we have at least twenty-five years more, because that is the only way I will ever be able to repay him for all the attention he devoted to this work.

Other people also reviewed the whole book. Mimi Abramovitz was wise, helpful, and unfailingly supportive in keeping me focused on its completion. Gordon Mehler asked excellent questions; Paul Colson and David Wagner willingly shared their knowledge and substantive insights. And, in addition, at a critical point in its development, the comments of Michael B. Katz, Peter Marcuse, Majorie Hope, and James Young had a major influence.

For their help with particular chapters, I want to thank Emily Cohen, Marcia Cohen, Michael Kimmel, David Sciarra, Sandy Siegel, and Ann Withorn. Together with my colleagues on the faculty of the School of Social Welfare at SUNY Stony Brook—Ellen Bogulub, Mary Ann Burg, Steve Rose, and Jerome Schiele, each contributed, in his or her own way, to greater clarity of language and ideas.

While gathering information about homelessness in various localities, I benefited enormously from the good will of people in cities around the country. For this reason, I want to thank everyone who sent me a news clipping or a study of homelessness in their municipality and, in particular, acknowledge the assistance of the following: in New York, Robert Altman, Steve Banks, Abe Gerges, Robert Hayes, Herschel Kaminsky, Robert Levy, Keith Summa, and Nancy Wackstein; in Los Angeles, Toni Reinis, Gary Squier, and Paul Tepper; in Santa Barbara,

Alice Hasler and Richard Appelbaum; in San Francisco, Bob Prentice, Michael Reisch, and Randall Shaw; in Seattle, Martha Dilts and Sylvia McGee; in Boston, Peter Dreier and Barbara Sard; and in Phoenix, Fred Karnas. Research in the West Coast cities was funded by a grant from the Lilly Foundation, for which I also want to express my appreciation.

At Oxford University Press, I want to thank Valerie Aubry, who had both foresight and patience: foresight to see the glimmerings of a worthwhile book in the original manuscript, and the patience to wait for that book to be born; and Carole Solis-Cohen, who was equally exceptional in her willingness to answer my questions and shepherd the book through the process of editing and production.

I am indebted to Ted Berkman for his editorial suggestions and guidance; to Bettyann Kevles, for her early support and assistance; and to Daniel Kevles for a title. Of course, neither they, nor anyone else, is responsible for any errors of fact or interpretation.

My parents, Raphael and Helen Blau, gave me, at an early age, an appreciation of writing and a respect for language. I value this gift more deeply with the passing years.

Beth Baron deserves a special note of thanks for her careful review and insightful criticism of the first chapter, which helped me to clarify some important issues. Emily Baron was wonderful, too, because in addition to providing moral support, she was always willing to turn the stereo down.

Finally, I want to express my profoundest gratitude to my wife, Sandra Baron-Blau, who read every draft, commenting acutely on each and making many valuable suggestions. It was always her feeling that the book should speak to the broadest possible audience. For this vision, for her editorial skills, and for her understanding of my busy schedule these past few years, she has both my love and my appreciation.

Contents

Introduction

Why are so many Americans homeless? Widespread homelessness should not exist in a country as rich as the United States. But it does, and the reasons why it does are the subject of this book.

These reasons are, or should be, of compelling interest to all of us. Although we tend to emphasize the differences between the housed and homeless, most of us who are housed remain so because we receive a regular paycheck and avoid catastrophic illness. A serious illness or the loss of a job would not automatically cost us our housing. It would, however, put that housing at considerable risk.

Because so many share this risk, I have tried to make this book accessible to the general reader. The issues are sometimes complex, the solutions even more challenging. But homelessness affects too many of us to allow it to remain obscure. This book is therefore written for those who know something about the issue of homelessness. But it is also written for those who, after seeing homeless people on the street, cannot help but wonder about their own prospects, as well as the prospects of the country in which they live.

To talk intelligently about these prospects, we must first discredit several myths. One myth is that most homeless people are mentally ill. Another is that drugs and alcohol are the primary causes of homelessness. A third is that the homeless are lazy misfits who brought their plight upon themselves. All these explanations share the common American belief that poor people are somehow responsible for their own poverty. The rapid growth of the homeless population represents a wonderful opportunity to test this proposition, because it requires believers to argue that for some mysterious reason, a sizeable group of citizens suddenly became irresponsible at the very same time.

This book offers a different interpretation. While acknowledging that the choices people make may well lead them to become homeless, it sees the rise of modern homelessness as the product of the political and economic changes that have occurred in the United States over the last generation. Three changes were particularly significant: the shift from an industrial to a service economy, a business-led effort to contain wages, and a corresponding governmental push to reduce social welfare. As a result of these developments, middle-income people ran harder to stay in place, the working poor tried not to lose too much ground, and those at the bottom of the income scale struggled to retain their housing. To be sure, some people made bad decisions, but when so many people make "bad decisions," it suggests that something else is going on.

Two hypothetical scenarios can help to illustrate this point. First, imagine the United States today with housing costs and income distribution unchanged, but without drugs, mental illness, or "bad decisions"—the personal factors often cited as the true causes of homelessness. Does homelessness decline under these circumstances? Yes, but not by much. This scenario eliminates some symptoms of individual frailty and social disorder, but still leaves too many people with too little money to obtain the available housing.

Now imagine another set of circumstances. This time, instead of eliminating the drugs, the mental illness, and the "bad decisions," make sure that there are comprehensive social services, a generous supply of affordable housing, and no one earns less than $25,000 a year. A miraculous development occurs. Not only does homelessness decline sharply, but the so-called personal factors that have come to be associated with it also experience a significant drop. Whatever problems people in the United States have, nothing exacerbates them faster than the lack of money, food, and housing.

If homelessness is primarily a product of political and economic causes, a sense of history is essential to place those causes in context. This book stresses that history, emphasizing patterns in the relationship of work and welfare, of the market and the provision of housing for the poor, that have contributed to the rise and decline of the homeless population. Having long been associated with skid row, it is easy to forget that homelessness has a history. Yet that history is vital if we are to understand homelessness as a contemporary social phenomenon.

Part I of this book begins by focusing on the visibility of the homeless, because even though people on the street make up just one part of the homeless population, it is their public poverty that has shaped virtually everybody else's response to them. In the description of the homeless that follows, I have sought to distinguish carefully between a reasonable interest in the population's characteristics and the rather obsessive preoccupation with those individual traits—drugs, alcoholism, or mental illness—which some use to explain their current status. Once we acknowledge that these personal characteristics are not sufficient explanations of homelessness, we can begin to explore the real causes.

This is the task of Part II. Chapters on the economic transformation of the United States, with its increasingly split wage structure, are linked, through the principle that work must pay more than welfare, to a comparable decline in government benefits. The combination of less money from work and less money from the government disenfranchised an entire class of people from a rapidly inflating and highly speculative housing market. Among the most conspicuous subgroups to be so disenfranchised were the mentally ill. Did their mental illness cause them to become homeless? Undoubtedly, for some it did, but to talk about how many and under what circumstances, it is necessary to pinpoint the precise relationship between deinstitutionalization and mental illness on the one hand, and homelessness on the other.

In Parts III and IV of this book, I explore what has been, and what should be, done in response to the growth of the homeless population. Although people without housing have sometimes advanced their own cause, lawyers and political activists dominate the social movement for the homeless. In the courts as well as in the streets, they have pressed solutions on governments at the federal, state, and local levels. An examination of these responses, with a particular focus on New York as the most comprehensive of any city, constitutes the core of this section.

After an analysis of homelessness as an issue of social policy, the book concludes with some recommendations. These recommendations are sure to prove controversial because they fall outside the relatively narrow confines of mainstream political discussion. By that time, though, I hope readers will recognize what homelessness means, both for the homeless and for themselves, and will be willing to entertain solutions that they might have otherwise rejected before they read this book.

PART I

Without A Home

1

The Visible Poor

The homeless as a group represent a menace, not only because of the high crime rate which exists among them, but also because of their psychological impact on those brought into contact with them.
DENNIS MITCHEM, chairman of the Phoenix, Arizona
Downtown Crime Task Force

The morning rush hour. A homeless man stands, hand outstretched to passers-by, on the curb across from the construction site of a downtown office building. His clothes are torn. His hair, which was parted in the middle when he last combed it several days ago, now hangs limply over his forehead. This is his spot. For over a month, he has been there nearly every morning.

People walk by. Some look away, including a few who have already given to the woman on the preceding block. Others grimace; in their eyes, the man is a failure, or he would not resort to begging. The more sympathetic give two quarters, then feel helpless at the inadequacy of so small a gift. Among frightened commuters who fear for their own safety, there are several who worry that they could end up in similar straits. Cynicism and indifference show in those pedestrians whose gait changes the least. These pass the homeless man as if they were walking through a glass tunnel. Above all, many cannot help but wonder: isn't there something profoundly wrong with a society that has so much poverty amidst so much wealth?

This small tableau is quite ordinary—and quite remarkable. Certainly, it has become a set piece of American life. A 1990 *New York Times* poll reported that 68 percent of urban Americans see the homeless in the course of their daily routine; nationally, the figure was 54 percent, an 18 percent increase in just four years.[1] All over the United States, the housed encounter the homeless many times each day.

The frequency of these encounters has provoked a strong public response. The homeless have been compared to urban graffiti and reproved for their begging. Cities such as Santa Barbara, New Orleans, and Clearwater, Florida, have passed laws against sleeping outdoors in parks, on beaches, or other public property; Fort Lauderdale has banned rummaging through garbage. In Burlington, Vermont, a group of businessmen formed an organization called Westward, Ho! to buy one way plane tickets for their downtown's most conspicuous beggars. And long before New York City police evicted the homeless from Tompkins Square Park in 1991, janitors spread ammonia on the floor of Grand Central Terminal to prevent the homeless from sleeping there.[2]

Whatever a municipality's usual response to the homeless, the prospect of any newsworthy public event is certain to bring about a major crackdown. Political conventions and important football games are especially noteworthy for reviving the littering and public nuisance statutes. When New York, San Francisco, and Atlanta hosted the Democratic National Conventions during the 1980s, each tried to hide its homeless population before the delegates arrived. Likewise, the Miami police initiated street sweeps in the week before the Orange Bowl.[3] If an event draws both tourists and media, the poverty that is public is the poverty that is sure to be concealed.

These responses suggest that perhaps the single most significant attribute of homelessness is its visibility. Visible poverty disrupts the ordinary rhythms of public life. It undermines the rules governing the use of public space. Although the written set of rules are well known—do not double-park your car, do not litter the sidewalk, another, equally powerful set of rules never appears in writing. These rules assume, for example, that one stranger in public does not come too close to another, and that public displays of poverty are somehow improper. Since only the most desperate people exhibit their poverty, the slightest glimpse of their desperation makes others feel uneasy. Witnesses to homelessness then become like the unwilling spectators of an intimate domestic quarrel. They know these things occur, but firmly believe they should be kept private if it is at all possible.

If one encounter with a homeless person is awkward, the cumulative effect of many such encounters is discordant. Some people are generous and do not mind occasional requests for money. Too many requests, though, soon exhaust their generosity. Losing their capacity to engage in single charitable acts, they are increasingly inclined to see homelessness as a disfigurement of the landscape, and begging as a personal assault. After a while, public opinion sours, and demands intensify to get the homeless off the street.

Yet there was a time, in the early 1980s, before these demands became quite so insistent, when the homeless were the favored subgroup among the poor. To some extent, they acquired this status by default. Since the Reagan administration cut back other programs for the poor, the investment in new social services and shelters made homeless people the only group to benefit from additional welfare spending. Some of this help was undoubtedly intended to make the homeless less visible. But another potent dynamic was also at work.

The Reagan administration justified its cutbacks of social programs as an attack on the bureaucracy of the welfare state. But poor people on the street were different from welfare clients. The public knew they were poor, not because a bureaucracy certified them as poor, but because it saw them on the street. This personal knowledge contributed to the reemergence of the gift relationship. In a gift relationship, the giver is benevolent, the receiver is grateful, and the positions of both parties are confirmed. A throwback to the old tradition of voluntary giving, the gift relationship meshed nicely with the concept of public welfare that President Reagan urged. The homeless might have been a nuisance in the early 1980s, but at least for those who shared his viewpoint, giving to the homeless on the street was the way giving really ought to be.[4]

Still, it would be wrong to exaggerate the relative importance of the gift relationship. Even at its height, giving on the street coexisted with, rather than displaced, the traditions of organized private charity and public support. So, when the growth of the homeless population took the glow off individual charitable acts, these traditions again came to the fore.

The Traditions of Social Welfare

Organized private charity and public supports are the two main social welfare traditions in the United States. Each of these traditions has formulated its own distinctive response to the growth of the homeless population.

Tracing its heritage to the Charity Organization Societies of 100 years ago, organized private charity espouses an ideology of individualism, self-reliance, and minimal government. Fearful that any kind of social assistance will only perpetuate dependency, it has often placed conditions, such as tests of the willingness to work, on those receiving welfare. Over the last century, exponents of this tradition have described the homeless as beggars, tramps, and the deinstitutionalized mentally ill. In each instance, though, they have carefully excised any hint of economic difficulties from these labels.

This ideology, which conservatives skillfully revived in the 1980s, is very powerful.[5] Whether charity has been provided privately or by the state, the fear of perpetuating dependency pervades virtually every aspect of social policy and crops up in incongruous places. In the 1949 Wechsler Children's I.Q. Test, for example, examinees are asked "why is it generally better to give money to an organized charity than to a street beggar?" The correct answers come straight out of this tradition: "assures that money goes to a really needy person; public charities are in a better position to investigate the merits of the case; a more orderly way of contribution for the donor." Children who simply assert that giving to a beggar makes them feel better demonstrate a lack of innate intelligence and lose valuable I.Q. points.[6]

The ideology of public supports has a somewhat different orientation. Its advocates have expanded the scope of social policy in slow, incremental steps, seeking to mollify those who worry about catering to the poor while simultaneously trying to manage demands for political and economic change. Usually, advocates of this ideology have handled these demands by giving movements on behalf of poor and working people part of what they wanted. Thus, when these movements campaigned for social security legislation during the 1930s, they got a Social Security Act, financed by a regressive tax, that omitted public housing and health insurance. Similarly, when trade unions fought for full employment, the outcome was laws like the Full Employment Act of 1946 and the Humphrey-Hawkins Act of 1978, both of which made rhetorical commitments to full employment without guarantees of adequate jobs. Pressured by conservatives, and guided as well by their own beliefs, exponents of the ideology of public supports have frequently taken the most drastic changes that social movements desired and turned them into modest reforms of current policy.[7]

Within this ideology, benefits and services do not promote dependency, and it is therefore possible to use social policies to address social problems. Yet politics sets severe constraints on what these policies can do. In housing, for example, governments are willing to construct temporary facilities for the homeless, but are still quite uneasy about expanding the supply of permanent housing. Where the need is pressing and the supply of funds adequate, permanent housing may be provided. Even when this housing is authorized, though, great care is taken to ensure that no harm comes to private interests.

The Debate Over Modern Homelessness

These two ideologies frame the conflicting social meanings of contemporary homelessness. Organized private charity defines it as a violation of the social order, the product of failed policies such as rent control, deinstitutionalization, and the permissive treatment of welfare clients. From this perspective, the problem is simply that the homeless are out there in public. Those interested in expanding public supports have a different view. They believe that homelessness is a problem of governmental legitimacy, an issue whose visibility raises uncomfortable questions about the relationship of poverty and wealth. For them, the problem of the visibility of the homeless is compounded by the need to remove them with political finesse and provide some social services.

Differences between cities complicate the issue of what homelessness means. In New York, the homeless are spread throughout the city, and people see them wherever they go. Los Angeles, by contrast, is a cluster of suburbs. Although its homeless population is almost as large as New York's, it is dispersed differently. The only major concentrations of the homeless are in Santa Monica and in a small downtown area near City Hall; 40,000 other homeless people live unnoticed in garages.[8] Like homelessness in any suburb, this diminished visibility defuses the urgency of homelessness in Los Angeles and alters its social meaning.

Some of this meaning has been derived from the way in which homelessness has been conceived as a social problem. In the 1960s, poverty was the dominant category for issues relating to the poor, and homelessness, to the extent that it existed at all, was a marginal subcategory for the inhabitants of skid row. Now the categories have been inverted: homelessness encompasses poverty more than poverty encompasses homelessness. Gradually, attention has turned from the invisible poor of the 1960s, with its uncomfortable discovery that the affluent society still had poor people, to the visible poor, those whose public poverty undermined claims of our having regained the old security and affluence.

Yet poverty is not the only social problem that lies within the domain of homelessness. Deinstitutionalization, low wages, and the scarcity of low-income housing have also come to be viewed as part of the problem. The point is not that these issues are unrelated to homelessness, but rather that they could be understood on their own or as part of a number of other categories—mental health, poverty, or cutbacks in social welfare. That the predominant tendency has been otherwise is an indication of the power of visible poverty to shape the construction of homelessness as a social problem.

This power may be traced to two distinct features of the public mood. The first is the belief that every individual's private pursuit of wealth will bring about "the good society." As public poverty, homelessness runs counter to the privatism of this ethic. By making a statement that not everyone is equally successful, it becomes such an insistent problem that many other social issues come to be subsumed under it.

The second reason for the current construction of homelessness as a social problem flows from a different aspect of this ethic. In its most ideal form, the ethic assumes that citizens retreat daily to home and family after they have succeeded in the pursuit of private gain. Indeed, the world outside the home is considered fit only for private gain; otherwise, it is a frightening place full of crime, drugs, and merciless competition. The relationship of the homeless to this world exerts a special fascination. Although their presence contributes to the sense of social disorder, they intrigue people who have homes precisely because the homeless live without a refuge. Their condition—homelessness—may have long had a name of its own. Not until recently, though, did it become the name for many other social problems.

The Politics of a Definition

How should homelessness be defined? In what ways is it different from, and similar to, the homelessness that has occurred before?

Defining homelessness is deceptively easy. According to the official government definition taken from the Stewart B. McKinney Act and used here, a homeless person is "one who lacks a fixed permanent night-time residence or whose nighttime residence is a temporary shelter, welfare hotel, or any public or private place not designed as sleeping accommodations for human beings."[9] Inclusive and reasonably precise, this definition contrasts with other definitions of homelessness that appear inclusive, but have actually excluded some significant segment of the population. In the controversial 1984 Housing and Urban Development (HUD) report, for example, a person is defined as homeless where, in addition to other living arrangements, "temporary vouchers are provided by public or private agencies."[10] The survey organization that conducted the study for HUD acknowledged that this definition prompted them to exclude families in welfare hotels, presumably because their residence was long-term, and no temporary vouchers were involved.[11]

Since only 32,000 people were in welfare hotels during 1983 when the study was conducted,[12] this omission would not have significantly altered HUD's much disputed national estimate of 250,000 to 350,000 people. The issue is, of course, not the comparatively small increase, but the subtle definitional twist that let this entire segment of the population slip by. Definitions are wonderful for this purpose. In keeping with the definer's political agenda, they can be easily used to decrease or increase the reported size of the population.

More generally, in discussions of homelessness, three different usages of the term correspond to three different political agendas. In ascending estimates of the population, these usages include people in shelters; people in shelters and the streets; or people in shelters, the streets, and at risk of losing their current housing. Since the first usage refers to the population served, it is ordinarily a favorite of public officials who would like to stress the adequacy of their programs and minimize the number of street people. The second usage represents a description of the population in need. This use is most common, but it does encounter some resistance when advocates employ it to advance the notion that large numbers of homeless people remain on the street. Lastly, there is the third, and broadest, usage. It is this usage that includes the population at risk, those who, though not currently on the street, are doubled up or might otherwise lose their housing. Typically found in projections of housing needs and other prospective policy analyses, it produces the biggest number of all.

Obviously, misunderstandings are most likely to arise when definitions are imprecise and one usage is substituted for another. Political agendas often enter into these misunderstandings, but it should also be noted that at least for individuals, the dividing lines between these definitions are not very clear. Cold weather may force a street person to take refuge in a shelter; alternatively, after a violent incident, a shelter resident may prefer the sidewalk. Imprecision, the influence of political agendas, and the blurring of individual and group behavior all add to the confusion about terminology. For this reason, whenever somebody mentions the issue of homelessness, it is generally wise to ask them exactly what they mean.

Homelessness: A Historical Overview

Homelessness has a history. Modern homelessness both diverges from, and conforms to, the phenomenon of homelessness in the past.

Of course, the popular view of homelessness is thoroughly ahistorical: the homeless, it is said, like the poor, have always been with us. Even when stripped of its weariness, resignation, and political uses, this statement is true, but at a level of generality that makes few historical distinctions about the way human beings have lived. Whatever the popular view, homelessness has not always been the same.

In fact, homelessness may be said to have passed through five major periods. During the first, preindustrial phase, there was an absolute shortage of shelter. Although resources were maldistributed in this period, even the most equitable distribution of resources would have left some portion of the population without housing. Perhaps the term *homelessness* is a misnomer, but the concept is not, for this was the "homelessness" of ancient and medieval societies and of the first American settlers.

Early industrialization in the late eighteenth and early nineteenth century marked the second phase. In London and Paris, workers who came from the countryside to labor in the factories were often homeless. Sometimes, they were unemployed for a while, or the pay was inadequate; at other times, there was just not enough shelter to house everyone who had migrated. Though their predicament was usually temporary, a period of homelessness was frequently part of their transition from the rural to the urban workforce.

The third period extends from the initial colonialization of the less developed world up to the present day. As in the second phase, homelessness in this period is at least partly attributable to an early form of industrialization. This industrialization, however, subordinates the needs of local people to an international system that values cheap labor and the export of raw materials. Providing either poorly paid or very occasional work, it has produced cities of the homeless in many of the great metropolitan areas of Asia, Africa, and South America.

Mature industrialization characterized the fourth period. In the United States, this period began with the first major upsurge of tramping in the 1870s and ended 100 years later with the alcoholics of skid row. Highly sensitive to the business cycle, homelessness spread most rapidly during or immediately after what Kevin Phillips has termed "capitalist heydays." In these periods—the Gilded Age of the late nineteenth century as well as in the 1920s and the Depression that followed—an un-regulated capitalism produced a two-tier economy, great disparities of income, and a sharp increase in the number of people without shelter. In between, though, during times both of affluence and of war, there was enough housing for poor people, and homelessness virtually disappeared.[13]

Another capitalist heyday, beginning in the 1980s, marked the fifth period of homelessness. Distinguished in the first instance by deindustrialization and the transition to a service economy, it has been powerfully fueled by a number of other factors including social welfare cutbacks, reductions in affordable housing, and the proliferation of low-wage jobs. All these factors are important. Nevertheless, viewed in the broadest historical perspective, they are not what truly differentiates the latest upsurge of homelessness.

Contemporary Homelessness: What Is Different, What Is the Same?

Contemporary homelessness has five especially distinctive characteristics. The first, and perhaps most remarkable, was its growth during an economic recovery: every previous expansion of the homeless population has occurred in a weakened economy. Whether it was the repeated downturns of the Gilded Age, with its closely spaced slumps of 1873, 1877, 1882–86, and 1893, business cycle slumps such as the recession of 1914–15, or the Great Depression of the 1930s, homelessness always grew in step with the number of unemployed people. By contrast, modern homelessness began in the economic difficulties of the 1970s, ballooned in the 1981–82 recession, and kept on growing despite an economic recovery that lasted until the recession of the early 1990s. This time, there is no simple correlation between homelessness and unemployment, and the recovery has been profoundly skewed along income lines.

Bad times have happened before, and they have made people homeless. But the risk incurred by poor and working people in this economic recovery has been significantly increased by a second distinctive factor, the decline of social networks and the loss of community. In the past, when workers lost jobs, there were people to take them in—friends, neighbors, and family. Now, however, these networks have shrunk, and people who are at risk of homelessness have much less to fall back on. Among the homeless themselves, for example, one study found that 22 percent of homeless mothers could not name a single supportive adult, as compared with only 2 percent of mothers who were housed.[14]

These findings are hardly surprising, given a whole series of developments that cut people off from one another. In cities, tall buildings seal residents off from the street, air conditioners substitute for verandas, and the videocassette recorder has taken its place beside the community movie theater. Neighborhoods with a high percentage of minorities are emptying themselves of middle-income residents, leaving their poorer citizens to struggle against the combined impact of drugs, crime, and unemployment. In this environment, people naturally tend to ration the aid they provide, because their own physical and emotional resources are already stretched to the limit.[15]

There is, in this analysis, a faint echo of the sociological literature of the 1960s, which also argued that people became homeless because they had severed their community ties. Then, sociologists used the concept of *disaffiliation* to explain the phenomenon, and they were fascinated by skid row as a world where people did not respond to the usual rewards and constraints.[16] Of course, these sociologists were imputing a defect to a small segment of the population. In contrast, homelessness now is more pervasive, and the process of disaffiliation is occurring within the community itself.

The third distinctive characteristic of modern homelessness is the relatively large segment of the population who are mentally ill. A controversy rages about this subgroup: authorities debate its size, its relationship to deinstitutionalization, and whether it is more likely to precede or follow homelessness. These questions will all be discussed at greater length in chapter 6. For the present, it is enough to note that despite tendencies to exaggerate their significance, the mentally ill do play a larger role in the homeless population than in previous periods. In a 1988 U.S. General Accounting Office report, nine research studies gave estimates of the number of mentally ill among the homeless that varied from 10 to 47 percent.[17] By comparison, in Alice Solenberger's 1911 Chicago study of 1,000 homeless men, only 52, or 5.2 percent, are described as insane.[18] Psychiatric classifications may have changed over the years, but there is nothing in this portrait to suggest even a rough correspondence between populations.

Just as there are more people who are homeless and mentally ill, so are there also more women and children. Families have not yet displaced the single adult male as the most common demographic type. Their prominence, however, suggests a greater vulnerability to a changing labor market as well as to gaps in social welfare. These changes have certainly made some educated women economically independent. Unfortunately, though, for those with less valued skills, the freedom to become independent has also meant the freedom to live unhoused.[19]

Finally, there is the new phenomenon of rural homelessness. Apart from natural disasters like the Oklahoma dust bowl of the 1930s and the occasional inhabitant who came upon hard times, homelessness in the countryside used to be rare. The rural economic crisis compromised this immunity. Low salaries, debt-ridden farms, and a shortage of local housing produced homelessness on a scale that overwhelmed the local support network of friends and family. Suddenly, the homeless could be found in cars near Coventry, Vermont, under bridges in Des Moines, Iowa, and in caves near Glenwood Springs, Colorado. Many small communities have scrambled to fund shelters for this new population, but they, like their counterparts in the big cities, have been unable to keep pace with the burgeoning demand.[20]

Although these characteristics of modern homelessness are all distinctive, there is much in the population's present growth that follows the historical pattern. To begin with, homelessness has most frequently occurred in periods of economic transition, like the current shift from an industrial to a service economy. There is, for instance, the case of the Industrial Revolution in Britain, where the Enclosure Acts denied rural laborers access to common lands, thereby depriving them of their livelihood and forcing them to migrate to an uncertain, and sometimes homeless, future in the cities.[21] Similarly, in this country, the transition to an industrial economy in the post-Civil War era left as many as 3 million men unemployed in the 1873–75 depression and brought about a great upsurge of tramping.[22] While homelessness has plainly mushroomed during depressions that were not the product of a transition to a new economic order, this trend is quite prominent in its history.

Two principles underlie this pattern. First, new economic eras establish a different set of relations between employer and employee—more favorable to employers in some periods, less favorable in others. Although these arrangements may subsequently be altered, generally, it is to the advantage of employers if transitions can be carried out on favorable terms. Usually, these terms entail keeping relative wages down, so that profits will remain high, and business will have more money to invest. Sometimes, though, the resulting wage levels have left workers without enough money to obtain the available housing.

The second principle is the concept of *less eligibility*, which holds that a person on welfare must have a lower standard of living than a person who works. While this principle has deep roots in U.S. social policy, its most recent implementation has been both consistent with the historical pattern and especially harsh. The current economic transition has witnessed a decline in the working poor's standard of living. Well into the 1960s, a welfare client could receive less than a poorly paid worker and still afford housing. But as the cost of housing began to rise in the 1970s, welfare benefits were reduced to correspond to the working poor's declining income; that is when the risk of homelessness grew—slowly for the working poor, more rapidly for those on welfare. If, in the 1960s, getting less than the working poor meant poor housing, by the 1980s, it often meant the streets.

For welfare recipients, the risks associated with the principle of less eligibility are part of a long tradition. As long as less eligibility requires a lower standard of living, measures will be taken to ensure that welfare is different from work. Historically, the two measures that have most often been used for this purpose are indoor relief and work programs. Indoor relief makes assistance conditional upon the welfare recipient's entrance into an institution; it can either coexist with, or be exclusive of, outdoor relief—assistance in the recipient's own home. Work programs make a similar demand; they condition the receipt of assistance on proof of the willingness to labor.

At first glance, a policy of indoor relief seems Dickensian, evoking memories of paupers in an almshouse, of nineteenth-century social policies that have nothing to do with modern homelessness. Yet the refusal to maintain people in their own home is hardly restricted to the nineteenth century. In the United States today, the comparable institutions for indoor relief are emergency shelters and welfare hotels. True, people do not have to enter these institutions until they have exhausted the possibilities of outdoor relief. But the institutions are very much there, helping to implement the principle of less eligibility and carrying into the present day the same deterrent functions.

To see old historical debates about indoor versus outdoor relief from this perspective is to look in a mirror. During the winter of 1878–79, for example, the city of Brooklyn reacted to concerns about the deleterious effects of assistance in poor people's own homes by abolishing outdoor relief. Dr. Thomas Norris analyzed the effects of this experiment in a report to the county superintendents.

> As to the entire withdrawal of temporary assistance, the experience of last winter showed that it would have been a saving to afford some. Many families were obliged to break up, the parents or parent going to the poorhouse, and the children to the asylums for care, at the expense of the county, costing in some instances, forty dollars a month; whereas one or two dollars' worth of food a week, during the winter, given by the public, would have sufficed to keep them together in their own little homes.[23]

Then, as now, poor people who needed relief were forced into institutions. Then, as now, authorities insisted on indoor relief even when, as with shelters and welfare hotels, it would have been cheaper to maintain them at home. There is great continuity in this tradition. While contemporary social policy is willing to undertake the cost of maintaining some people in their own homes, it is no less worried than its nineteenth-century ancestor about a total severing of the relationship between work and shelter. Salaried employees are supposed to be able to pay for their housing, and so are welfare recipients, on the grants they are given. Those who cannot will become homeless and can receive assistance solely in an institution.

The historical tradition for work programs is equally well-established. In Washington, D.C., when the Municipal Lodging House opened in 1893, chopping wood was required in exchange for shelter. Such arrangements were common at Charity Organization Societies throughout the country. In New York, it was necessary to work for a day in order to obtain two meals and a night's lodging; in Indianapolis, the 1911 annual report of the Charity Organization Society extolled the virtues of the woodyard.[24] More recently, cities like New York have again introduced work programs when they became concerned that too many homeless people were taking advantage of their newly secured right to shelter.

Of course, work programs vary from helpful referrals and job training to punitive make-work. Moreover, an insistence on work as one element of a municipal response to the spread of homelessness may simply reflect a greater degree of programmatic development: when cities expand their social welfare system for the homeless, they naturally tend to include work programs. In practice, however, current programs, like those in the past, often have a deterrent function: New York's pays $12.50 a week for twenty hours of work. The quality of life in a shelter may be poorer than in paid housing, but it is free. With a work program in place, a city ensures that the prospect of this free housing does not become too appealing to its own poor.

Homelessness and Social Policy

The homeless are visible, and the response to that visibility has been filtered through the history and traditions of social welfare. From this perspective, the most pressing questions concern the nature of these responses and why, given their very limited success, more has not been done. To answer these questions requires first, a description of the population, and second, an examination of the causes of homelessness. These analyses will clear the way for a discussion of how people in communities all over the country, as well as governments at every level, responded to the growth of the homeless population. New York receives special attention in this section because of all U.S. cities, it had the most developed response.

The pattern emerging from this analysis shows the U.S. economy to be so dependent on the production of widespread homelessness that it could not, in its current form, tolerate the necessary remedies. But the analysis also suggests that together with other common human needs such as health care and an adequate income, the failure to address the issue of homelessness creates the political conditions for the formation of a progressive coalition. This coalition, in turn, could well spearhead the next great period of social reform.

2

Who Are the Homeless?

Statistics is a grim business. Most of the time, it seems to me, people resort to counting when they find things too horrible to describe any other way.

A social service researcher for the state of Michigan, in response to a question about data on the homeless

Who are the homeless? It is not easy to say. Faced with the problem of describing a mobile and diverse population, researchers have employed a variety of techniques to help them obtain an accurate portrait. They have counted people in shelters, estimated the size of the population on the street, and tried to enumerate the homeless in the 1990 census.[1] Studies of the population have become one of the more prestigious forms of social research. Yet despite their increasing sophistication, agreement among these studies has been spotty, and consensus has been reached about just a few demographic trends.

In fact, from the publication of new findings to the reception of these findings by other researchers, the pattern has been remarkably uniform. One set of researchers announces that their study presents a true portrait of the homeless population; other researchers then promptly attack the study for its methodological flaws. When a group led by Peter Rossi searched for the homeless in the streets of Chicago, they found an average of only 2,722 people. Rossi claimed that the study represented a distinct improvement: the census was an actual count of people on the street, done twice to minimize seasonal differences. Counterpoising his census to the much larger numbers cited by homeless advocates, Rossi accused them of wildly inflating the population's size. Critics soon pounced. The study, they said, omitted families who were doubled up, even though such families are estimated to constitute as much as 40 percent of the Chicago homeless population. Besides, plainclothes police officers accompanied the interviewers. Easily identified by the streetwise, their presence caused respondents to be less forthcoming and seriously compromised the integrity of the research.[2]

Reactions to other studies have followed a similar course. A 1986 report by Richard Freeman and Brian Hall of the National Bureau of Economic Research developed a sophisticated mathematical formula to estimate the total homeless population. Individuals in New York shelters, the authors asserted, spent 55 percent of their time homeless there; the rest of their time homeless they spent on the street. By contrast, those on the street spent only 20 percent of their time in shelters. Applying these figures to national data from the controversial 1984 HUD study, this report determined that HUD's estimate of 250,000 to 350,000 people was essentially correct.[3]

Despite its use by some conservative critics,[4] several important objections have been raised about these calculations. First, as the National Academy of Sciences has argued, data from New York cannot be employed to generalize about the rest of the country. Second, unlike the Chicago research, this analysis is based on a single count without adjustment for seasonal variations.[5] It is, moreover, methodologically dubious to employ the very data under question in the HUD study to confirm that study's validity.

Objectifying the Homeless: Turning Numbers into Causes

Consensus about the composition of the homeless population is important, and its absence has undoubtedly hindered the development of sensible policies. The size of the population, and the subgroups within it, do make a difference. If the population is large, it deserves a bigger share of resources. If it consists mostly of the mentally ill, it needs different services than if workers who have recently lost their jobs make up the majority. The debate about the demographics of the population is useful at this level of distinction. It helps to shape social policy and choose among the programs that should be funded.

Yet the debate also possesses a far less attractive side. It is one thing to make some basic distinctions about the population's makeup; it is quite another to substitute the pursuit of these distinctions for significant policy interventions. The formation of commissions to study social problems has long been an established technique for managing politically difficult issues. Often, the public outcry subsides while a commission studies a problem, making it easier for the branch of government that authorized the study to implement the recommendations without opposition, or if it chooses, to ignore them entirely. With or without any formal mandate from government, much of the social research on homelessness has served a comparable function.

This outcome is more the product of the funding and orientation of social science research than the intent of individuals. It occurs because at a time when government officials repeatedly emphasize the lack of money for new domestic spending, social science researchers are inevitably caught up in the growing tension between studying an issue on the one hand and doing something about it on the other. Most research-ers want to help the homeless, and they understandably want this help to be based on the best possible data. But data that show the need for major new commitments of funds run up against the usual budgetary constraints. Money can be spent for temporary shelter, but not per-manent housing, for emergency psychiatric care, but not long-term stays in a mental hospital. The budgetary constraints transform the function of the research. Blocked by the financial obstacles to change, the research has often fed the national inclination to objectify poor people.

A reliance on numbers exacerbates this tendency. Numbers are ob-viously useful, and in circumstances where there are significant monies to be spent, knowledge of the homeless—how many and of what type and condition—is enormously valuable in spending that money wisely. But where there are budgetary constraints, statistical data can become a weapon in a campaign to prove that homeless people are different from the rest of the population. The homeless, this data implies, are not like you and me; they have this or that defining characteristic in too little or too great abundance.[6]

Seen through this lens, the homeless become a collection of attributes. Researchers do not gather information about *them*; they gather infor-mation about their characteristics—age, gender, race, mental health, or job status. This information does not always work against the homeless; clearly, even in the current period, fundings sources have used it to establish, on a modest scale, some innovative programs. Yet the existence of these programs does not offset the far more powerful tendency by which characteristics come to displace the people who possess them. The homeless as people need money. Their characteristics, however, signify a telling deviancy: for people like *that*, it would be wrong to make a major commitment of funds.

Curiously, although this search for individual defects typifies much mainstream social research, it conflicts quite explicitly with orthodox economic analysis. Most introductory economics texts feature discussions of the *natural unemployment rate*—the rate of unemployment that is said to be inherent in the operation of a market economy.[7] Some texts are more careful than others and make distinctions between kinds of un-employment: frictional, for workers between jobs, structural for those lacking the needed skills, and cyclical, for those whose status responds to changes in the business cycle.[8] But regardless of their subtlety, these texts all acknowledge the necessity of unemployment, and by implication, accept its systemic origins. Even if everybody had the "correct" demo-graphic attributes, some people would still be unemployed.

Social science research ignores this orthodoxy; it consistently turns demographic characteristics into causes of homelessness. Many alcoholics live in houses, and some housed people are emotionally disturbed. In neither case is a demographic attribute—substance abuse or mental ill-ness—used as an explanation of their housing status. Any careful analysis of the power of these attributes to "explain" homelessness requires a comparison of their incidence in the rest of the population. It also demands proof that they are actually causes of homelessness and not one of its consequences.

This latter demand runs contrary to the usual reasoning, which proceeds automatically from attribute to cause. It presumes that if someone is emotionally disturbed, it is their emotional disturbance that made them homeless. But homelessness is itself extremely disturbing, and few people could be homeless for any length of time without it affecting their behavior.

Several research studies illustrate this point. In Detroit, for example, researchers found 9 percent of the homeless to have a documented history of mental illness. After a period of homelessness, however, 25 percent of the sample reported severe stress and disorientation.[9] Likewise, in Minneapolis, the first hospitalization for one quarter of those hospitalized occurred *after* a spell of homelessness.[10] And, in New York, when Freeman and Hall examined the relationship of homelessness and time in jail, they found that in fully 39 percent of the cases, incarceration followed, rather than preceded, the time spent homeless.[11]

Of course, the correct sequence alone is not enough, because a causal relationship must still be demonstrated. Whether it is homelessness and mental illness, criminality, or substance abuse, sequence is a necessary but insufficient demonstration of cause. This standard of proof is especially arduous in the social sciences, where phenomenon are not discrete, and it is very difficult to say conclusively that one condition *caused* another. Research about the homeless may never be able to attain this level of proof. Nevertheless, the loose imputation of causality to particular demographic attributes does represent a big drop-off from this standard.

While demographic research makes it possible to prepare a portrait of the homeless population, its assumption that the characteristics people have explain their own plight leads to unjustifiably individualistic interpretations. Portraits of the homeless should combat this view. This task is, however, only one of many problems that researchers about the homeless face.

Obstacles to Research About the Homeless Population

The homeless population is diverse. The homeless population is mobile. For understandable reasons, homeless people may not always tell the truth about themselves. Every researcher tries to overcome these obstacles, but they are always there to raise some doubts.[12] Does the sample reflect the whole population? Were families, children, people on the streets, or people in the shelters left out? Doubts like these may spur further efforts, but their overall effect is unsettling. Researchers like to have confidence in what they know. Unfortunately, with research on the homeless, that is not always possible.

The most important conceptual barrier to research about the homeless is the lack of an adequate theory. An adequate theory of homelessness would give full weight to social factors, but it would also be able to explain why one person rather than another became homeless. In other words, it would specify the interaction between the political/economic and the psychological.

This imprecision has troubled observers for a long time. Looking at homelessness during the Depression in Chicago, the authors of the study *Twenty Thousand Homeless Men* recognized the importance of economic factors and made a prescient comment:

> This interpretation describes properly the situation out of which shelter relief developed. It helps explain why there were twenty thousand men in Chicago shelters in 1934 and practically none in 1924. On the other hand, it does not explain why some men were unemployed and others employed, why some were unattached and others lived with their relatives, why some accepted relief in shelters and others refused to accept that relief.[13]

The problem has not been resolved in the intervening years. Nor has any other theory gained wide acceptance. It is true that at its height in the early 1960s, functionalist theory did reach a point of nearly unquestioned dominance.[14] But functionalist theory was not concerned with the problem of specifying the relationship between political/economic and psychological factors. Instead, what these sociologists wanted to know was why homeless people on skid row existed outside the boundaries of a society that had incorporated virtually every other group. Researchers today would probably reject their sharp distinction between normal and deviant, even if the distinction returns in subtler forms. Since, however, they have been no more successful in elaborating an adequate theory, many might well envy a time when at least those who studied homelessness all spoke the same language.

One of the main consequences of this theoretical vacuum in current research efforts is an absence of shared definitions. The definitions of terms like *temporary, shelter,* and *mental illness* are so sensitive to changes in the political milieu that they have never shown much staying power. What is temporary, for example, at one time may seem fairly permanent at another. Similarly, nearly every generation has redefined shelter and mental illness in politically congenial ways. Over time, redefinitions of such ambiguous terms are to be expected. But when social scientists in the same period cannot agree on the meaning of these terms, that is a far more unusual phenomenon.

The absence of shared definitions is a major obstacle to the accumulation of knowledge. Researchers accumulate knowledge most rapidly when they can compare studies that ascribe the same meaning to the same terms. If studies in five cities find 40 percent of their sample population to be temporarily homeless, the statistic is not a meaningful one when temporary is defined as a month in one city and twelve months in the others. Whatever their individual validity, studies stand alone in these circumstances because researchers cannot aggregate data.

This absence of shared definitions naturally reinforces the tendency toward counting. It may not always be clear exactly what researchers are counting, but at least numbers give the appearance of a convincing portrait. If this activity seems almost ritualistic, it is nonetheless easy to understand: the problem is complex, the size of the population is daunting, and researchers know that funding constraints are likely to obstruct the implementation of any recommendation they might make. So, hemmed in on all sides, they count the homeless.

The homeless population is ideally suited for this ritual because they are so difficult to count accurately. Since doubts will always hover over the accuracy of the numbers in the last study, it is easy to justify the need for another census. The interviewer could have missed the man who lives under the bridge; gone to an abandoned building the day after the police evicted a family of squatters; or conducted the study in late June instead of early February. Subsequent counts may only be slightly more accurate, but the mobility of the homeless population tantalizes researchers and fosters illusions about the value of these marginal improvements.

Equally tantalizing is the prospect that the homeless may not be telling the truth. Seeking to allay this concern, some studies have asserted that the homeless are not necessarily less truthful than any other people.[15] Certainly, many have reason to dissemble, because their past experiences with those in authority have not been reassuring. The questions researchers ask reinforce their subjects' wariness: inquire about somebody's history of drug use, and a well-meaning interviewer begins to sound like the police. The interviewer wants information, but the ex-psychiatric client may not be willing or able to recall the entire history of her hospitalization. Likewise, when the substance abuser describes his participation in a methadone program, his story may not match the official record. As with the other issues in research process, self-reported data are not invalidating, but they do undermine somewhat the confidence that can be placed in the accuracy of any portrait.

Researchers are therefore caught in a standoff between the larger society and the homeless population. The society wants a portrait of the homeless that both informs policy and rationalizes limited intervention. Counting is, in part, the response of the social sciences to this dilemma. Numbers usually show that the problem is big; demographic attributes usually prove that the problem is their own fault. The homeless complicate this research because they are such a difficult population to study: mobile, wary, and understandably not always telling the truth. Any portrait of the homeless that emerges from these circumstances is going to be less scientific than the purest laboratory research. Nevertheless, it is, at least for the time being, the only portrait we have.

The Size of the Homeless Population

Two numbers are usually employed to frame discussions of the size of the homeless population. The smaller number, 250,000 people, derives from the 1984 HUD report.[16] The larger number, 2.2 million, stems from the 1980 congressional testimony of Mitch Snyder and Mary Ellen Hombs, adjusted upward by their book *Homelessness in America* to a 1983 total of 3 million people.[17] Both numbers were, for different reasons, problematic, but it is typical of the confusion surrounding the issue of the population's size that they should have so often been joined together. The HUD figure represents an estimate based on the number of homeless during one night; the 2 to 3 million number projects a total of those believed to be homeless over the course of one year. One source of the confusion about the size of the homeless population therefore derives from the imprecision created by the linkage of a nightly to a yearly number.

The problem of obtaining an accurate census is further complicated because both these estimates possess other significant flaws. The Snyder/ Hombs estimate takes the 1 percent of the population said to be homeless in major metropolitan areas and applies it nationally. Central cities contain the highest incidence of homelessness. There is, however, no evidence justifying the application of this rate to the United States as a whole.

The HUD report sparked such a major controversy that a congressional committee even held hearings about its findings.[18] The study asserted that homelessness was temporary, included few formerly middle-class people, and did not result from Reagan's 1981–82 recession. Together with its small national estimate, these conclusions led critics to declare that the report was the product of a transparent political agenda. Over the years, the cumulative effect of these attacks on the report have seriously damaged its credibility.[19]

Three major criticisms have been made about the methodology of the HUD study. The first involves the question of *snowball sampling*, where interviewers contact shelters already known to them and then ask for the names of other shelter providers. In theory, this technique leads to the development of a complete shelter list; in practice, however, several interviews are required to ensure that the list is complete. HUD did not attempt these interviews, and its study suffered accordingly.[20]

HUD also failed to specify the nature of the estimate it was requesting. In the congressional hearings, for example, Ronald D. Pogue, pastor of the Bering United Memorial Methodist Church in Houston, Texas, testified about his surprise at the misuse of the 5,000 to 7,000 person estimate provided by him and three other members of the Mayor's Task Force. Thinking they had given their best estimate of the number on the street, they were disturbed to see that the number had been cited by HUD as the estimate for Houston's entire homeless population, including those in shelters and jails.[21] Providers in Boston, Hartford, and Phoenix all made similar complaints.[22]

Lastly, and perhaps most devastating, is the criticism of the report's use of Ranally Metropolitan Areas (RMA). RMAs are larger than central cities; they were, in fact, developed by Rand McNally for use in its annual commercial marketing atlas. The New York City RMA, for example, includes seventy-four cities in twenty-four counties in three states. It had a 1980 population of 16.6 million people, of which New York City proper contributed only 43 percent. Likewise, the city of Los Angeles accounts for less than one-third of the local RMA, which has 10.6 million people in five counties. Altogether, the twenty largest RMAs researched by HUD include 78.3 million people in 455 cities involving 141 counties across thirty-two states.[23]

The HUD interview protocol has been obtained under the Freedom of Information Act. It did not specify the geographic area in question, and certainly made no attempt to define an RMA. Instead, it merely asked knowledgeable observers, "How serious a problem is homelessness in your city?"[24] HUD claims that in the New York RMA, it actually asked this question in New York City, Newark and Paterson, New Jersey, as well as in Bergen, Westchester, Nassau and Suffolk counties.[25] But inquiries in these localities can hardly be expected to capture the total number of people homeless in the whole New York RMA. Just from its handling of this issue, the weight of the evidence suggests that HUD significantly understated the population's size.

Flaws in both the Snyder/Hombs and HUD estimates illustrate some of the problems in counting the homeless population. There are, in reality, only a limited number of options to choose from for those who wish to undertake such a count. The first option is to conduct a one-time survey of shelters, institutions, and the streets. This method is probably the most accurate, but it is also the most expensive. Second, it might be possible to develop a more elaborate reporting system. The problem with this option is, of course, that the count would be limited to those who use the service. The third option combines the first and second—a street survey plus a reporting system. It would be more complete, but might confuse those who use the shelters and those who do not, especially when that use occurs sequentially. Finally, some other social indicator such as poverty or unemployment could be drafted as a substitute measure. This option would be cheapest of all.[26] So far, however, the only indicator of homelessness we have is homelessness, and even direct counts using this indicator have yielded but limited success.

Each of these options points toward a different population size. According to a U.S. General Accounting Office (GAO) summary, census-based studies—actual counts of the population—yield lower rates of homelessness, a median of 13 per every 10,000 people. By comparison, the median rate for utilization studies is 18 per 10,000, and escalates to 29 per 10,000 for studies based on expert judgment. The range of all twenty-seven studies varied from an incidence of 6 to 95 per 10,000. In general, the GAO found that studies of high technical quality produced a 40 percent lower incidence of homelessness than those of more questionable merit.[27]

This summary certainly constitutes a caution against greatly inflated numbers. Yet there are several reasons why the GAO median for the lowest, census-based figures should not be applied nationally. First, one of the census-based studies dates back to 1975 and estimates the homeless population of Sydney, Australia. Its inclusion in this summary is simply inexplicable.[28] Second, the other twenty-six studies—census, utilization, and expert—were conducted during the period from 1983 to 1987, when virtually everyone agrees that the population increased rapidly. Plainly, incidences of the population from 1983 cannot be used to obtain a current estimate.

Another problematic issue in gauging the population's size is the ratio of those in the shelter to those on the street. Once again, the data vary widely. Estimates range from 2.23 people on the street in Freeman and Hall's *Permanent Homelessness in America?*, to 1.78 in the HUD study, 1.3 in the 1984 report *Homelessness in New York State*, and on down to 0.06 in a study of Fairfax County, Virginia.[29] Variations also exist within as well as between localities. In Chicago, for example, the 1.44 ratio that the Rossi study found in summer dropped to only 0.35 during the winter. A similar pattern was evident in Nashville, Tennessee where summer reduced the 0.21 winter street-shelter ratio to a mere 0.07.

Because factors like regional differences, seasonal effects, and shelter bed capacities all enter into the street-shelter ratio, it must be used judiciously to project a national total. Low street-shelter ratios can be the product of providing many shelter beds in a northeast city, where winter drives many homeless people indoors, or it could be the outcome of the homeless policy in a warm suburb, with limited emergency shelter and a relatively invisible street population. By contrast, in a temperate climate such as Santa Barbara, California, the street-shelter ratio is likely to be high because many homeless people live outside, and the number of beds in shelters is limited to about 150.[30]

Despite all these obstacles and complications, the 1990 census tried to conduct an actual count of the homeless population. On the night of 20–21 March, 1990, the Bureau of the Census sent 15,000 interviewers to 11,000 shelters and an equal number of open-air sites all over the country. Faced with the prospect of a low estimate, advocates for the homeless engaged in a heated debate about their own participation. A strong minority led by Mitch Snyder insisted that any attempt to enumerate the homeless represented collusion with an undercount. The majority, however, reasoned that advocates who had taken part in the census would have much greater credibility explaining its flaws.

The final number of 230,000 left a good many flaws to be explained. The Census Bureau had excluded almost all cities of less than 50,000 population. It had also prohibited workers from including homeless people who were not at the designated sites. A study commissioned by the Census Bureau estimated that it had missed 70 percent of the population in Los Angeles and 47 percent of the population in New York. With the Bureau itself admitting that "[the census] was not intended to, and did not, produce a count of the homeless population," advocates were well-positioned to argue that the hidden homeless—as much as two-thirds of the population—may have been lost.[31]

A few experts believe that capture-recapture techniques can overcome the difficulties that made the 1990 census and other actual counts of the homeless so inherently problematic. Statisticians, though, developed the capture-recapture technique to enumerate animals in the wild, and some doubt that it can be used to count the homeless population.[32] As a consequence, until researchers demonstrate its accuracy, future estimates will continue to be obtained through less sophisticated means.

There are, nonetheless, some base figures. In 1988, Samuel Pierce, who was secretary of HUD throughout the Reagan administration, acknowledged that an update of the 1984 HUD study would yield a nightly figure in the 500,000 to 600,000 range. One year later, S. Anna Kondratas, assistant secretary of Housing for Community Planning and Development in the Bush administration, also estimated the nightly total at 600,000 people.[33] Both these revised figures represents annual growth rates of about 17 percent. In its 1988 report, the National Academy of Sciences cites with evident approval a study by the National Alliance to End Homelessness. By reinterpreting the HUD data and assuming a suburban rate one-third of that in cities, the Alliance hypothesized that 735,000 people were homeless on any one night, and 1.3 to 2 million people were homeless during the course of an entire year.[34] Amid all the methodological problems, the claims and counterclaims, this estimate represents the best considered judgment.

The Composition of the Homeless Population

There is a greater degree of consensus about the composition of the homeless population than there is about its size. Admittedly, no single study has been accepted as definitive, and some significant differences do exist between regions. Yet the information obtained from a variety of studies on some attributes does present a fairly consistent portrait. The highlights of this portrait indicate that the homeless population is younger than its skid row predecessors and consists of about 50 percent minorities. Families are its fastest growing subgroup. Although a surprisingly large number of homeless people work, some studies also show that an even larger number have spent time in foster care, and many are veterans.

Age

Most studies place the average age of the adult homeless at about thirty-five years old. There is, moreover, remarkably little divergence among regions. Three New York City studies all group the average around this age, as does research from Ohio, St. Louis, Minneapolis, and Los Angeles.[35] Two significant deviations from this average are the thirty-nine years old found in Rossi's Chicago study, and the general tendency for homeless women to be somewhat younger.[36]

Because the age of the population is probably the attribute about which there is the least controversy, it usually leads researchers to remark on the unmistakable trend that the average represents. The typical resident of skid row was noticeably older. A special 1930 census of New York's Bowery District is illustrative: almost 59 percent of the population was older than forty years of age.[37] Their age suggests that the residents of skid row were often retired, superannuated workers whose relationship to the job market had become increasingly tenuous. The last remnants of a transient hobo culture, their presence on skid row testified to that culture's demise.

By comparison, the prototypical homeless adult today is younger and belongs to the sizeable class of urban poor people. Lacking the occupational skills required for employment in a changing labor market, the homeless must survive on poorly paying jobs or the deflated value of their public assistance checks. The difference in the ages of skid row and contemporary homeless people therefore stems from the effects of economic change on the two groups. Skid row residents became economically superfluous when the railroads and mines had been built, the need for transient workers declined, and the residents were too old to perform hard physical labor. In contrast, the transition from an industrial to a service economy occurred at a time when a younger group of urban poor people—often people of color without the newly required technical skills—were vulnerable to further exclusion from the job market. Economic change affected both groups, but it interacted with the homeless of today when they were on average about ten years younger.

Gender

Single men make up slightly more than half—51 percent—of the total homeless population. While unaccompanied women account for only 12 percent, females predominate as the caretaker among the 34 percent of the homeless composed of families. As a result, the total percentage of women is almost as much as the men's. Unaccompanied children—3 percent—make up the rest.[38] Localities vary considerably in this breakdown by gender.[39]

Information about the sheltered population confirms the accuracy of this breakdown. A 1988 HUD survey found unaccompanied women to constitute 14 percent of the sheltered population. Once again, however, with women largely heading the 40 percent of the sheltered population in families, their total number undoubtedly rivals the 45 percent of the population composed of unaccompanied homeless men.[40]

Families

The growth in the number of families has been the most striking change in the demographics of the homeless population. The 40 percent of the sheltered population in families during 1988 was almost twice the proportion of 21 percent who were homeless four years earlier.[41] Although the U.S. Conference of Mayors does not show quite so rapid an increase in its annual survey—27 percent in 1985 to 34 percent in 1990—families probably make up a bigger share of the homeless population than at any other time in recent American history. In fact, in some cities such as Chicago, Kansas City, and New York, homeless families total more than 55 percent of the population.[42]

Some disturbing data about children are implicit in these statistics. The National Academy of Sciences estimates that if 735,000 people are homeless on any given night, upwards of 100,000 of them are children. Since this figure excludes runaways, throwaways, and children on the street or in institutions, it shows just how much homelessness has changed from the times when the population consisted of white, male alcoholics who inhabited skid row.[43]

Race

Slightly more than half the population are people of color. In 1986, the Robert Wood Johnson Foundation, which sponsors health care projects for the homeless in sixteen cities, reported that together, blacks and Hispanics totaled 51 percent of their clients.[44] This number is consistent with the 54 percent found in both the Urban Institute study and HUD's 1988 shelter survey.[45]

In keeping with the long tradition of portraying the poor as somehow different, a few writers have cited these data to accentuate the contrast between the homeless and the rest of the society. People of color do make up a disproportionate percentage of the poor, and the poor are naturally the group most at risk of becoming homeless. According to these writers, however, if people of color are overrepresented among the homeless, then homelessness becomes that much easier to explain away.[46]

Substance Abuse

Substance abusers constitute about one-third of the homeless population. This estimate is derived from local studies such as those in Ohio and the San Francisco area, as well as the U.S. Conference of Mayors' synopsis of data from thirty cities.[47] While a wider range of numbers does exist—in excess of 50 percent for cities like Boston, Cleveland, New

Orleans, less than 20 percent for Chicago, Nashville, and San Antonio[48]—the one-third estimate still represents the most plausible middle range.

Some substance abusers have difficulty keeping a job. Their dependence on drugs and/or alcohol may anger family and friends, who eventually grow tired of giving them money and throw them out of the house. This and many other similar stories feed the popular belief that substance abuse causes homelessness. It does, and it does not.

Substance abuse may be the proximate cause of some homelessness, but the real cause lies in other underlying factors. People abuse drugs and alcohol because their economic and emotional needs are not being met. In any analysis of homelessness, it is these factors, rather than the substance abuse *alone*, that need to be addressed.

Mental Illness

About one-quarter to one-third of the homeless population suffers from severe mental illness.[49] Many methodological problems impinge on this estimate. First, mental illness must be defined. Less inclusive definitions consist only of psychosis and schizophrenia, but depressions and personality disorders have also been included. Second, there are always questions about what constitutes evidence of this symptomatology. Separately or in combination, the judgment of the interviewer, the receipt of outpatient services, and prior hospitalization have all been used. Finally, the extent of interviewer's training and differences between self-reported data and official records introduce additional complications.[50]

Whatever number is obtained must then be compared with the incidence of mental illness among the general population. Few studies have made this comparison, lending credence to the notion that the homeless as a group are uniquely impaired. Yet the Midtown Manhattan study, perhaps the most famous epidemiological analysis of mental illness, discovered significant mental disturbances among 23 percent of the population.[51] More mentally ill people are found among the homeless, but if the proportion is compared to the population at large, the difference is not nearly as much as is widely believed.

Education

The proportion of homeless adults with high school diplomas is about 45 to 50 percent. The National Academy of Sciences cited 45 percent as the overall average, the same figure found in Ohio; however, three New York studies ranged from 47 to 52 percent, and Chicago's average reached 55 percent. Studies in both Memphis and Los Angeles have obtained percentages as high as 66.[52]

These numbers run slightly lower than local averages for the rest of the population. While the differential for Chicago is only 1 percent, it is 4 percent in Los Angeles, and 9 percent in Ohio.[53] Yet, as with the rest of the population, the general trend toward greater education is decisively upward. By comparison, in Nels Anderson's 1934 study of homeless men in New York, the average level of education was about the eighth grade.[54] Although the actual level of functioning nowadays is often several years below the last grade completed, the homeless have indisputably spent more years in school.

Employment

A significant minority of the homeless are employed. In a 1990 survey conducted by the U.S. Conference of Mayors, 24 percent of the population were engaged in either full or part-time work. In some cities— Charleston, Phoenix, and Alexandria, Virginia, for example—more than 40 percent of the population was employed. But 15 percent or less of the population was employed in Chicago, Philadelphia, and Kansas City, and Trenton had the lowest proportion with between 2 and 3 percent.[55]

Casual labor is consistent with the tradition of homelessness in the United States. Typically, men on skid row hired themselves out for short-term employment, for a day's work performing physical labor. Part of the homeless' current work falls within this tradition. Certainly, the jobs have changed, and employment as kitchen help is more likely than employment as a farm hand. Yet one segment of the homeless population has always worked, and despite myths about the population's shiftlessness, it is no different now.

On skid row, work supported a single man who, with a few extra dollars in his pocket, could sleep indoors or buy a pint of liquor. Among the homeless today, however, are an increasing number of employed men and women who work but are not paid a salary large enough to support their families. Their presence among the homeless is a new phenomenon.

Transiency

By and large, the homeless population that cities have is their very own. An indigenous homeless population has made it easier to invoke the tradition of localism in U.S. social policy. Whatever their initial resistance, taxpayers have usually relented in the face of evidence that help for the homeless is help for their poorest neighbors.

Most studies cite similar data. Nationally, 76 percent of the sheltered population have lived for more than one year in the area where the facility was located. Local studies confirm this trend. In a 1984 New York City study, more than 85 percent of the sample listed New York State as their usual place of residence. In Los Angeles, 86 percent of the population had been in the county for two or more years; 72 percent, according to the Rossi study, had spent ten years or more in Chicago. It is only the occasional report—in Portland, Oregon, for example—that shows figures as low as 59 percent for two years of residency.[56]

Length of Stay

The information on length of stay reflects considerable variation among localities. For families in New York City, eleven months is the average, down from thirteen months in previous years. In Los Angeles, however, the average length of stay is just thirty-four days.[57] The average for other cities generally lies between these extremes. In most cases, the median is less than the average, which has been inflated by one segment of the population that has been homeless for a very long time.

Sometimes, information on the length of stay is erroneously interpreted as evidence that homelessness is a short-term phenomenon. For instance, HUD data collected in 1988 indicate that while 23 percent of the population has been homeless for more than three years, 49 percent has been homeless for less than three months.[58] Even though the latter figure includes information gathered from more than one shelter, it still captures only time spent homeless *to date*. Moreover, like other shelter surveys, the 1988 HUD study does not collect data from the population on the street. And finally, as the population grows, tabulations at one point in time are usually going to underestimate the length of the typical spell.[59] Together, all these factors suggest that the average time spent homeless is considerably longer than most shelter surveys indicate.

Veterans

Veterans make up about one-third of the homeless male population. Proportions of exactly one-third have been reported in New York and Los Angeles.[60] Enough other studies have been close to this figure to establish a consensus about it: 28 percent in Milwaukee, 32 percent in Ohio, and 37 percent in Boston.[61] These proportions are actually less than the 41 percent of the male population who are veterans.[62] Nevertheless, one might reasonably expect service in the armed forces to lead to a better life.

Adjustment has been especially difficult for the 16 to 43 percent of these men who served in Vietnam.[63] Many of these veterans have service disabilities, and some suffer from posttraumatic shock syndrome. Having failed to get the help they needed, their homelessness now is a sign that somehow, they have never really come home.

Foster Care

Although it has only occasionally been noted, several studies have found that a substantial minority of the homeless population spent some time as a child in foster care. These studies include 38 percent of the sample identified in Minneapolis, and 29 percent among homeless youth, ages eighteen to twenty-five years, in New York. Similarly, 29 percent of the adults living in the San Francisco area who had spent some time in foster care lacked permanent housing.[64] Despite all the efforts to promote self-sufficiency, foster care did not adequately prepare these children for independence or equip them with the requisite skills.

Any correlation between foster care and subsequent homelessness is particularly disturbing because many children are placed either just before or soon after their families lose their housing. In a New Jersey study of 690 children, 40 percent of the families were homeless at the time of placement.[65] Conversely, from the mothers' perspective, of the 1,635 women in the New York City shelter system whose records were reviewed, 26 percent had children in placement. With an average of 2.16 children in placement per mother, this group, alone, had the startling total of 490 children in foster care.[66] Since some surveys also show that as many as 22 percent of homeless mothers have been investigated on charges of neglect or abuse, it demonstrates that just as it has with so many other policy issues, the problem of homelessness has merged with the problem of child welfare.[67]

AIDS

Homelessness and AIDS overlap, too. New York City has more than 10,000 homeless people with AIDS. In Chicago, 25 percent of the city's 50,000 to 70,000 HIV-drug users described themselves as homeless. Similarly, in Dallas County, advocates estimate the incidence of homelessness among newly diagnosed persons with AIDS at 20 percent.

Sometimes, people who are already homeless contract AIDS. Sometimes, people with AIDS become homeless because they cannot support themselves any longer. Either way, the proportion of homeless people with AIDS is bound to increase, because just a few cities like San Francisco and New York have any supportive housing, and even in these cities, the number of beds are far from adequate. New York City is typical. It has just 1300 housing units available for people with AIDS. If anywhere near 13,000 homeless New Yorkers really do have AIDS, this provision is nowhere near enough.[68]

A Concluding Look

This description of the homeless population makes for a somewhat clearer portrait. But while this portrait contains important data on each attribute, its main theme is broader and more striking: the homeless population encompasses so many subgroups—unaccompanied men, female-headed families, children, substance abusers, the mentally ill, veterans, and the employed. If it were not for their lack of shelter, one subgroup within this cluster might be linked to another—children with families, or substance abusers with the AIDS, but there would be no overarching problem that all of them had in common. Homelessness provides that dismal unity.

Their shared plight demands careful examination. But it also requires balancing the knowledge of their homelessness against an understanding of the distinctive issues within each subgroup. Then it will finally be possible to address the truly crucial question: how did so many different kinds of people ever become homeless?

PART II

Causes

3

The Economic Causes
of Homelessness

I was at a very fancy cocktail party—wealthy, wealthy people—and
they thought I was just wonderful: "Oh, he helps the poor and he
works with them" and all that stuff. One woman asked me, What
would I do if I could change any law or take just one big step to
help the homeless? I said I would raise the minimum wage to $5.
She wouldn't talk to me; she said at $5 she couldn't afford her maid.
Brother Paul Johnson, Camullus House, Miami, Florida

[S]uch an extraordinary income inevitably raises questions as to
whether there isn't something unbalanced in the way our financial
system is working.
David Rockefeller, on the news that junk bond specialist Michael Milken
had earned $550 million in 1987.

Every upsurge in the homeless population has prompted an
intense debate about its causes. The basic positions in this debate have
changed very little over the years. One viewpoint describes the homeless
as lazy, shiftless, and prone to criminality, the other as victims of political
and economic forces beyond their control. The latter argument is a
legacy of the Progressive Era, when American social thought underwent
a major philosophical transformation and began to qualify its presump-
tions of individualism and personal responsibility. Once the "natural
outcome" of laziness and inferior skill, poverty and unemployment were
gradually reconceptualized as a social condition, the product of institutions whose power dwarfed any single individual's drive and
resourcefulness.

Of course, the origins of the belief in individual responsibility go back
much further, to the older tradition of the Protestant ethic in American
politics and culture. When proponents of this ethic first encountered
the explosion of tramping in the 1870s, their depiction of tramps ac-

quired certain conventions that have persisted to the present day. Speaking before the 1877 Conference on State Charities, Yale Professor Francis Wayland defined a tramp as a person without a home who was unwilling to labor. He then went on to describe them in the following terms:

> He fears not God, neither regards man. Indeed, he seems to have wholly lost all the better instincts and attributes of manhood. He will outrage an unprotected female or rob a defenceless child or burn an isolated barn or girdle fruit trees, or wreck a railway train, or set fire to railway bridge, or murder a cripple, or pilfer an umbrella, with indifference if reasonably sure of immunity. Having no moral sense, he knows no graduation in crime.[1]

Some homeless people committed crimes in the 1870s, just as they do now. This description, however, sensationalizes the issue. Accusations about the immorality of all tramps may be less common today. But in every other respect, this speech foreshadows the modern letter to the editor that charges the homeless with "turning our streets into cesspools of lawlessness and crime."[2]

While there is no sign of any permanent closure to this debate, a reanalysis of historical data suggests that from Francis Wayland to the present, charges of shiftlessness and pervasive criminality have seriously mischaracterized the homeless population. In his *Poverty and Policy in American History*, Michael Katz reexamined 5,000 questionnaires filled out by tramps applying for public aid in New York State during the 1870s. What Katz found out about these people bears little resemblance to their public image. Among the men, some 57 percent reported that they were unemployed, and 37 percent said they were destitute. More women—54 percent—described themselves as destitute, though a significant number—37 percent—still asserted that they were unemployed. These figures are about what one would expect in a depression. As Katz explains:

> Tramps, it is true, were largely single, young, or middle-aged men. They also were often foreign born, but they were not recent immigrants, and most of them had started tramping within New York State. Nor, by and large, were they either drunks or illiterates. Nor did they constitute a permanent class. All but a fraction had been tramping less than 1 month. Most had a trade. They were circulating between cities, stopping most often in country towns, looking for work. Given these characteristics, it is hard to imagine that most tramps were dangerous, a threat to the honor of women, the security of property, and the relations between labor and capital.[3]

The mischaracterization of tramps was probably not intentional. Rather, as Katz argues, tramping was linked in the public mind with other manifestations of political disorder such as the Paris Commune, the 1877 railroad strike, and the growth of a labor movement. The collective hysteria brought about by these events blurred real, and not so real, threats to property. The contemporary portrait of tramping emerged from this confusion. The portrait might not be accurate, but surely those who popularized it were genuinely convinced of its accuracy.[4]

The "Causes" of Homelessness

Over the years, the debate about homelessness has contributed to the preparation of some extraordinary lists about its causes. In 1886, William L. Bull reported the results of a questionnaire on the causes of tramping to the thirteenth National Conference of Charities and Correction in St. Paul, Minnesota. The public officials and various charitable organizations who responded identified the following factors:

> Drinking, lack of employment, laziness, war, example, ignorance, lack of home training, dime novels, tobacco, discontent, poverty, shiftlessness, vice, love of roving, heredity, indiscriminate almsgiving or false charity, inability, dishonesty, strikes, depravity, disappointment, worthlessness, immigration, existing type of civilization, improvidence, force of habit, low wages, loss of self-respect, fees made by officers and magistrates, aggregation of capital in manufacturers, socialistic ideas, overpopulation, lack of manhood, lack of a trade, our jail system, imbecility, defective system of education in our public schools, hospitality of jails and almshouses, uncomfortable homes, high temper, industrial causes, ex-convicts, specialization of labor, lack of Wayfarers' Lodges, Chinese, the devil.[5]

Some of the items on this list may seem archaic, but the list as a whole is no less random than its modern counterpart. A comparable list of recent causes would identify all the most commonly cited reasons: economic change, poverty, low wages, the scarcity of affordable housing, social welfare cutbacks, deinstitutionalization, alcoholism, drugs, and the disintegration of the family, as well as the decline of social networks and the loss of community. But it would also include less conventional explanations. The high quality of shelter services have been associated with homelessness. So has rent control, family size, and the birth order of homeless people.[6] After 100 years, some items on the list are the same, and some are different. Yet whatever the merits of each cause, the list itself seems equally fragmented.

This historical record is enough to humble anyone who searches anew for the causes of homelessness. Seeking to narrow the scope of this search, some authors have focused on "proximate rather than ultimate causes ... on the homeless individual rather than on the larger social structures and norms that sustain, tolerate, and justify homelessness and other severe kinds of deprivation."[7] That is unequivocally not the perspective adopted here. The actions of individual homeless people certainly contribute to their plight. But the causes of homelessness are also political and economic, and these causes deserve an analysis of their very own.

The Economic Transformation

Modern homelessness is, to a great extent, a product of the trans-formation of the U.S. economy. Broad economic changes have swept the United States in the last quarter of the twentieth century, and these changes have either caused homelessness, or created the preconditions for its growth.

From the end of World War II until the late 1960s, the United States was the world's dominant economic power. But the American century that some envisioned in the 1950s lasted barely twenty-five years. Instead of being able to set the terms of its leadership, the United States gradually found itself confronted by economic circumstances beyond its control. Business suffered as a result, and in the subsequent economic downturn, government lost tax revenues. Working together to halt these trends, business and government adopted policies that transferred income up-ward and spurred the growth of the homeless population.

Heightened international competition played the single most impor-tant role in upsetting the old equilibrium. When Germany and Japan reconstructed after World War II, they built a more modern industrial plant than the United States. Countries like South Korea, Taiwan, and Brazil soon followed their lead. Employing cheaper labor and using the technologies of the postwar era, these countries could now undersell American industries hampered by higher labor costs and rapidly obso-lescing technology. Steel, automobiles, shoes, electronics, textiles, and machine tools: as American corporations lost their competitive edge, the value of manufacturing goods imported in the United States soared from 14 percent of domestic production in 1969 to 38 percent just ten years later.[8] The economic power of American business was clearly on the wane.

The U.S. military build-up contributed to this loss of competitiveness. U.S. military spending was a powerful economic stimulus as well as an instrument of political containment in the Cold War. But protected by the American build-up from the expense of financing their own military budgets, Germany and Japan invested in nonmilitary research and tech-nology that paid significant economic dividends. By the mid-1970s, Ger-many and Japan were devoting 25.8 percent and 35 percent, respectively, of their real national output to capital investment, while the United States was allocating just 17.5 percent.[9] The paradox was slowly, but insistently, devastating: the same military spending that kept the U.S. economy going funded its economic decline.

The loss of access to a supply of natural resources added to the economic difficulties. Such access had been another crucial element in the era of postwar prosperity. But as a resource-dependent economy steadily depleted the supply, its replenishment became more costly. This was particularly true of oil and other energy resources. Wells drilled in deep water off the Louisiana coast replaced those on the Texas panhandle; more expensive oil imported from the Organization of Petro-leum Exporting Countries (OPEC) substituted for cheaper domestic pe-troleum. The combination of increased costs and greater international competition generated obstacles to continued growth that the United States had not previously faced, and these obstacles crystallized in the economic stagnation of the 1970s.

Changes in the world marketplace were hardly the only changes that business faced. The decline of the capital-labor accord also reverberated throughout the economy. Under the terms of this informal understand-ing, business and labor set aside the antagonisms of the 1930s and de-clared a truce. Business would suspend its campaign against trade unions, and labor would no longer seek to usurp the prerogatives of business. In exchange for accepting the terms of this truce, labor received wage hikes tied to its improving productivity. The mutual benefits flow-ing from this arrangement anchored the business-labor partnership and sustained the growth coalition of the postwar era.[10]

The capital-labor accord, however, did not include everybody. Small businesses—the Taft wing of the Republican party—were excluded, as were those employees, generally women, younger workers, and people of color, who belonged to the nonunionized and less upwardly mobile segments of the labor force. As the success of the capital-labor accord widened the gap between unionized and nonunionized workers, social movements arose among the excluded, and these movements placed new pressures on the business community. Whether women, welfare recipients, and people of color fought for equal treatment or distributive justice, new mechanisms had to be established for addressing their grievances.[11]

These mechanisms were costly. They included the whole array of Great Society programs dealing with poverty, civil rights, and social welfare, and they intruded on business prerogatives in ways both large and small. Poverty and social welfare programs raised the cost of labor by improving the standard of living of the poor and unemployed. To get and keep a labor force, business had to pay its workers more. Sim-ilarly, to the extent that civil rights and affirmative action programs eliminated the old distinctions among employees, they tended to con-solidate wage levels around a higher minimum. Business, which once had to contend solely with labor unions, had been outflanked.

A growing regulatory movement also troubled the private sector. Between 1964 and 1979, Congress enacted thirty-two laws to regulate energy and the environment and another sixty-two laws for the protec-tion of consumers and workers.[12] By trying to protect the air, water, and overall quality of life, regulatory movements challenged the premise that business could lay off the social costs of its operation on other sectors of society. Business had always assumed that while its profits were private, losses in the form of any social cost should be public. When a chemical plant dumped its carcinogenic waste on nearby land, local residents covered their own medical expenses—some, perhaps, with government aid, and the government itself used revenue from taxpayers to pay for the cost of the cleanup. The environmental movement rejected such double-entry bookkeeping. Its argument that business should accept greater responsibility for the consequences of its activities was yet another factor costing business money—as much as $55 billion by some estimates.[13]

Together, these new programs brought about a substantial increase in the size of government. In 1948, federal, state, and local expenditures amounted to 19.5 percent of the gross national product. By 1979, this number had risen to 31.2 percent.[14] A debate has long raged about the meaning of this increase, with some contending that it was the cause of the U.S. economic difficulties. That seems unlikely. The most rapid expansion of government in the postwar era has always occurred in good economic times, suggesting that government expansion is as much an effect of economic growth as it is a cause. Moreover, since government occupies an even larger role in all the major Western European countries, it is quite implausible to claim that the size of government alone explains such wide variations in economic performance.[15]

Yet setting this debate aside, there is no gainsaying the importance of the transformation that had taken place. From financing the construction of the Erie Canal to the contribution of land for the building of railroads, the actual role of government in the economy has always towered over its image in the popular mind. Nevertheless, the growth of the government after World War II did signify a different level of economic involvement. The government stimulated business activity, as spending on the military and spending on social welfare worked synergistically, to keep the economy from falling back into its pre-World War II state. At the same time, though, the deficit spending required to inject this stimulus gave the economy an inflationary bias. As a result, when both unemployment and inflation reached postwar heights in the 1974–75 recession, government lay open to the charge that its policies had slowed rather than stimulated the economy.

Perhaps nothing better captures the new conditions facing American business than its declining rate of profitability. Intensified competition pressured business in the international economic arena. Social movements, social regulation, and a labor force demanding immunity from inflation pressured business on the domestic front. These developments reduced the average net after-tax profit of domestic nonfinancial corporations from nearly 10 percent in 1965 to less than 6 percent during the last half of the 1970s.[16]

Clearly, business had to do something. The transition to a new economic era cost corporations some of their power. Setting out to regain what they had lost, they sought to ensure that when business was conducted in the future, it was certain to be conducted on more favorable terms.

The Corporate Response

Making American business competitive meant making it "mean and lean." It meant removal of all the obstacles to successful competition. Most of all, though, it meant channeling more money into the hands of wealthy people, even if that made others poor and homeless.

The latter notion resonates powerfully through a private enterprise economy. Investments by wealthy people make the economy go. When wealthy people stop investing because demand lags and there are insufficient opportunies for profit, the economy slows. From the capital formation crisis of the mid-1970s, to the supply-side remedies of the 1980s, and continuing on through to the pleas for economic growth in the 1990s, getting more money into the hands of wealthy people has been a fundamental objective of business.

This analysis of the remedy for the decline of American economic power is, of course, patently self-interested. Yet many Americans accepted it. Part of the reason they accepted it stems from an instinctive reliance on what had worked before. Amid stagflation and a gnawing sense of decline, it was easy to argue that business had somehow been deprived of the tools necessary to fulfill its proper economic role. The argument was made all the more seductive by business advocates who consistently disguised its form. There was talk of "pain," and a "new social contract,"[17] but enough Americans were confident of their own impunity to believe that the victim of this pain could only be somebody else. Since the mid–1970s, it is this segment of the American electorate that has given the corporate response its political viability.

The linchpin of this response was the campaign for tax reduction. In 1981, Congress enacted the Economic Recovery Tax Act, a modified version of the Kemp-Roth bill that cut taxes a total of 25 percent in three successive years. The formulation of Kemp-Roth illustrates the skill with which conservatives took a goal that had very limited appeal—reducing the top rate on the richest taxpayers—and broadened its political base. As David Stockman, director of the Office of Management and Budget later admitted in a famous interview,

> the hard part of the supply-side tax cut is dropping the top rate from 70 to 50 percent—the rest of it is a secondary matter. The original argument was that the top bracket was too high, and that's having the most devastating effect on the economy. Then, the general argument was in order to make this palatable as a political matter, you had to bring down all the brackets. But, I mean, Kemp-Roth was always a Trojan Horse to bring down the top rate.[18]

Having structured the act to obtain sufficient political support, the wealthy benefited far more than poor and middle-income people from its provisions. A fixed percentage tax reduction distributed income upward because it gave those with more money relatively larger post-tax incomes. Hence, by 1984, the average tax reduction attributable to the 1981 tax cuts for those in bottom quintile was $3; for the top quintile, it was $2,429.[19]

The act had a similar effect on corporate taxes. Although the statutory tax rate remained unchanged at 46 percent, the effective marginal tax rate was reduced from 32 percent in 1980 to just 18 percent in 1981. In practice, the law was so generous that many major businesses—General Electric, Boeing, and Pepsico, among them—paid no taxes, and the federal government actually owed money to some corporations. Among financial institutions, in particular, the rate declined from 5.8 percent in 1980 to −3.8 percent in 1982.[20] At tax refund time as well as the rest of the year, Americans were giving the banks money.

The return to corporate profitability also depended on an improved capacity to compete with other foreign countries. Several major policies were advanced for this purpose. First, and perhaps most harsh, was the Federal Reserve Bank's tight money policy of 1981–82, which induced the single biggest recession of the postwar era. Determined to drive inflation down to more tolerable levels, Federal Chairman Paul Volcker clung to a monetary policy that produced a 10.8 percent unemployment rate and the failure of 24,900 businesses, the highest number since 1933.

Despite these business failures, the pain was not distributed evenly. Softening the labor market weakened the bargaining power of workers. As a consequence, labor absorbed 59 percent of the $570 billion lost in output from 1981 to 1983; farmers and small proprietors shouldered the burden of another 25 percent. No one knows exactly how many of these people became homeless; however, an Urban Institute study estimated that in the period 1979–82, these tight money policies produced a $148 billion transfer of income upward to the 10 percent of American families who owned 86 percent of the nation's net financial wealth.[21]

To enhance its competitiveness, the business sector also fought hard for social deregulation. Reagan quickly implemented many of the policies it favored. Between 1981 and 1985, he cut 8 percent (in constant dollars) from the budgets of the regulatory agencies. His administration reduced personnel at the Consumer Product Safety Commission by more than a third and pared the Occupational Safety and Health Administration (OSHA) staff by almost a quarter.[22] Enforcement slackened immediately. At OSHA, for example, complaint inspections declined 58 percent, while subsequent inspections dropped 87 percent. With total penalties down 78 percent, manufacturers could expect to pay an average of just $6.50 per violation.[23] For those seeking to reestablish the principle that profits are private and losses are public, $6.50 a violation was a bargain indeed.

The Reagan administration also tried to alter the regulatory environment by changing the membership and policies of the National Labor Relations Board (NLRB). The administration's appointees were often explicitly antiunion. They included people like Donald Dotson, a man-

agement lawyer for Wheeling-Pittsburgh Steel and formerly labor counseling for Westinghouse and Western Electric. Dotson opined that "collective bargaining frequently means labor monopoly, the destruction of
individual freedom, and the destruction of the marketplace as the mechanism for determining the value of labor." Hugh Reilly, the NLRB's
new solicitor, had previously been staff attorney for the National Right
to Work Legal Defense Foundation and continued to work for the foundation after he accepted his government appointment.[24]

These appointments had a direct effect on policy. In 1983–85,
charges of unfair labor practices were sustained 50 percent of the time,
down from the 84 percent rate in 1975–76 when, for a while, all the
board members were Republicans. Employers also won two-thirds of all
representation cases, compared to a simple majority won by the unions
under Ford and Carter. In addition, the NLRB case backlog rose from
400 to an all-time high of almost 1,700 cases. As the likelihood of a quick
positive decision evaporated, so did much of labor's power within the
government bureaucracy.[25]

Labor did not do any better in direct contract negotiations with business. In 1980, no union signed a contract in which it accepted a wage
reduction for the agreement's first year. By 1982, though, 44 percent
of the unionized workforce had signed such contracts. Even in 1985, at
the height of the recovery, management was still compelling 33 percent
of the unionized workforce to agree to these terms.[26] Two-tier wage
agreements for new and current workers also proliferated, until they
covered one-third of the employees in unions. Lastly, in response to the
corporate demand for "flexibility" and low benefits, the number of contingent laborers, including temporary workers, involuntary part-timers,
and home employees, grew from 8 million people in 1980 to 18 million
in 1985, or almost 17 percent of the workforce.[27] Squeezed by business,
labor could neither organize effectively nor face its adversaries on equal
terms at the bargaining table.

One indication of labor's diminished political clout was the long
drought between increases in the minimum wage. The minimum wage
only covers about 5.5 percent of the labor force, or 4.7 million people,
but it does establish a floor for salaries. Any increase would boost this
floor and send ripples upward through the labor market. When Congress
raised the wage in 1977, it set the floor at $2.30 an hour and phased in
gradual raises until the minimum reached $3.35 in 1981. By 1989, how-
ever, inflation had reduced the value of the minimum to the equivalent
of about $2.00, the lowest rate since 1956. Despite growing concern that
people could be working, poor, and possibly even homeless, President
Bush initially vetoed a bill that would have raised the minimum to $4.55
wage before agreeing to $4.25 an hour in 1991. At the lower wage and
with a subminimum for teenagers, the legislation represented a very
modest victory for labor.[28]

Homelessness, Deindustrialization, and
the Growth of the Service Economy

Deindustrialization and the growth of a service economy were crucial factors in the largely successful drive waged by business to increase its power over workers. In a period of economic transition, they helped business to reduce the leverage and income of its salaried employees. This loss of income was, indisputably, the prime economic cause of homelessness.[29]

The process of deindustrialization has its roots going back to the height of American economic dominance in the postwar era. In 1960, before competition intensified from other countries, the manufacturing sector employed 28.2 percent of all American workers. But as the efficiency of the domestic industry declined, goods were either purchased from increasingly competitive producers overseas, or American companies, in an attempt to regain their competitiveness, transferred production to other, lower-wage countries.

The high deficits run by the Reagan administration quickened this process. The administration bought the uneven prosperity of its years in office by borrowing $20,000 on behalf of each family of four. But only an overvalued dollar could entice the foreign capital necessary to finance these deficits. When this inflated dollar increased the cost of exports and made imported goods relatively cheap, a weakened manufacturing sector was simply unable to sell its products. As a result, by 1987, the trade deficit had reached $159 billion, and the manufacturing sector employed 19 percent of the American workforce. It is expected to decline to 14 percent by the year 2000.[30]

Deindustrialization effected a true economic transformation. In its most rapid phase between 1979 and 1984, 11.5 million workers lost their jobs because of plant shutdowns, relocations, rising productivity, or shrinking output, including 5.1 million who had held their jobs for more than three years and were officially designated as displaced. By 1984, 1.3 million had still not found jobs but were looking, another 730,000 had dropped out of the labor market, and at least half of those who found jobs were forced to take cuts in pay. The same trend persisted even when the economy recovered later in the 1980s. Deindustrialization might be exacerbated by the business cycle, but it did not merely mirror it. Even as it lowered wages and jeopardized peoples' housing, deindustrialization remained, in every respect, a phenomenon all its own.[31]

Just as over the course of a century or more, industry gradually came to replace agriculture, so the current decline of industry has been matched by the explosive growth of an economy based on services. Most popular analyses make only the most casual connection between these two kinds of economic activity. The central assumption in this mode of analysis is interchangeability. If the economy used to be industrial and is now more service-oriented, one can be painlessly substituted for the other, because every economy, after all, has to be organized around something. There is, in these analyses, little sense that the decline of industry is somehow related to the rise of a service economy.

The connection, though, is an intimate one. Growth in the size and complexity of industrial corporations have themselves fostered the growth in services. As products have become more differentiated and markets have steadily diversified, the need for technical workers to man-age the corporation—to plan, develop, and market goods—has expanded accordingly. Indeed, a major part of this expansion has occurred in order to provide the services required by these better paid corporate employees. With both parents in the workforce, many functions that used to be handled in the home have been parceled out to a second tier of lower-wage service jobs: one service worker cleans their clothes at the neighborhood laundromat, another waits on them in a restaurant when the adults are too tired to cook after a long day at the office, and a third takes care of their children. The family is securely housed, the workers, somewhat less so. Hence the service economy has evolved out of the transformation of the modern *industrial* corporation, and this corporation has transformed the jobs of its workforce, just as surely as it has transformed their lives at home.[32]

The appearance of the global office represents one of the more striking indications of this trend. Linked by telecommunications, corporations have begun to ship some of the less technically skilled jobs overseas to cheaper labor markets. One insurance company, New York Life, moved its claims division to Castleisland, Ireland, where labor costs at $14,000 annually are half the U.S. rate. In making the move to Ireland, New York Life joined the McGraw-Hill Publishing Company, which had already started to process subscription renewal and marketing information from Galway. Similarly, American Airlines has established Carribean Data Services, whose 1,050 employees in Barbados and the Dominican Republic handle reservation information for itself and other interested airlines.[33] These moves demonstrate that service industries have begun to follow manufacturing companies in their search for cheaper labor outside the United States. By putting greater wage pressures on the lower rung of technically skilled workers, this search further splits service industry employees into high and low-wage groups, into the well- and poorly housed.

Overseas and at home, the growth of a service economy is closely associated with the need for a more educated workforce. As education becomes ever more closely tied to the needs of the labor market, the corporate sector has expressed great concern about the skills that applicants possess. In 1987, for example, the *Wall Street Journal* reported that when New York Telephone gave a fifty minute basic reasoning test to 21,000 applicants for entry level jobs, only 16 percent passed. Since more than half the jobs created in the 1984–2000 period will require some education beyond high school, applicants who failed such tests severely limit their prospects in the job and housing markets.[34] By the year 2000, there will be 2.5 million new workers in restaurants, bars, and fast-food outlets, another 500,000 in hotels and motels, and almost 400,000 in department stores. These jobs pay low wages. Optimists like to point out that professions like computer technician, with 250,000 new positions, are among the fastest growing. But they fail to emphasize that the biggest increase in absolute numbers will occur in those low-wage jobs to which most people with poor educations are headed.[35]

More generally, the suspicion that the process of deindustrialization has contributed to a split labor market has sparked a vigorous debate. Bennett Harrison and Barry Bluestone, the best-known proponents of this view, maintain that deindustrialization correlates one-to-one with an increase in the size of the low-wage group: for every 1 percent decline in the number of industrial workers, there is an equivalent increase in the number of low-wage workers. Harrison and Bluestone's most famous study, which was prepared for the Joint Economic Committee of the U.S. Congress, found that 44 percent of the new jobs created from 1979 to 1985 paid less than $7,400 in 1986 dollars, as compared to 20 percent in the 1963–73 period.[36]

When some critics disputed this study, Harrison and Bluestone tried to respond to their criticism.[37] They checked for indications that either the entry of the baby boomers into the labor market or the influence of the business cycle might have unduly altered their conclusions. They also recalculated the data, substituting the less inflationary Personal Consumption Index (PCE) from the Bureau of Economic Statistics for the Consumer Price Index. In this reanalysis, the numbers changed somewhat, but the pattern remained fundamentally the same. Between 1973 and 1979, 20 percent of new workers earned less than $11,103 a year in 1986 dollars. Between 1979 and 1986, however, the figure rose to 36 percent.[38] Since data also show that the median hourly wage for all U.S. workers dropped, from $8.52 in 1973 to $7.46 in 1990,[39] their thesis has become ever more convincing: deindustrialization and the growth of a service economy does correlate with the proliferation of low-wage labor.

While the effects of this transformation pervade every sector of society, it has had particularly traumatic consequences for people of color in the central city. Their unemployment rate has always been higher than among whites in other geographic areas. Still, the good jobs that did exist were industrial: they paid relatively well and demanded little formal education. Deindustrialization has eliminated these jobs and replaced them with positions that have higher educational requirements. Central city residents cannot secure these positions because although their education has improved over the last twenty years, educational requirements have advanced at an even faster rate.[40]

These changes in the social structure of the central city have initiated a process of what sociologists William J. Wilson and Lois Wacquant call *hyperghettoization.* Hyperghettoization concentrates the poorest people of color in small geographic areas. It destroys all the major social structures of the inner city and sends ghettos, whose social institutions once hung by a slender thread, into a free fall. As unemployment rises, housing deteriorates, and students fail to graduate from the local public schools, hyperghettoization begins to gnaw away at the system of social supports that previously sustained life in the inner city. Now when residents lose their jobs or are evicted from their apartments, neither local institutions nor local people are themselves strong enough to halt their descent into the streets.[41]

The Effects of the Economic Transformation

Both in the ghetto and elsewhere, the business campaign interacted with deindustrialization and the growth of a service economy to create the preconditions for the contemporary upsurge of homelessness. Manifesting themselves in every major indicator of income and wealth, these preconditions show a significant decline in financial resources for people well up the income scale.

Yet people at the very top of the economic pyramid benefited considerably from this shift. By bringing about an economic transformation on their terms, they got the money that was supposed to spark an economic recovery. Unfortunately, the only kind of economic recovery it could spark was income-polarizing, and an income-polarizing economic recovery placed many poor people at risk. Their risk of homelessness, their deepening poverty, is therefore less a random occurrence than the direct consequence of these specific political and economic policies.

The extent of this income polarization has been thoroughly documented. In one typical study, the Congressional Budget Office (CBO) estimated that between 1980 and 1990, the income of the poorest tenth of U.S. households decreased by 8.6 percent, to an average of $4,695. At the other end of the income range, families did much better. The top fifth increased its income by 29.8 percent; the top 5 percent by 44.9 percent; and the richest 1 percent by 75.3 percent, to an average of $548,969. As a result of this trend, the top 1 percent of U.S. households—some 2.5 million people—have nearly as much after tax income as the 100 million people who constitute the bottom 40 percent.[42]

Something fundamental has been happening to income distribution in the United States, because this skewing is not merely restricted to the extremes. The proportion of middle-income people has also been falling. Census data show that in 1989, the middle 60 percent of U.S. families received only 50.8 percent of the national income, the lowest percentage recorded since the Census Bureau first began collecting this information in 1947. Since the poorest fifth of the population received just 4.6 percent of all U.S. income, these data meant that in the aggregate, the bottom four-fifths of all U.S. families were receiving less, proportionately, than ever before.[43]

A parallel trend has also occurred in the data on the distribution of wealth. A study by the Joint Economic Committee of Congress—later modified under political pressure—revealed that in 1983, the top 0.5 percent of American households owned 35.1 percent of the wealth held by families, up almost 10 percent from the 25.4 percent figure of twenty years earlier. The distribution is still more skewed if personal residences—the single most common, nonliquid asset of nearly everybody else—is excluded. The top 0.5 percent then hold 45 percent of all private wealth in the United States. Increasing 38 percent in the preceding twenty years, this figure also stood at the highest concentration ever recorded.[44]

This transfer of income and wealth inevitably evokes the powerful American myth that money appears magically, without being taken from anybody. When new wealth and income materialize among the richest segment of the population, this myth says their gain was nobody's loss. Instead, the money they got was earned, ever bigger pieces of an infinitely expanding pie.

The experience of the last two decades should disprove this myth. Tracing the source of this transfer of money upward, researchers have found that greater inequality accounts for 55 percent of the doubling in the number of rich people, from 3.1 percent of the population in 1973 to 6.9 percent in 1987. They defined *rich* as nine times the poverty level, or about $95,000 in 1987 dollars. An increase in the earnings of family members other than the head of the household are said to explain the rest.[45]

Amid all this data about the upward shift, there is one statistic that has especially direct implications for the homeless. During the period from 1973 to 1987, additional revenue from property constituted 45 percent of the income growth among the top 1 percent of the population.[46] The upward shift in income affected many individuals, but it is still difficult to assert with confidence that it did any more than create the preconditions for widespread homelessness. The link with the data about the role of property income, however, is much more direct. Since revenue from real property significantly increased the income of the wealthy, it is highly likely that these increases in income actually caused homelessness among some people.

The Economic Causes of Homelessness

An industrial plant closes. Despite vigorous opposition from the local union, the company moves its assembly line overseas to Taiwan. Some employees who had bought houses in the vicinity lose their jobs. A few get other lower paying jobs and manage to eke out a living. Several, though, cannot make the mortgage payments. After six months staying with family and friends who are themselves struggling to cope with a depressed local economy, these employees end up homeless in an emergency shelter.

This is a "purest case" example of an economic cause. Some people have surely become homeless in this way, but paths to homelessness that are much less direct may still be fundamentally economic in their origins. After all, housing is a commodity in this society for which people are expected to pay. Unless public assistance intercedes, those who cannot pay become homeless.

In surveys of the homeless, this lack of money takes many forms. Unemployment is the most obvious. Twenty-one percent of the homeless people in a Ohio survey cited it as the reason for their predicament. Yet this statistic contains only part of their story; another 13.9 percent blamed their homelessness on "problems paying the rent."[47] They, too, were apparently suffering from a shortage of funds.

Ambiguities like this pervade studies all across the country. By locality, unemployment figures among the homeless range from 28 percent among women in New York up to 76 percent in Salt Lake City, Utah.[48] But alongside this statistic, there are usually other categories in the surveys masking an inadequate income. As with any other cause of homelessness, these explanations are not unicausal, and cannot be taken too literally. Nevertheless, they probably account for about half of the homelessness described in a typical survey.[49]

Ultimately, though, surveys tend to fragment the economic causes of homelessness by creating a set of false distinctions. Certainly, it is useful to specify the precise form that a lack of money takes. But too often the form—whether it be unemployment or eviction for nonpayment of rent—gets confused with the cause. People become homeless because they cannot afford housing. That so many people can no longer afford housing is a consequence of the response of business to changing economic conditions. Business sought to regain its competitiveness, but it did so by lowering everyone else's standard of living. From deregulation to tax policy and the assault on labor unions, this response left the bottom four-fifths of the U.S. population with less money. Hence, whatever form the lack of money takes, this business response is the true economic cause of contemporary homelessness.

4

The Contraction
of Social Welfare

The fundamental principle with respect to the legal relief of the poor is, that the condition of the pauper ought to be, on the whole, less eligible than that of the independent laborer.
The British Poor Law Reform of 1834

Welfare should be treated as a response to a temporary emergency, not a permanent way of life. Our goal should be to get people off welfare, not to encourage them to remain on public assistance by giving them options working people don't have.
EDWARD KOCH, mayor of New York, 1988

Welfare must pay less than work. The principle of *less eligibility* held true in nineteenth-century England; it is equally true more than 150 years later in the United States. Britain first established the principle in the Poor Law Reform of 1834. To this day, it would be hard to improve upon the Poor Law Commissioners' original rationale. They wrote that

> ... in proportion as the condition of any pauper class is elevated above the condition of independent laborers, the condition of the independent class is depressed; their industry is impaired, their employment becomes unsteady, and its remuneration in wages is diminished. Such persons, therefore, are under the strongest inducements to quit the less eligible class of laborers and enter the more eligible class of paupers. The converse is in effect when the pauper class is placed in its proper position below the condition of the independent laborer. Every penny bestowed, that tends to render the condition of the pauper more eligible than that of the independent laborer, is a bounty on indolence and vice.[1]

People must work to support themselves in a market economy. For those who do not, there must be consequences.

Although some countries such as Sweden, Norway, Denmark, and the Netherlands reject this policy and give benefits to everyone regardless of income, their universalistic approach has never been integrated into the Anglo-American tradition of social welfare. The Anglo-American countries have instead stressed means-tested programs and the principle of less eligibility.[2] Harsher in practice, this principle nonetheless remains defensible as long as the working poor are paid enough so that those on public assistance can survive with an even lower standard of living. Serious problems arise, though, when the lowest paid worker's standard of living declines, and the principle dictates that a person on public assistance must receive still *less*. At this level of subsistence, most people juggle payment for the barest necessities, and the decision to skimp on food or skimp on housing is largely a matter of individual preference.

Such a downward trend has been operative in the United States since the early 1970s. In keeping with the principle of less eligibility, the decline in the cost of labor brought about by the economic transformation necessitated a reduction in the adequacy of social welfare. As always, wages and welfare operated in tandem. Unless the government cut back on social welfare, any effort to make the United States competitive by reducing labor costs would push the going wage for poor working people below the welfare standard. In both the industrializing Britain of the past and the deindustrializing United States of the present, it was only by limiting social welfare that business could manage the workforce.

The budget deficit aggravated the demand for the resulting cutbacks. The public had always been ambivalent about programs for the poor, wanting to help the needy but fearful that welfare sometimes squandered money on many who were perfectly able. The new economic conditions intensified these feelings. Under the pressure of the budget deficit and the need to make the economy competitive again, many voters temporarily lost their ambivalence. Social programs, they said, too often served the wrong people. Before long, this view drove them to the conclusion that the cost of social programs was beyond what the budget could bear.

The social programs cut back encompassed more than just public welfare. In popular terminology, welfare is usually equated with public assistance, primarily Aid to Families with Dependent Children (AFDC). The reductions, though, affected virtually every social program. Some policy analysts refer to the *social wage* as a concept for describing social welfare programs in the aggregate. In this usage, the social wage represents the combination of cash and services that government provides to its citizens. By providing an alternative means of support, the social wage frees people from their reliance on personal earnings.

From the outset, the Reagan administration did not merely attack AFDC. Rather, it sought to reduce the entire social wage. David Stockman, director of the Office of Management and Budget, clearly articulated the philosophy underlying this policy: "The idea that has been established over the last ten years, that almost every service that anyone might need in life ought to be provided and financed by government as a matter of right, is wrong. We reject that notion."[3] The Reagan administration acted forcefully on this perspective. Throughout its years in office, it tried to get people to substitute a dependence on the labor market for a dependence on government.

The growth of the social wage weakened the effect of unemployment on labor. It threatened to erode the concept of less eligibility. Comparatively low unemployment in the postwar period contributed to this erosion. From 1946 to 1979, unemployment averaged just 6.2 percent, compared to 10.4 percent from 1890 to 1914, and 14.9 percent from 1920 to 1939.[4] Between a decline in the rate of unemployment and an increase in the social wage, workers had too little to fear. More than ever before, they could get a job when they wanted one and quit if they were poorly paid or did not like the working conditions. The number of employees who actually exercised this option might vary, with fewer people taking advantage of it in bad economic times. But independent of the business cycle, the option itself was always there, undermining labor discipline and hampering business efforts to reorganize the economy for the world marketplace.

The Reduction of the Social Wage

Declining salaries make it harder for the working poor to pay for housing; a declining social wage heightens the risk of homelessness among its recipients. Although the most obvious method of reducing the social wage is to decrease the amount of the benefit, this reduction can actually take many other forms.

Obstructing the receipt of social benefits is one traditional strategem for reducing their value. A long waiting line is typical of this kind of reduction. Government can also reduce the value of the social wage by attaching conditions to benefits, such as an insistence on work. Lastly, when the program in question provides not cash but a service, the same effect may be achieved by degrading its quality. A homeless man, for example, is less likely to use a shelter where there are 700 beds crowded into a space meant for 400. Whether these methods are used separately or in combination, they contract the social wage and reduce the living standard of the poor. They may also compel that portion of the poor population which can work to do so for less pay.

All of these techniques have been used recently. But while officials often publicized cutbacks in income security programs, they have been far more reticent in describing the equally dramatic effects of changes in welfare practice. By denying people access to benefits, these changes have significantly deflated the value of the social wage.

The Southern Governor's Association and the Southern Legislative Association sponsored a study that underscores the importance of these changes. Conducted by Sarah Shuptrine, this research discovered that although agencies rejected 7 percent of the public assistance applicants for owning or earning too much, 16 percent were turned down for problems with their applications. Even more significantly, the study found that in the period from 1980 to 1986, there was a 75 percent increase in the number of welfare applications rejected for procedural reasons. The state of Texas had the worst record. In fiscal year 1985–86, it denied 45 percent of all AFDC applications and classified 69 percent of these denials as a failure to comply with procedural requirements.[5]

The closing and reopening of welfare cases has also become a common practice. Called *churning*, this practice has grown as a consequence of some of the administrative requirements introduced in the 1970s, including greater documentation and face-to-face recertifications of need. In New York City, for instance, cases may be reopened when the client complies with these administrative requirements, files a change of address, or persuades the agency that its actions were erroneous. New York credits administrative closings with bringing down the New York City error rate from nearly 19 percent in 1975 to about 3.6 percent in 1985. But this statistic is biased downward. It captures only those who were paid when they should not have been, not those legitimate applicants whom the new procedures deterred. It also fails to acknowledge the havoc that the procedure wreaks. Clients experiencing thirty-day administrative closings do get retroactive benefits. Yet with administrative closings affecting an estimated 47,980 cases in 1983, some clients undoubtedly went hungry and faced eviction because they had no money for thirty days.[6]

The timing of this crackdown is, of course, broadly consistent with the historical pattern, which Piven and Cloward have described in their classic *Regulating the Poor*. Before the economy slowed, the extensive welfare rights organizing of the 1960s contributed to the growth of the social wage. But once this organizing dissipated, the social wage declined, and the poor faced a harsher version of less eligibility. As usual, the government retrenched some public assistance programs. There was an important difference in this crackdown, however. By now, many other social benefits and services had been established, and these welfare state programs remained largely intact.[7]

Cutbacks in Income Security Programs

Five income security programs absorbed the brunt of the reduction in the cash portion of the social wage. These programs are AFDC; Old Age Survivors Insurance (OASI, commonly called Social Security); disability benefits (Social Security Disability Insurance, SSDI, and Supplemental Security Income, SSI); food stamps; and unemployment insurance. The federal government adopted several different strategies to carry out these retrenchments. Sometimes, it slashed the amount of the benefit; sometime, it sought to cut back on the number of recipients; and sometimes, it did both. But regardless of the specific strategy, the outcome left many people who had depended on these programs with less income.

AFDC

AFDC was the prime, and perhaps the easiest, target. It provides assistance to families with children. In fiscal year 1990, the national AFDC caseload numbered about 3,967,000, or a total of slightly more than 11.4 million people, at a combined cost—federal and state—of 18.5 billion.[8]

AFDC was an easy target because it is a stigmatized program. This stigma has at least three distinct sources. First, although two-thirds of all recipients are children, AFDC is perceived as assistance to the unworthy poor because in half the cases, the parents were never married. Second, since women constitute the vast majority of caretakers, the public has often been eager to punish them for their failure to work. Lastly, there is the racial composition of AFDC: 38 percent white, 40 percent African-American, and 16 percent Latino.[9] While the white population is probably larger than popularly thought, it has never been large enough to counter the myth that the vast majority of AFDC recipients were people of color.

Adroitly blending these vulnerabilities with the new demands for a lower social wage, the Reagan administration immediately set out to slash AFDC. During its years in office, it altered eligibility and payment standards three times, cutting a total of $3.6 billion and eliminating 442,000 people from the national caseload.[10] Many of these reductions were specifically directed at working families, 250,000 of whom lost their eligibility, while another 200,000 had their benefits reduced.[11] In its study of this issue, the General Accounting Office found that these families lost an average of $124 to $216 monthly, or $1,500 to $2,600 a year, a substantial decrease in purchasing power for people of limited means.[12]

These cutbacks come on top of the long-term deflation in the value of AFDC benefits. From 1970 to 1991, the median decline in benefit levels adjusted for inflation was 42 percent; just one state—California—raised benefits in this period. In no state does the value of AFDC benefits for three people exceed 82 percent of the official poverty line, and in half the states, it pays less than 42 percent. At this level, Illinois, the median state, grants a one parent family of three persons $367 a month, or $4,404 a year. In all, thirty-five states have maximum AFDC benefits that do not even meet their own standard of need.[13]

Although a reduced AFDC grant put welfare families at risk of homelessness, it was not the only method of reaffirming the principle of less eligibility. Work programs were also necessary in order to ensure that families receiving AFDC had a lower standard of living. There is, of course, a long history of using work for these ends, a history which reflects a national ambivalence in the attitude toward work.[14] Americans believe that work redeems, but they also think that work punishes: work can make people whole, but it can also break them of their willfulness. If some people are poor, and work offers the promise of both punishment and redemption, then work programs are going to be implemented whenever poverty spreads. For Americans, this is almost an instinctive response, one with both culture and history on its side.

In eighteenth-century Boston, the poor chopped wood at a workhouse on the Commons in exchange for shelter. In New York City, social reformers tried to deter vagrants by installing a treadmill at the Bellevue Complex in the early 1820s. Later, in New York, there were work programs for the poor at Blackwell—now Roosevelt's Island—in the 1840s, and long discussions about the possibilities of labor camps for the homeless during the early part of this century. In many cities throughout the country, work tests for the homeless were a fact of shelter life.[15]

Modern work programs now encompass a wider range of activities, from voluntary participation in a job search to compulsory work equal to the cost of a recipient's welfare grant. Yet short of changes in the labor market and a well-funded job training program, none of these activities are, nor are they likely to be, very successful. Arising out of the conflict between the desire to impose labor discipline and the pressure to reduce welfare costs, work programs consistently founder on the failure to achieve one, or sometimes, both of these objectives. But this history does not prevent successive generations of public officials from rediscovering work as a policy tool and trying once again. The latest example of this pattern is the Family Support Act of 1988.

The product of a widespread dissatisfaction with the welfare system, the Family Support Act of 1988 made a number of important changes in the AFDC program.[16] First, and perhaps most significantly, the act required that by 1995, states develop job search, training, or work programs for 20 percent of its AFDC recipients, including women with children younger than three years of age (one year or less if the state chooses). The AFDC-UP (Unemployed Parent) program, which was operative in only twenty-eight states, will become mandatory, though states can limit the participation of two-parent families to six months a year. By 1992, 40 percent of these AFDC-UP recipients must spend sixteen hours of work weekly in exchange for their benefits, with the proportion rising to 70 percent in 1997.

The act also emphasizes parental responsibility by legislating automatic child support deductions from the paychecks of absent fathers. With the states required to establish paternity in an escalating number of child support cases, the CBO expects this provision to save state and federal governments a total of $1.039 billion by 1993. No one would quarrel with the moral imperative underlying this provision: obviously, fathers should support their children. The problem is that many fathers of children receiving AFDC are poor, and their failure to contribute to their child's support stems as least as much from their own meager paycheck as it does from a faulty sense of moral responsibility: if full payment had been made to all women owed child support monies in 1985, the average woman would still have received less than $2,500. True, in 1988, the collection of child support payments did gain the states $381 million. But since the effort cost the federal government $357 million, a more measured judgment would suggest that expectations of sizeable financial savings have been greatly oversold.[17]

Transitional child care and medicaid payments have been widely touted as the two most progressive aspects of the legislation. In the past, the absence of child care and the loss of medicaid benefits have obstructed the path of many AFDC parents who sought private employment. Even if one could obtain child care, medical coverage was rare in the low-paying jobs most likely to be open to a welfare mother. To remove these economic disincentives, the bill offers one year of transitional child care and medical coverage. Despite the likelihood of limited income at the end of this year, employees are then expected to join the ranks of the working poor who struggle on their own to obtain these benefits.

Proponents of the Family Support Act relied heavily on studies conducted by the Manpower Demonstration Research Corporation (MDRC). Funded jointly by private foundations and the state governments operating the workfare programs under study, MDRC monitored the outcome of workfare experiments in eight states: Arkansas, California (San Diego), Illinois (Chicago), Maine, Maryland (Baltimore), New Jersey, Virginia, and West Virginia. These experiments showed very slight results. Employment among workfare participants increased an average of about 5 percent over control groups who did not participate. In San Diego, for example, 61 percent of the experimental group left AFDC within fifteen months, as compared to 55 percent among the control group. Increases in earnings were also very small, in the range of $110 to $560 a person, except in West Virginia, where there were no gains at all.[18]

One would hardly expect findings like these to spur a significant piece of social legislation. Yet both Congress and the media packaged this research as the justification for a major social reform. Senator Daniel Moynihan, one of the leading sponsors of the bill, praised the study as "rigorous scientific research" and "the best work of its kind ever done." And while the *New York Times'* expectation of modest savings tempered its enthusiasm, *Fortune* claimed that the research showed "states can reduce spending by propelling welfare recipients into the workforce."[19] The approval with which the study was greeted confirms the moment we have reached: once again in American history, work has been determined to "cure" welfare.

In fact, based on the research alone, there is little evidence for such a belief. The experimental programs studied the effects of workfare on women with school age children who were applying for welfare; The Family Support Act targets current welfare recipients with children younger than three years of age.[20] Whatever results were obtained for the experimental population are sure to evaporate as the states implement the program for the latter, more difficult group.

The replication of eight experimental programs nationwide will also dilute the outcome. The Reagan administration's Omnibus Budget Reconcilation Act (OBRA) of 1981 authorized the experiments that MDRC studied. They were special programs, designed to show that making work a condition of welfare could reduce the size of the AFDC population. Although the results of this experiment were scarcely spectacular, they are certain to be further muted once the program is implemented in every state.

Lastly, even after they participated in the program, the test group continued to be desperately poor. This fact tended to be minimized amid the talk of 8 to 37 percent increases in earnings. Participants in San Diego received the most income, and their yearly total from both work and welfare amounted to just $5,313. At the other extreme, in Arkansas, the total yearly income after participation in the program was $1,611— $582 from work and $1,029 from AFDC. Arkansas was, in fact, the site of the 37 percent increase in earnings—the difference between $213 and $291 over a six-month period.[21]

In another political climate, a seventy-eight dollar increase over six months would not have merited the attention of the president and both houses of Congress. But that was not the case with the Family Support Act. If AFDC recipients had simply kept up with inflation since 1970, they would have received an additional $5.88 billion in 1988. The act effectively ratifies this reduction in the social wage by taking 57 percent of this money, or $3.34 billion, over five years and spending it on a workfare program.[22] In essence, the act returns some of this lost social wage, but uses the money to fund a program that places conditions on the future receipt of AFDC.

The decision to place conditions on the receipt of AFDC is closely related to changes in the U.S. labor market. The United States is faced with a potential shortage of workers in the 1990s, especially for poorly paid jobs in the service sector.[23] Needing a pool of workers to fill these jobs, business has looked with increasing favor on the prospect of employing welfare recipients, who, as the National Alliance of Business stated, "represent an important source of labor."[24] The Family Support Act of 1988 enables employers to draw more readily from this pool.

The recasting of welfare recipients as employees represents a decided shift in federal policy. AFDC originally gave federal sanction to the task of poor people raising children in their own home. But now that the needs of the labor market have intensified, child-rearing—at least the child-rearing of poor children—has lost some of its legitimacy. This legitimacy has instead been transferred to the labor market, where welfare clients, in a classic application of the principle of less eligibility, will increasingly be channeled into low-salary jobs. Once again, the rediscovery of work as a policy tool will expand the supply of labor by cheapening its cost. At this wage level, though, it will not make the lives of the laborers themselves or their housing any more secure.

Social Security

The reduction of social benefits extended beyond AFDC to include modifications in OASI, SSDI, and SSI. As social insurance programs to which beneficiaries make contributions, OASI and SSDI would ordinarily be exempt from attacks on public welfare. The Reagan administration, however, believed some beneficiaries of these programs could work and established stricter standards of eligibility. It also cut SSI, because SSI provides a uniform national grant to the aged, blind, and disabled, and disabilities in both the SSDI and SSI programs had come under particularly close scrutiny.

Passage of the OBRA of 1981 had an immediate effect on OASI. The act eliminated the $122 minimum monthly allowance granted since 1975 to poor and sporadically employed social security recipients. This change affected 3 million people, three-quarters of them women, whose low pay and widowed status often left them without any other income. OBRA also stopped payments to spouses of deceased workers when the youngest child turned sixteen years of age, two years earlier than regulations had previously established.[25] By depriving recipients of government support, both these changes forced people to depend on the labor market, where their salary was sure to be meager and their need to work was likely to defuse the pressure for further wage increases.

The cutbacks in SSDI have their roots in congressional concerns that precede the Reagan administration. In the period from 1970 to 1975, the number of disabled workers per 100,000 insured grew by 45 percent, from 2,062 to 2,988.[26] While the rate of growth began to shrink in 1978, a 1979 Social Security pilot audit claimed that as many as 20 percent of all recipients might be ineligible. A full validation study subsequently reduced this figure to 11 percent. Although even this figure was later found to result from factors such as inadequate development of medical evidence and simple disagreement among adjudicators, Congress used this information in 1980 to authorize triennial reviews of each case.

The Reagan administration took these data very much to heart. Projecting a five year savings of $3.45 billion, it added SSI recipients to the list of cases to be monitored and removed 491,000 people from the disability rolls. Critics insisted that some of these people were still seriously disabled. But when the political fallout became intense, the administration asserted it was merely carrying out the intent of the 1980 legislation. Congress soon responded. Rejecting this interpretation of the legislation's purpose, it enacted Public Law 98–640, the 1984 Social Security Disability Benefits Reform Act. This law forbids the termination of benefits unless improvements in the medical condition of recipients enable them to work.[27]

Along with the changing political climate, the 1984 reform did slow the pace of terminations. It was not until 1986, however, that the courts, ruling in the New York City class-action suit, *City of New York* v. *Heckler*, declared the federal government to have acted in an arbitrary and capricious manner. The decision forced the reinstatement of half of those who fought back, or 200,000 people. The number of SSDI recipients climbed thereafter, but even in 1990, with more than 4.26 million recipients, it was still 192,000 below the 1981 level. SSI recovered more rapidly. Having benefited 4.2 million people in 1978, it reached that level again eight years later.[28]

Even more than with cutbacks in other social programs, there is a well-documented relationship between contractions in disability benefits and the spread of homelessness in the early 1980s. Public officials in Denver, Columbus, and New York have all attributed some of the new homelessness to overly zealous enforcement of the 1980 legislation,[29] which showed itself most conspicuously among the homeless mentally ill. The data suggest why, although the mentally ill made up just 11 percent of those receiving SSDI, they constituted almost one-third of cases terminated in the first year.[30] While mental illness may have a less definitive effect than physical ailments on the capacity to work, it is the vulnerability of the mentally disabled that accounted for their overrepresentation. Mentally disabled people possessed neither the skill nor the resources to appeal termination of their benefits. As a result, many joined the homeless population, where they noticeably altered the population's demographics.

Food Stamps

The federal government also retrenched the food stamp program. First, in 1981, the Reagan administration ceased funding for outreach. Then, between 1982 and 1986, it cut $6.8 billion from the budget. These cuts pushed 1 million recipients out of the program and reduced benefits for the remaining 20 million.[31] By the time Reagan left office in 1988, the 18.7 million people still receiving food stamps reflected a decline in the participation rate (recipients as a proportion of poor people) from 65.6 percent in 1980 to 58.9 percent.[32] This figure was the lowest ever since the elimination, in 1977, of the requirement that the stamps be purchased. In effect, it meant that another 12 million individuals were eligible for benefits that they were not receiving.

Food stamps are not intended to provide anything more than a minimally nutritional diet—nor could they, at an average cost of 49 cents a meal. But they do feed the poor, and they do have an impact on hunger in this country. When food stamp provision is reduced, the need for emergency food assistance grows, and there is a general squeeze on necessities. The U.S. Conference of Mayors found, for example, that in 1990, the demand for emergency food assistance had increased by an average of 22 percent in twenty-seven out of thirty cities.[33] The people who received this assistance may have been homeless and hungry, or they might have required it so that they could retain their housing. In either case, the increase epitomizes the sacrifices that an increasing number of people must make. Pay for food, or pay for housing: that is the dilemma they face.

Like other cash programs, the cutbacks on food stamps represent another attempt to shrink the social wage. By forcing people to choose between food and housing, the cutbacks do their part toward exacerbating the conditions of life on welfare. Recipients, then, have a choice. They can either resign themselves to a life on welfare, or accept a job in the hope that the wages, however low, will nonetheless provide a marginally higher standard of living.

Unemployment Insurance

Perhaps the most dramatic evidence of the shrinking social wage is the reduction in the percentage of jobless workers who are covered by unemployment insurance. In 1990, unemployment insurance covered only one-third of the unemployed, just marginally above the record low of 31.5 percent in both 1987 and 1988. In fact, throughout the 1980s, the trend was downward, rising but twice, in 1989 and in response to the 9.7 percent unemployment rate of the 1982 recession.[34]

The evidence of this decline is even more striking when comparisons are made between years with similar levels of unemployment. The 1988 unemployment rate of 5.5 percent in 1988 closely approximated the 5.8 percent unemployment rate of 1979. Yet unemployment insurance covered 42.1 percent of workers in 1979, almost 11 percent above the 1988 level. By itself, then, the smaller number of unemployed workers does not explain the diminished coverage.[35]

Several of the strictest states accentuate the contrast between low coverage and high unemployment rates. Louisiana, for example, had the highest unemployment rate of any state in 1988—10.9 percent—but it was ranked forty-fourth in coverage among the states, because only 20.2 percent of its unemployed received insurance benefits. Likewise, West Virginia, the state with the second highest rate of unemployment at 9.9 percent, provided coverage to 23.8 percent of its unemployed workers. Yet even with so little coverage, it was still the thirty-seventh ranked state.[36]

The value of the benefits has dropped, too. Although 12 percent more people were unemployed in 1988 than in 1979, the inflation-adjusted value of all unemployment insurance benefits declined by 11 percent.[37] Tightened eligibility standards have keyed this reduction. Some states have increased the amount of money that must be earned in a given period. Others have minimized the number of eligible workers by disqualifying certain forms of income such as dismissal payments and back or holiday pay. Not surprisingly, when Mathematica Policy Research conducted a study for the U.S. Department of Labor, it found these new eligibility requirements to be the single most important factor in the decline of unemployment coverage.[38]

States have tightened their benefits to reduce the unemployment tax on employers and make their states more attractive to business. They have also sought to avoid the levy, initiated in 1981 by the federal government, of as much as 10 percent on loans from the unemployment insurance trust fund. Although this penalty was eased somewhat in 1983, states disregarded the evidence of declining coverage and continued to make it harder to receive unemployment insurance.[39] In 1990, for example, thirteen states raised, and none lowered, the minimum earnings in the base year. Similarly, while three states reduced the requirements for the maximum weekly benefit, thirty-eight states increased the standard.[40] In sum, the states have behaved just like the federal government, because they, too, have tried to shrink the social supports that permit unemployed people to survive.

Homelessness and Cutbacks in Social Welfare

The principle of less eligibility still holds, but at the price of spreading homelessness among the people who receive social welfare benefits. Just as business restrained wages to bolster its international competitiveness, the government, acting in conjunction with business, sought to reaffirm the principle that social welfare benefits should provide a lower standard of living than the poorest paying job. As the number of these jobs grew, and the wages they paid bought less, the principle of less eligibility demanded that those receiving any form of public assistance be treated in an even harsher manner. This the government did. Whether it was procedural harassment, the addition of a work component to an entitlement program such as AFDC, or the variety of cutbacks that pared cash programs such as social security, disability benefits, food stamps, and unemployment, the effect was the same: make living on social welfare so uncomfortable that the standard of living on paid labor, even at the lowest wage, had to be an improvement.

The relative decline in salaries at the lower end of the labor market combined with a corresponding decline in social welfare to imperil a whole segment of the population. Some people accepted jobs at the prevailing wages. But if a low-paying job could no longer provide enough money to cover the rent, the principle of less eligibility meant that those receiving government benefits were still more vulnerable. Their vulnerability stemmed from their loss of purchasing power: money had been taken from their hands. It was highly likely, then, that they would become homeless when low-cost housing became scarce, and housing costs soared in the 1980s.

5

Housing

We're getting out of the housing business.
A HUD deputy commissioner

The housing policy of America has sought the integration of the poor with the poor—which is to say, the segregation of the other Americans from the society at large.
MICHAEL HARRINGTON

Housing for the homeless is part of the larger problem of housing for the poor. Yet federal subsidies to poor people have always played a relatively minor role in the national housing market. In fact, only 5.6 million of all households in the United States, or slightly more than 6 percent of the total, benefit from direct, public subsidies.[1] By comparison, the public sector in most Western European countries is considerably larger, amounting to one-third of the housing market in Britain and slightly less than 40 percent in France and Sweden.[2]

In the United States, the public housing sector has always been marginal. No strong political and economic forces support it, and the real estate industry has been consistently successful in limiting its role. This domination left its mark. From the Public Housing Act of 1937 to the housing voucher programs of the 1990s, even its most heralded reforms reflect the power of the private sector. Perhaps no other outcome was possible in a battle between opponents of such unequal weight. Nevertheless, the result permanently tarnished public housing policy. Since public housing could only become politically legitimate by accepting the concept of "less eligibility," conspicuously *poorer* housing was all housing for the poor could ever mean.

Under the principle of less eligibility, public housing could not compete, and it could not succeed. This stricture caused public housing to be blamed for many problems that were not of its own making. It could not be attractive, and when it was of decent quality, the supply had to be limited. Segregated by class, race, and location, and easily identifiable as a distinct architectural style, public housing got the problems inherent in carrying out the task assigned to it. And, when, in the early 1980s, the Reagan administration used these problems to reduce its subsidies, the cutbacks combined with an escalation of costs in the private sector to create a crisis of affordable housing.

The Private Housing Market

Private ownership is the dominant form of residence in the U.S. housing market. In 1940, 44 percent of U.S. households owned their own home.[3] By 1980, easy mortgage credit and its accompanying suburbanization had driven the proportion up to a peak of 66 percent. At this level, three-quarters of the American Federation of Labor and Congress of Industrial Organizations (AFL-CIO) members lived in private homes, as did 85 percent of two-person households headed by a forty-five to sixty-five year old, and 95 percent of whites in small cities. This two-thirds rate was double that of Germany, Switzerland, France, Great Britain, and Norway; indeed, only in Canada, New Zealand, and Australia, all countries with small populations, a frontier tradition, and an inherited British dislike for cities, was homeownership equally common.[4]

The 1980s, however, saw a reversal of this upward trend. Despite one of the most sustained housing recoveries on record, the homeownership rate had declined to 64 percent by 1987 and remained at that level into the early 1990s.[5] Frozen out of the housing market by large down payments and high interest costs, the 2 percent decline meant that 2 million families could not afford to buy their own homes. These families were geographically dispersed: they did not just live in those regions like the West and Northeast where rising housing costs have received the most publicity. They were, moreover, often younger people who have had difficulty purchasing "starter homes." In the twenty-five to twenty-nine year old age group, for example, the percentage of homeowners fell from 43.6 percent in 1973 to 35.9 percent in 1987; those under twenty-five years of age experienced a similar drop, from 23.4 to 16.1 percent.[6]

The U.S. real estate market has always prided itself on these buyers, and their exclusion does not bode well. First-time buyers represent both current and future business, as homeowners ride the inflationary wave and trade up to more expensive houses. The real estate industry certainly needs their business, but it also needs something else: the belief on the part of most U.S. citizens that homeownership remains part of the American dream. If the decline in homeownership extinguishes that belief, something more than mere sales may be lost.

One element of this belief was, of course, always based on an erroneous popular assumption; namely, that an autonomous, freestanding marketplace had given rise to private ownership. Somehow, people retained this belief even when they had relied on a government-subsidized mortgage to buy a house in a new development, and the development was itself possible because local authorities had allocated tax revenues to build roads, install gas pipes, and dig sewer lines. Although such a purchase was hardly reflective of Adam Smith's "invisible hand," the faith that government had little to do with this transaction dies very slowly.

The involvement of the state in housing is actually extensive and far-reaching. The government regulates the materials that are used in construction; plans and builds streets, with all their accompanying infrastructure—gas, electricity, sewer, and water; and establishes a system of transportation that makes it economically feasible for residents to live there. Through its legal system, it both defines the terms for a lawful housing sale and specifies the punishment for interference with, or damage to, private property. Its fiscal policy determines the tax rate on real estate profits; its monetary policy has a vital influence on the availability of credit for mortgages. In short, without the government, the private housing market would shrink to a fraction of its current size.[7]

As this list of activities suggests, more is involved here than the conservative prescription that the state should only establish "the rules of the game." While some of the state's involvement may be attributed to its increasingly prominent role in monetary and fiscal policy, it has long influenced the market's development. In fact, at least since the New Deal, this shaping of the housing market has been the chief housing policy of the U.S. government.[8]

Modern housing policy emerged out of the Great Depression. The growth of the housing market in the 1920s was like other booms in the industry—fueled by debt, and heavily dependent on continuous economic growth. Mortgage debt grew four times faster than the overall economy in this decade. So when the Depression came, millions lost their homes, depositors whose banks had provided mortgages lost their savings, and the entire housing finance system needed revamping.[9]

Fundamental to this restructuring were such new institutions as the Federal Home Loan Bank System, the Federal Housing Administration (FHA), and ten years later, the Veterans Administration. These institutions were intended to stabilize the banking system, protect lenders against default, and not so incidentally, stimulate employment in the construction industry. Together with the Federal National Mortgage Association (1938) and the Government National Mortgage Association (1968), they transferred much of the risk in mortgages from the lender to the government. A boom in the private housing market was the predictable result.[10]

Federal housing laws also fed the boom. Title VI of the National Housing Act of 1934 permitted a builder to insure up to $9,000, or 90 percent of a housing mortgage. Since the FHA made prior commitments to insure a mortgagor, developers could use this commitment to obtain production advances for a large number of houses and put up very little of their own money. Although the real boom in construction only came after World War II, it was this kind of financing that endowed suburban pioneers like William Levitt. Levitt secured an FHA commitment to finance 4,000 houses before he even cleared the land for Levittown, Long Island.[11]

The 1949 Federal Housing Act had similar consequences. While Title I funded urban renewal, Title II subsidized the flight to the suburbs. By insuring the mortgages of middle-income buyers and guaranteeing mortgages for veterans, the act enshrined the single family home as the centerpiece of federal housing policy. The act failed to challenge racially discriminatory practices in the real estate industry and thereby excluded people of color. But it did give whites a ticket to escape the cities, and they fled in pursuit of the single family suburban home.[12]

Great Society legislation like the Civil Rights Act of 1968 outlawed the most egregious examples of housing discrimination. The government now officially supported middle-income people of color who could buy their own homes. But the government's preference for private ownership remained unchanged. Perhaps nothing demonstrates this preference better than the subsidies homeowners receive in the form of tax expenditures.

Tax expenditures are taxes that would normally be collected, but whose collection the tax code specifically forgoes. The oil depletion allowance is obviously a tax expenditure. So, too, though, are the deductions on mortgage interest and property taxes for owner-occupied homes, which dwarf the oil depletion allowance in size. All told, in 1987, there were 108 such tax expenditures amounting to $376.9 billion, or 37.5 percent of direct outlays. Tax expenditures are popular because money not collected is less visible than money that is actually spent. Ideal in a conservative political climate, they enable the government to confer its benefits, while simultaneously appearing to do nothing.[13]

In 1989, the mortgage interest and property taxes foregone totaled almost $39 billion. They will exceed $50 billion by 1993.[14] Not only was the 1989 figure more than six times the $6 billion spent in direct outlays, but most of it was distributed among upper income taxpayers. The Congressional Joint Tax Committee calculated, for example, that 67 percent of housing-related tax subsidies went to households earning more than $50,000 a year. At an even higher income level, it is estimated that the 5 million homeowners earning more than $75,000 get a larger tax subsidy than the 5 million poorest households receive in direct outlays.[15]

Tax expenditures are politically popular. They are the perfect instrument for a country that makes mass purchase of private homes the main goal of its housing policy. Nor are they inherently wrong. After all, governments often use taxes as a tool of social policy. Tax credits, for instance, constitute a key ingredient of our daycare policy, just as tax deductions for each dependent encourage parents to have and raise children. In the shorter term, at least, the problem is not that tax expenditures subsidize the purchase of private homes; it is, rather, that the subsidy benefits wealthy people at a time when direct aid to the poor has been so severely reduced.

These cuts only make sense in the context of a national housing policy built around the goal of the private dwelling purchased in the private marketplace. This goal may well represent a convergence of interests and wishes—of business, for profit; of consumers, for their own home; of politicians, for a successful, uninterrupted career.[16] But its effect has always been to marginalize those for whom a private home was never a real possibility. By comparison with what government has offered the private homeowner, it has given them very little.

Housing for the Poor

The provision of housing to the poor and the homeless encounters the same obstacles as the provision of free benefits and services. One of the most basic assumptions of a market economy is that there is a relationship between work and the purchase of commodities such as food, clothing, and shelter. Both free benefits and housing at subsidized or below market rates undermine this relationship—the benefits from the purchase side, housing from the supply. Besides its effect on the work ethic, housing at subsidized or below market rates creates an alternative to the market. For these reasons alone, the opposition to any form of public housing goes back well over a century.

A sketch of the earliest attempts at housing reform in New York illustrates the fundamental dilemma. New York's housing problems began to draw attention in the 1840s, when Dr. John Griscom, city inspector, reported to Common Council that 33,000 people, or one-tenth of the city's population, lived in damp, poorly ventilated cellars and filthy backyard tenements. Leading the first of New York's periodic efforts at housing reform, Griscom used his membership in the Association to Improve the Condition of the Poor (AICP) to convince the organization to sponsor a model tenement. The AICP tried unsuccessfully to get state legislation chartering it as a housing company. Philanthropic capitalists were also reluctant. Eventually, though, in 1855, the AICP constructed a six story model tenement in the vicinity of Mott and Elizabeth Streets. Designed to earn a 6 percent profit, the building was intended to appeal to enlightened self-interest, "a business investment tempered by justice."[17] The experiment was a failure. Its rooms, which rented at $5.50 to $8.50 a month, cost more than the $4.00 monthly that the poorest New Yorkers could afford. And after thirty years, the building itself had deteriorated so completely that the AICP declared it unfit for human habitation.[18]

Between business and "justice": the AICP's model tenement epitomizes the basic conflict in the provision of housing for the poor. Attempts to provide housing for the poor in a market economy always produce some dissonance because the system is simply not designed for this purpose. The dissonance may be more or less, depending on the magnitude of the effort, the nature of its interaction with the private market, and the breadth of political support for the program. But whether it is early philanthropic experiments such as the AICP's or later attempts by the public sector, the provision of housing for the poor demands that the market behave abnormally. In the AICP's model tenement, success depended on a lower rate of profit. Subsequent public sector attempts affirmed private enterprise by using public monies to stimulate the housing industry, but they also exempted a growing number of people from paying market rates. The controversy surrounding these exemptions is an indication that even when public housing programs appear to have been successfully grafted on to the economy, a conflict lurks just below the surface.

It has never stayed there for long. In the Progressive Era, housing advocates such as Lawrence Veiller and E. R. L. Gould sided firmly with the market. Believing that better regulation could solve the problems of urban housing, they opposed both public subsidies and public construction. Most European countries committed themselves to significant public housing programs after World War I, but in the United States, it was not until the New Deal that either the states or the federal government enacted similar legislation.[19]

This legislation clearly bears the imprint of the conflict from which it arose. Persistent doubts about the appropriateness of a federal role could only be overcome by granting substantial concessions to private interests. In 1937, passage of the first major federal public housing legislation depended on defining its purpose not as the production of housing but rather as the alleviation of "present and recurring unemployment." A promise to destroy one substandard unit for every unit that was constructed ensured no net increase in the supply; an understanding that the law targeted a different consumer created the distinction which, after World War II, would firmly establish less eligibility as its guiding principle. Finally, to further minimize its inroads into the private housing market, only localities could certify need and create the municipal housing agency necessary to request federal funds. Since no public housing could be constructed without these actions, compliance was in some sense voluntary.[20]

The Housing Act of 1949 perpetuated this conception of the federal government's role in building housing for the poor. Although it recognized the existence of a housing shortage and promised decent housing for everyone, the act funded just 322,000 units in eleven years, instead of 810,000 in six as Congress originally intended. Moreover, despite requirements that families displaced by urban renewal be temporarily relocated into "decent, safe, and sanitary dwellings," municipalities tended to bulldoze first and ask questions about resettlement later. The act was a potent stimulus to the suburbs, the real estate in-

dustry, and downtown business interests. Yet between the lack of funding
and the highhandedness of local implementation, it ultimately destroyed
more housing in the central cities than it ever built during the period
from 1949 to 1965.[21]

The segregation of public housing in the housing market led inevitably to racial segregation, to a demographics of public housing where
the most impoverished segment of the minority community constituted
a majority of the residents. Holding these demographics partly to blame
for the ghetto riots of the 1960s, politicians abandoned their commitment
to large-scale public housing projects and switched to smaller scale *private*/public partnerships. But as always, there was a catch: in order to
get the private sector to build housing for poor people, these partnerships had to be made sufficiently attractive.

The first financial package the government offered was the Section
236 housing program. Enacted in 1968, Section 236 granted developers
low-interest loans, tax breaks, and an occasional rent subsidy. These
inducements did not materially change the demographic makeup of
subsidized housing. But by putting the profits up front, they left developers with little incentive to manage the project. As a result, HUD had
to repossess one-third of the half million units built under Section 236.
In 1973, President Nixon ordered an end to the program.[22]

The federal government then tried another method of inducing private developers to provide housing for the poor. This program was the
famous Section 8 of the 1974 Housing and Community Development
Act. Section 8 reserved some money for developers of new housing, but
it also authorized vouchers to tenants. Vouchers were issued on the
reasonable assumption that poor people lacked purchasing power. Yet
they were never issued in sufficient quantity to make a measurable dent
in the number of poor people looking for housing, and their subsidy of
market rates had the unfortunate consequence of inflating rents. In
addition, since, like Section 236, they were also time-limited, a developer
could opt out of the program if a neighborhood gentrified. Section 8
temporarily equips poor people to obtain housing, but consistent with
its market orientation, it makes no permanent contribution to the supply
of affordable apartments.[23]

From private philanthropic ventures to the construction of public
housing and the subsidization of market rates, the history of housing
for the poor in the United States is a history of trying to get the economy
to do something for which it is basically ill-suited. The market dominates:
it will build housing for profit, but its power is such as to disable any
stratagem that does not share its conception of housing as a commodity.
Whatever their defects, the 4 million units of housing for the poor that
have managed to survive in this environment constitute a valuable resource. They need to be protected, and they need to be protected, above
all, against the myths that the market generates.

The first myth that the market generates is the myth about public housing. This myth has three interrelated ingredients, all wrapped in a larger misunderstanding. First, most public housing projects are popularly believed to be in poor condition. Second, it is generally thought that public housing is a hotbed of criminal activity, at least in part because it shelters the least functional poor people. Third, public housing is said to be more expensive than housing that is privately supplied. What ties these myths together is the belief that they are all true merely because the housing is public.

Starved for funds, some public housing projects have stinted on maintenance. But the popular belief in their deterioration derives from confusing the condition of public housing generally with that of the most overtly debilitated projects in the central cities. As the CBO has stated, "while some public housing is in need of substantial improvement . . . , available evidence suggests that, by and large, public housing is in reasonably good condition and could, with additional investment, continue for some time as a source of decent housing for low-income households." To support this view, the CBO quotes a HUD study that categorized public housing by project and by unit. By project, the developments were classified as two-thirds untroubled, one-quarter relatively untroubled, and 7 percent troubled. By unit, the comparable statistics were 55, 30, and 15 percent. In keeping with the CBO's interpretation, the figures by unit are higher because troubled projects typically consist of large buildings with many units in the central cities.[24]

It is these buildings that have tarnished the national reputation of public housing and given rise to misperceptions about its inhabitants. Although poverty and crime are generally linked in this misperception, they need to be separated. It is true that over the years, public housing has come to shelter an ever poorer population. One half of the public housing population earns less than 30 percent of the metropolitan median income; in fact, the median income of public housing tenants—at $6,000 to $9,000—is low even in comparison with the median income of participants in other HUD programs.[25] But given the shortage of housing for the poor, these demographics are to be expected. There are, quite simply, very few other places for poor people to go.

Poverty, in itself, does not lead to crime, and we can only conjecture about just what other factors—feelings of anger, isolation, and hopelessness—drive people to criminal activity. Nevertheless, it does not require much of a speculative leap to hypothesize that public housing's policy of racial and economic segregation feeds and exacerbates these feelings. In essence, there are two related truths here: first, crime *is* common in many big city housing projects, and second, its presence cannot be adequately discussed without fully recognizing the role of public policy.

Then there is the matter of cost. Public housing is said to be more expensive than a policy of income supplementation because it requires both capital outlays and money for upkeep. But this comparison is unfair.

Income supplementation pays for shelter in existing units; construction increases the supply of the housing stock. In a more equitable comparison, President Reagan's Commission on Housing reported that maintenance of public housing was either equal to or slightly less costly than the expense of operating existing housing in the Section 8 program. As for a direct comparison of construction costs, the evidence is mixed. While the General Accounting Office found public housing to be the least expensive option over a twenty year period, another study completed for HUD by Urban Systems Research and Engineering, Inc. (1982) asserted that the development of public housing entailed as much as $10,000 more per unit. Any final judgment is risky, however, since none of these studies controlled for variables such as larger units, a bigger investment in land and site development, and the expense of constructing high-rise elevator buildings.[26]

A critique of the public sector is the common strand that unifies these beliefs about the quality and cost of public housing. The litany is invariably the same: public housing is poor, crime-ridden, and expensive, all because it is public. In making these allegations, the market presides as both antagonist and judge. First, it fights against every possible expansion of the public sector. Then, having successfully defined the responsibilities of the public sector to keep them as compatible as possible with the operation of the market, it strips government of the resources necessary to do the job. Lastly, after withholding the requisite funds, it declares its performance to be unsatisfactory. Not surprisingly, by these standards, public housing has failed. But other, more dispassionate criteria yield a different verdict. If public housing has some defects, it is, to a large extent, because it was never permitted to succeed.

Defending the Private Housing Market

A defense of the private housing market accompanies most critiques of public housing. Two theories are typically set forth. One is the real estate market's version of trickle down: the belief that as people move up to better housing, they leave their old residences to the poor. According to this interpretation, in the housing market as in the labor market, upward mobility prevails. The second is a critique of rent control, both in general and as a cause of homelessness. Rent control, it is alleged, impinges on the freedom of the market to set prices. With rents set at below market rates, landlords cannot recoup their investment and lose their incentive to build housing. In this respect, the argument goes, rent control is rather like the minimum wage. Intended to help poor people, it ends up hurting them.

Although both these interpretations have serious defects, at least trickle down can claim to be a partially accurate description of the way in which the housing market used to work. Before family income began to stagnate in the early 1970s, upward mobility in the housing market

did reflect upward mobility in the labor market: workers who got higher-paying jobs had some choice of better housing. But this process has slowed considerably in recent years, as family income stopped growing and the supply of low-income housing declined.

Between 1973 and 1983, demolitions and structural conversions permanently removed 4.5 million units from the housing stock. Low-income households occupied almost half these units. Without an increase in income, these households could not keep up with the price hikes that ensued from improvements in some of the older housing. Moreover, as the process of trickle down began to slow, rental rehabilitation expenditures, which had remained constant in annual terms from 1970 to 1982, more than doubled from 1982 to 1986.[27] Improved and upgraded, this housing was gentrified out of the poor's reach.

The changes of the last two decades have bisected the real estate market, so that trickle down seldom operates.[28] In effect, the housing industry has erected an invisible barrier. A middle-income person may move up from a modest to a more substantial dwelling, but few poor people improve their living standard so dramatically that they can afford the vacated residence. In the meantime, demolition and rehabilitation have eliminated much of the old housing for the poor. With their upward mobility blocked and housing in their price range becoming scarcer, the poor do not benefit from trickle down. Instead, they face a housing squeeze.

Naturally, among those analyzing the issue as it is defined by the real estate industry, this housing squeeze has another explanation. Blaming the prevalence of rent control for the cessation of trickle down, many of these policy analysts argue that such regulations take the profit out of the construction of new housing and consequently reduce the supply. Since a constantly expanding supply of housing is supposed to free vacated residences for occupancy by the poor, trickle down cannot work as long as rent control artificially depresses the return on real estate investment.[29]

The principal object of this criticism are the 200 localities in the United States that currently rely on some form of rent regulation. Altogether, these localities contain about 10 percent of the nation's rental housing, though it is estimated that in California, controls affect as much as one-quarter of all rentals.[30] While critics do not usually make the distinction, modern rent regulations differ from earlier, more restrictive measures in that they permit vacancy decontrol and allow annual increases to ensure a fair return. What constitutes a fair return, though, differs considerably by locality (4 percent in Los Angeles, 6 percent above the maximum local passbook savings account in Hoboken, New Jersey).[31]

Although rent controls have long been criticized for tampering with the market, the latest twist on this critique seeks to blame them for the spread of homelessness. The chief advocate of this view is William Tucker, a journalist whose research for the Manhattan Institute for

Policy Research, a conservative think-tank, has been published in *National Review* and the *New York Times*.[32] Tucker's study has been instrumental in propagating the notion that federal authorities should consider withholding funds from local governments which currently practice any form of rent control. Despite the flaws in his analysis, a number of U.S. senators, including D'Amato (R-New York) and Cranston (D-California), were quite receptive to this idea.

In his research, Tucker investigated the statistical relationship between nine different factors in fifty cities. Among the factors he examined were rent control, the incidence of homelessness, the mean temperature, and the poverty, unemployment, and vacancy rates. Tucker found that rent control was the single most powerful explanation of homelessness, accounting for 27 percent of the difference between cities.[33]

The truth is that these results cannot withstand a careful examination. Tucker's sampling method is rather dubious; it consists of some of the metropolitan areas in the much-criticized HUD study plus fifteen localities that he chose. Even more questionably, Tucker derived his own estimate of the homeless population in these areas by telephoning unnamed informants. Ignoring evidence that three of the four cities with the highest rate of homelessness do not regulate rents, Tucker's analysis confuses the causes of homelessness with differences in its incidence. As a result, he overlooks the possibility that another factor, the high cost of housing, might well account for the existence of both homelessness *and* rent control.[34]

Using HUD numbers, but correcting for these sampling and methodological errors, other researchers have reanalyzed Tucker's data. They found that rent control was a significant factor in the fifteen cities Tucker selected. In a truly random list of cities, however, homelessness was associated not with rent control, but with unemployment, the vacancy rate, warmer temperatures, and the percentage of rental housing. Any relationship with rent control was a figment of Tucker's research.[35]

The Housing Policy of Reagan and Bush

The market has never met the housing needs of the poor. This is an economic fact, not a moral judgment. The market provides housing solely to those people who can afford to pay for it; it is government intervention, alone, that enables some of the poor to obtain housing. Hence blaming government intervention for the failure of the market misreads history. It also implicitly attributes to the market a purpose for which it was never intended.

Housing policy in the 1980s sprung from this misreading. Confusing the failures of the market with its successes, the Reagan administration sought to infuse its housing policies with a market orientation. As articulated by the president's Commission on Housing, this orientation as-

sumed that "the genius of the market economy, freed of the distortions forced by government housing policies and regulations that swung erratically from loving to hostile, can provide for housing far better than Federal programs."[36] The commission recommended free and deregulated housing markets based on an enlightened federalism with minimal government intervention. Government, it stated, would retain a continuing role in ministering to the housing needs of the poor. In practice, however, the commission's reliance on the marketplace represented a further contraction of that role.

For critics, the best index of the Reagan administration's housing policy was its reduction in new appropriations. And, indeed, new appropriations did drop precipitiously, from $32.1 billion in 1978 to $9.8 billion in 1988, a decline of 80 percent after adjustment for inflation. Much of this decline occurred in fiscal years 1982 and 1983, when subsidized housing absorbed 50 percent of all domestic cutbacks in the administration's first two budgets.[37]

Yet this description of Reagan's policy angered conservatives. Citing the increase in housing outlays from $3.7 billion in 1978 to $13.9 in 1988, they consistently maintained that the Reagan administration spent more, rather than, less money, on housing.[38] Their argument is both technically correct and ultimately specious. Housing appropriations are often expended over a long period, and the Reagan administration cut the authorization for future housing expenditures at the same time that earlier commitments, including those made for capital construction during the Carter administration, boosted its own outlays. In truth, the most accurate gauge of housing assistance—the number of new households helped each year—did fall dramatically, from an average of 316,000 new households in fiscal years 1977–80, to 82,000 new households in fiscal years 1981–88, a decline of nearly three-quarters.[39]

New production figures under the Reagan administration reflect this drop. The federal government, which had added a total of more than 1 million new units in the periods from 1976 to 1982, was, by the end of the Reagan administration, producing only 25,000 units annually.[40] Instead of long-term capital commitments, the administration preferred housing vouchers as its favorite policy tool. Vouchers embody one of the market's main virtues: they encourage choice by giving money to people who do not have enough to obtain their own shelter. But without enough money and an adequate supply of housing, the concept of choice in the marketplace can easily turn into an empty abstraction.

Vouchers risk this judgment. They do not pay enough, especially in big cities where rents are high, and they do not add to the housing supply. In New York City, for example, three out of every four vouchers are returned because the holder cannot find an affordable apartment. This outcome is hardly surprising: in 1987, the voucher program granted just $134 per month for a four person family with an income of less than $14,750—far from what is needed in New York to help such a family obtain a suitable residence.[41] "Choice" therefore depends on money, and in the absence of both sufficient money and sufficient new units, vouchers too often mirror the market's inadequacies in providing housing for the poor.

Although less frequently noted, banking and tax reforms in the 1980s also contributed to a decrease in the supply of low-income housing. Deregulation of the savings and loan industry in the early 1980s led the way to a bailout which, between outright fraud and collapsing regional economies, may end up costing taxpayers as much as $500 billion. Yet deregulation did something else as well. By freeing the industry to pursue more speculative ventures, it severed the relationship between housing and the financial sector that had previously been assigned to it.

Before 1980, the savings and loan industry provided the chief funding for residential finance. When rising interest rates threatened it, however, two new laws were passed to enable the industry to compete on more equal terms with other financial institutions. The laws primarily responsible for this shift were the 1980 Depository Institutions and Monetary Control Deregulation Act and the Garn-St. Germain Act of 1982. The 1980 act authorized interest on checking accounts and allowed the thrifts to expand their consumer loan and credit card operations. Garn-St. Germain provided emergency assistance to the savings and loan, increased their investment authority, and gave them broad new lending powers. Once the thrifts were free to charge for the highest paying loans, the housing sector lost its cheap pool of mortgage money, and the financing of residential construction became more difficult.[42]

The 1986 Tax Reform Bill had similarly negative effects. The bill eliminated many tax deductions in exchange for lowering the top marginal rate. Unfortunately for the housing sector, though, some of the tax deductions it removed had previously been instrumental in encouraging construction of residential housing. These deductions include slowing the housing depreciation period to twenty-eight years, up from eighteen years for market rentals and fifteen for low-income; limiting losses from *passive investment* (property that homeowners do not actually manage) to profits from comparable investments; and terminating the tax status of Industrial Development Bonds, which state and local housing finance agencies often used to provide below market financing. Although a tax credit specifically targeting low-income housing may offset some effects of this reform, the initial returns were not encouraging, since the number of rental units started in 1987 was little more than half the number begun in each of the two preceding years.[43]

At the same time that banking and tax reforms helped to take the profit out of low-income housing, the HUD scandal demonstrated that there was still money to be made. In a spectacle that epitomized the relationship between housing policy and the growth of the homeless population, the Reagan administration cut the HUD budget, while HUD misspent as much as $6 billion on the housing projects of politically connected consultants and developers.[44] One of the most publicized beneficiaries was former Interior Secretary James Watt, who collected a $400,000 consulting fee for making eight phone calls and attending a single half hour meeting with HUD Secretary Samuel Pierce.

The HUD scandal caricatures both the politics and the policy of a market-based approach to housing. This caricature is revealing because the illegalities of the HUD scandal illuminate the legalities of a market-based approach. In essence, while political connections and private profit are legal, influence-peddling and profiteering are not. This distinction is not to be taken lightly. Nevertheless, there is a link. Despite, or perhaps because of, its illegality, the HUD scandal underscores who must benefit in order for the poor to get housing.

While President Bush has sought to clean up HUD and replace it with a HUD that operated legally, the policies that he advocates come from the same mold. The Homeownership Opportunities for People Everywhere (HOPE) program, which allocates funds to enable tenants in public housing to purchase their apartments, is the centerpiece of his housing policy. HOPE extols the benefits of poor people owning their own homes, but its failure to provide no-interest loans severely limits the number of potential purchasers. Moreover, in a result typical of the application of market principles, those who do succeed in purchasing their apartments will inevitably cream off the best of the public housing stock.

Although HOPE adds no new units to the supply of housing, its mystique of tenant ownership does offer a cover under which other low-income housing programs can be cut back. In his proposed 1991 fiscal year budget, Bush used this cover to pare an inflation-adjusted total of $359 million from the budget for all subsidized housing. While Congress eventually authorized another $1.7 billion for the final budget, its much-touted National Affordable Housing Act failed to appropriate money for both HOPE and another new program, HOME, which was designed to provide grants to states and municipalities for production and preservation of affordable housing. Reagan wanted fewer housing subsidies. Congress wants more, but does not appropriate money. In the face of this entirely resistible pressure, Bush seems inclined to accept some very modest increases.[45]

The Scarcity of Low-Income Housing

Over the last fifteen years, the deterioration of an imperfect system has led to a crisis of affordable housing. By nearly every measure, low-income housing is in short supply, and people are allocating steadily increasing shares of their income to obtain whatever is available. Most have somehow managed to accommodate themselves to these changes: they cut back on food, they wear clothing a little longer, they skip the few extras they previously enjoyed. Inevitably, though, there are some who cannot keep pace, and as the housing market rachets upward, they are the people who become homeless.

The supply of affordable housing contracted quickly. Between 1974 and 1983, the number of units renting for less than $250 a month in real terms shrunk by 2 million.[46] An increase in the number of poor people aggravated the effects of this decline. In 1970, there was a 2.4 million unit surplus for households with an annual income of $10,000 or less paying 30 percent of their income in rent. By 1985, however, this surplus had turned into a 3.7 million unit deficit.[47] Altogether, the number of rental units available nationally—both subsidized and un-subsidized—is only about one-half the number of people who earn less than 50 percent of the median income and are limited to paying 30 percent of that income on rent.[48]

Government assistance helps a relatively small part of this group. In 1987, just 29 percent of the 7.7 million renters with incomes below the poverty line lived in public housing or received a rental subsidy from any government assistance—federal, state, or local. This proportion is lower than for most other assistance programs. Seventy-one percent of poor households with school children receive free or reduced-price school lunches, and 42 percent of the poor receive medicaid. Yet more than 70 percent of poor renters, and 82 percent of all poor households, receive no housing assistance.[49]

Rent-to-income ratios are one of the best indicators of a tightening housing market. Between 1974 and 1983, the proportion of renters paying more than 35 percent of their income in rent increased from 25 to 37 percent.[50] Rent-to-income ratios also narrowed, because rents rose almost twice as fast as income. Over a somewhat longer period, from 1970 to 1983, the income of the median renter grew just 97 percent, while rents jumped 192 percent. Since housing helped to inflate the consumer price index 157 percent in the same period, it contributed significantly to a noticeable decline in the standard of living for the median renter.[51]

These rental increases persisted well into the 1980s. Between 1981 and 1986, real rents increased in seven of eight big cities, ranging from 11 percent in Detroit and 16 percent in Denver, to 25 percent in Boston and 36 percent in San Francisco. Only in Houston, where substantial overbuilding occurred, did rents decline—by 2 percent—during this period.[52]

As a small oasis of reasonably priced shelter, public housing has experienced a considerable expansion of its waiting lists. In 1987, 13,000 families were signed up for vacancies in one of Baltimore's 17,000 units of public housing. Similarly, in Chicago, 49,000 units of public housing had a waiting list of 44,000 people; in Sacramento, almost the entire public housing stock of 2,800 units would have to turn over in order to make room for the 2,700 families who were awaiting a vacancy.[53] Whatever the deficiencies of public housing, there is nothing quite like an acute shortage of other low-priced dwellings to heighten its appeal.

Public housing may be in short supply, but single-room occupancy hotels have almost disappeared. The transformation of the city economy from manufacturing to service industries created a demand for the up-grading of old housing stock. When urban professionals needed housing near the central business district, real estate developers initiated a process of gentrification that often targeted single-room occupancy (SRO) hotels. In the past, SROs had been the place where the elderly, the casual laborer, and the recently deinstitutionalized could find cheap housing. Yet once SROs could be turned into high-priced rentals and cooperative apartments, their stock diminished rapidly.

Nationally, a total of 1 million SRO units were lost during the 1970s. Everywhere, the pattern was the same. In the late 1970s and early 1980s, Phoenix lost forty hotels with 1,800 rooms. Between 1970 and 1987, Portland, Oregon lost 59 percent of its SROs, or over 2,400 units, and Atlanta lost 88 percent, or almost 1,800 rooms. In both percent and number, however, the single biggest loss occurred in New York City, where the 113,000 units, or 89 percent of the total, vanished between 1970 and 1983.[54]

With the decline in income and the increasing scarcity of affordable housing, the opportunities for the poor to secure shelter are blocked at every turn. More than any other single phenomenon, it is the interaction between the relative decline of income and the relative increase in hous-ing costs that explains the growth of the homeless population. Sadly, though, just as the proliferation of low-paying service jobs dampens the income prospects of the working poor, so, too, do predictions of future losses to the housing stock bode ill for the supply of subsidized housing.

The Future Loss of Housing

Inducing the private sector to build housing for the poor has long been one of the cornerstones of federal housing policy. Since poor people cannot afford rents high enough to enable a landlord to turn a profit, it is only the addition of government money that permits sufficient profits to be made. During the 1970s, however, the government added another incentive to this pool of public money: it permitted landlords to charge market rates after they had housed the poor for a limited period of time. In Alameda, California, a return to market rates meant that Clayton Guyton, a transportation dispatcher, paid $675 a month, up from $271, for the apartment that he shared with his wife and three children. The Guyton family managed to remain in their apartment. All across the United States, however, others will not be quite so lucky.[55]

At risk of a return to market rates are more than 900,000 units of privately owned housing whose federal subsidies will expire by 1994.

Some 720,000 units of this housing involves time-limited Section 8 contracts, usually of five to fifteen years. In addition, 247,000 vouchers of five years' duration are scheduled to run out during this period. To renew these contracts and continue funding them at the same rate, Congress would have to appropriate nearly $73 billion. While Congress made a downpayment on this bill by authorizing $7.7 billion in fiscal year 1991, a much larger sum is coming due when the contracts for another 750,000 Section 8 units expire between 1995 and 2005.[56]

Overall, it is estimated that by the year 2003, the combination of the shrinking supply of affordable housing and the growth in the number of poor families could produce a gap of 7.8 million units, which at the national average for household size, would shelter 18.7 million people.[57] Of course, this figure represents an index of risk that public policy can modify. And, surely, even with the most minimal intervention, all these people will not become homeless. The great majority will find some other kind of housing: they will live in substandard dwellings, double up with relatives, or fall back on any one of the many other coping strategies that the poor typically employ. Nevertheless, if just 5 percent of the at-risk population failed to find alternative arrangements, nearly another 1 million people would become homeless. Some poor people are very resourceful, but a spurious confidence in the resourcefulness of the poor is a bad starting point for housing policy in this country.

The Homeless Mentally Ill

A simple way to abate homelessness is reinstitutionalize the mentally ill.
JOSEPH PERKINS, in the *Wall Street Journal*

Fails to plan ahead, or is impulsive, as indicated by one or both of the following: a) traveling from place to place without a prearranged job or clear goal for the period of travel or clear idea about when the travel will terminate; b) lack of a fixed address for a month or more.
One of the characteristics of Antisocial Personality Disorder, 301.70,
as listed in the *Diagnostic and Statistical Manual* III-R,
the official reference book of the American Psychiatric Association

As the most conspicuous segment of the visible poor, the mentally ill have fostered the popular belief that deinstitutionalization caused homelessness. It is a comforting perception. If deinstitutionalization caused homelessness, then reinstitionalization is the obvious remedy. This analysis has its advantages. Diagnosing the homeless as mentally ill labels them as different and justifies their separation from society. No other solution leaves the political and economic institutions of the United States quite so intact.

What is at issue, then, is a question of proportion and, inevitably, of politics. Obviously, some homeless people are emotionally disturbed, and they constitute an important subgroup within the homeless population. But at a time when families are the fastest growing segment among the homeless, and the great majority of homeless people do not, *prior to their homelessness*, behave in notably bizarre or unusual ways, the label of "mental illness" tars the entire population with a very broad brush. The homeless are undeniably poor; it is just too politically convenient for them also to be crazy.

The Diagnostic Imperative: Inflating the
Percentage of Homeless Mentally Ill

Those who tend to inflate the percentage of mentally ill among the homeless population are most heavily drawn from two groups—conservatives and psychiatrists. Conservatives are naturally reluctant to emphasize the economic causes of homelessness, and they bridle at any hint of criticism that Republican domestic policies might have contributed to the growth of the homeless population. For them, the chief cause of homelessness is the failure of deinstitutionalization at the state level. An emphasis on mental illness and substance abuse permeates their characterizations of the homeless population.

These characterizations are legion. Prior to her assignment as director of homeless programs for HUD under President Bush, Anna Kondratas wrote a short monograph for the Heritage Foundation in which she asserted that between one-half and two-thirds of the population are mentally ill and/or substance abusers. Myron Magnet made similar claims for the readers of *Fortune* and the *New York Times*. And in the *Wall Street Journal*, Joseph Perkins depicts a homeless population whose mental incompetence usually prevents them from getting the help they need.[1] Virtually untouched by economic conditions, the homeless in these writings are captives of their mental illness, people who could never work regardless of the demand for their labor.

Among some psychiatrists, the estimates of mental illness are even higher. One research team in Philadelphia set their estimate at 84 percent. In Boston, Ellen Bassuk of Harvard Medical School designed a study that found a 90 percent incidence of mental disorders among the homeless in one shelter. The highest incidence yet, though, was the 96.6 percent rate of prior institutionalization uncovered in a New York study. In this case, researchers appear to have underestimated the extent to which the site—the Bellevue Psychiatric Emergency Room—biased their findings.[2]

Surgeons are trained to identify organic diseases, and they operate; psychiatrists are trained to see mental illness, so they prescribe drugs and psychotherapy. Diagnostic skills are useful, but they breed tunnel vision when they are employed without some attention to their social and economic context. The principal reference book of the American Psychiatric Association says that collecting garbage, hoarding food, and a marked impairment in personal hygiene and grooming are residual symptoms of schizophrenia.[3] Perhaps they are, but perhaps they are also the not-so residual symptoms of lacking a home.

Distancing themselves from their profession's tendency to label, other psychiatrists have conducted their research with due regard for the impact of social conditions upon mental health.[4] These researchers understand that while some homeless people are seriously disturbed, the cataloging of every symptom exhibited by the homeless mixes cause and effect and vastly overstates the true incidence of mental illness among the population. Homeless people who are depressed or withdrawn are not necessarily disturbed. Indeed, it would be indicative of a far more serious pathology for someone to react with complete equaniminity to the loss of their home and job.

On the other hand, since we know that some homeless people really are mentally ill, what are reasonable criteria for identifying them? The only practical standard of mental illness is extremely bizarre or aberrant behavior. Admittedly, such behavior could also result from spending a long time on the street. But at least this criterion partially corrects for labeling situational behavior as mental illness. A group of researchers who espouse this standard buttress their argument by quoting at length from a woman who clearly qualifies. Approaching one of them at a bus stop on the way to a church service for the homeless, she introduced herself by saying,

> I'm from one of 5000 planets which have beings superior to humans. People on those planets watch earthlings on TV, but they find them repulsive. You're ugly to me too.... I have been reincarnated on earth and trained to be a scientist so that I can inform God about scientific developments on earth. But earth science is bullshit! I know because I saw a picture on the front of *Scientific American* that was supposed to be a nebula in space, but I recognized it was a photograph I took a long time ago of a dirt clod under a microscope. [Asked if she knew for whom they were waiting, she added], We are waiting for the last pure descendants of the Romans who are going to feed us.[5]

This women, clearly delusional and hallucinatory, suffers from obvious mental disabilities. But other homeless people also sleep on the street, wear ragged clothes, and mutter to themselves while searching the garbage. The "mental illness" of those who behave in this way remains very much open to question.

A psychological approach therefore needs to be combined with an ethnographic one. Then the view is quite different, and behaviors that would otherwise raise the eyebrows of any clinician do not seem nearly so disturbed. At a symposium sponsored by the National Institute of Mental Health, Paul Koegel, a research anthropologist in the UCLA Department of Psychiatry, reported on some field work conducted from this perspective:

> Time and again, researchers met women who were clearly guarded, perennially frightened, confused, depressed, and perhaps even delusional. Were they chronically mentally ill or were they simply reacting very sanely to the enormous stress of an insane situation? Was the fact that they wore four pairs of pants during the summer a reflection of an inability to properly identify weather-appropriate clothing or was it a highly conscious strategy aimed at frustrating potential rapists? Was their confusion a function of psychopathology or was it a result of long standing sleep deprivation? Was their poor hygiene the result of poor self-management skills or their restricted access to sinks and showers?[6]

In other words, every behavior does not merit a diagnosis, and the conditions of life as a homeless person should themselves refute the automatic presumption of mental illness.

A History of Deinstitutionalization

The credo that mental illness is widespread among the homeless population flows from the belief that the people who are now on the street are the people who were, or should be, in an institution. Census data superficially appear to support this view. The census of mental hospitals in the United States dropped steadily from its peak of 558,922 in 1955, to 137,810 by 1980, and then to 118,647 in 1984.[7] The image this 79 percent decline brings to mind is of a thirty-year exodus, orderly and single file. That, however, is not quite the way it happened.

Prior to deinstitutionalization, the history of mental institutions in the United States had passed through three distinct periods.[8] In the first period, chronicled by David Rothman in his classic *The Discovery of the Asylum,* citizens of the Jacksonian era constructed the first institutions for the insane. The building of these asylums was an important social reform, one that derived its rationale from very particular ideas about the origins of insanity. The Jacksonians were proud of the youthful energy in the new republic. Yet, as they saw it, this energy was gradually destroying all the signposts of the old social order. From agricultural to urban, from stability to flux, the disappearance of these signposts caused people to lose their moral bearings and literally drove them insane, the disordered workings of their mind mimicking the disordered state of a rapidly changing society.[9]

The Jacksonian remedy for this condition consisted of an attempt to replicate the old social order: remove the insane from society, put them in asylums located in rural areas, and rigidly schedule their day. These principles lasted for a while, but by the second phase, in the 1850s, the asylum had become fundamentally custodial. In this role, asylums overflowed with both the poor and the insane, and their residents often suffered at the hands of a staff also drawn from the pauper classes.[10] Although institutions still separated the poor and insane from society, their loss of vigor combined with spiraling costs to strip them of their reforming function.

Reenergized by the prospect of scientific approach to mental illness, the forerunners of the psychiatric profession initiated the third cycle of reform in the last quarter of the nineteenth century.[11] Scientific research had already identified the bacterial origins of many serious diseases including, between 1882 and 1885, the organisms responsible for tuberculosis, cholera, tetanus, and diphtheria. These discoveries gave hope to those who thought that there might be a comparable explanation for mental illness. Their hopes remained unfulfilled. But throughout the early twentieth century, their interest in preventing mental illness through the mental hygiene movement keyed this era of reform.[12]

The census of state and county mental hospitals continued to rise throughout this period. In 1904, there were 150,151 residents of mental institutions in the United States. The census reached 255,245 in 1923, 318,821 in 1931, and 450,000 in 1943.[13] By the time the census topped 558,000 in 1955, mental institutions had become one of the bigger items on most state budgets. The stage was set for another major change, if only something would arise to give it impetus.

One impetus came from *Rauwolfia serpentina*, or serpent wood. Serpent wood is a foot tall shrub native to North India that Hindu doctors used to calm disturbed people. During 1953, Nathan S. Kline, a psychiatrist at New York's Rockland State Hospital, began trying to extract the active ingredient. His success gave psychiatrists reserpine, which, along with chlorpromazine, became one of the first tranquilizers. Kline published his findings in 1954, the same year that Governor Averill Harriman took office.[14]

Economics and medical science were soon wed. Apart from local aid, mental illness was the single largest expense in the New York State budget, and bonds were issued regularly for the construction of new hospitals. The discovery of psychotropic drugs presented Harriman with an opportunity to do something about this cost. In the spring of 1955, at the urging of his secretary, Jonathan Bingham, Bingham's assistant, future New York Senator Daniel Moynihan, and Paul Hoch, commissioner of Mental Hygiene, Harriman agreed to invest $1.5 million so that the new tranquilizers could be distributed systemwide. It proved to be a good investment. Drugs tranquilized not only the patients to whom they were administered but also the growth rate of the state's mental health budget. In combination with other factors, they contributed to a decline in the number of state hospital residents, from 93,314 in 1955 to less than 14,000 in 1991.[15]

In New York and other states, chlorpromazine soon replaced reserpine as the drug of choice. Marketed as thorazine, it benefited from the enormously successful campaign that the Smith, Kline, and French drug company conducted. As a result, by 1955, less than one year after its introduction, Smith, Kline and French could boast that thorazine was already being given to 2 million people.[16]

The availability of tranquilizers added a new tool to the arsenal of management techniques. Drugs could be used to manage behavior inside an institution, and they could also promote desirable behavior after a patient's release. Drugs stabilized patients; they made some symptoms disappear. But harnessed so tightly to the state budget, they lent themselves to easy abuse. An overreliance on drugs can prolong social dependency and produce neurological damage, most typically tardive dyskinesia, with its involuntary movements of the tongue. This outcome was all the more likely when budgetary pressures led them to be prescribed for a variety of economic, administrative, and other nonmedical reasons. In these circumstances, it was all too easy to forget the difference between the capacity of drugs to "cure" patients and the capacity of drugs to cure the institutional problems that difficult patients caused.[17]

The economic incentives to release residents gained momentum throughout the 1960s. First, after years of study dating back to the formation of the Joint Commission on Mental Health in 1955, President Kennedy signed the 1963 Mental Retardation Facilities and Community Mental Health Centers Construction Act. As one of the last bills his administration enacted, the act projected the funding of one community mental health center for every 100,000 people, or 2,000 centers by 1980. Yet only 789 were eventually funded. Both the state and federal government saved money: the states, by shifting the responsibility of care to the community mental health centers, and federal government, by failing to fund the centers in the quantity that were originally planned.

The community mental health centers contributed to this service vacuum by changing their client population. The nascent premise of the act was to serve chronic mental patients in the community and thereby reduce the hospital census. But chronic mental patients are hard to serve, and their share of the client population in community mental health centers dwindled steadily. As a result, by 1973, the percentage of admissions diagnosed with "social adjustment disorder" had exceeded those diagnosed with schizophrenia.[18] Hence, a mere ten years after passage of the act, chronic mental patients had too few places to go, and even in those places, they were not exactly welcome.

Changes in the regulations for Aid to the Disabled (ATD), a federal category of public assistance, further enhanced the economic incentives. After the rules were liberalized in 1963, the mentally ill were eligible to receive assistance in the community. ATD, which was later incorporated into SSI, never provided generous assistance, but it was sufficient to maintain the deinstitutionalized in a board and care home or an SRO hotel. ATD quickly became another way that states could save money by handing the cost to the federal government.[19]

The enactment of Medicaid and Medicare in 1965 and 1966, respectively, had a similar effect. Medicaid covered people who could be housed in a skilled nursing home or intermediate care facility; Medicare made its biggest contribution by covering patients in the psychiatric units of general hospitals. Community mental health facilities, the liberalization of the regulations for ATD, and the passage of Medicaid and Medicare: for the states, these developments transformed deinstitutionalization into a very low-risk strategy. They were sure to benefit if a lot of money was saved. But if the costs to the federal government meant that only a little money was saved, the states could be confident that it was they who would do the saving.[20]

This confidence was well-founded. Total expenditures by the federal, state, and local governments for the seriously mentally ill soared from

1 billion dollars in 1963 to 17 billion dollars in 1985, a 400 percent increase even after accounting for inflation and population growth. Far more significant, however, was the reallocation of expenses. In 1963, the federal government paid 2 percent of the expenses for the seriously mentally ill; by 1985, its share had risen to 38 percent. Local governments also bore more of the fiscal burden, as their share increased from 2 to 9 percent in the same period. Only the states, who cut their expenses from 96 to 53 percent, benefited.[21]

In addition to drugs and legislative developments, a third factor—judicial decision making—fueled the process of deinstitutionalization. Beginning in the 1960s, the courts began to apply civil libertarian principles to the mentally ill. These principles would not have been applied if hospitals had retained some measure of therapeutic legitimacy. Yet this legitimacy was exactly what they had lost. When drugs enabled people to maintain themselves in the community; when tales of horrendous conditions discredited the presumption of adequate care; and when mental hospitals confined people for long periods, but few patients seemed to improve, then hospitals were not really hospitals: they were much more like prisons.

Analogies to prison evoked another conception of institutional life, and with it, another set of laws. The first precedent-setting case, *Lake* v. *Cameron* in 1966, affirmed the right to treatment in the least restrictive environment. It was followed by *Wyatt* v. *Stickney* (1971), an Alabama ruling that declared a patient's right to adequate treatment, and a 1971 Florida decision, *O'Connor* v. *Donaldson*, which established "dangerousness" as the criterion for involuntary commitment.[22] Despite variations in specifics, these cases shared the common premise that without the rehabilitative care which is supposed to distinguish a hospital from a prison, mental institutions had no right to deprive patients of their liberty.

The court rulings had predictable effects. While drugs and new social welfare legislation merely encouraged states to release patients, judicial decisions gave deinstitutionalization the force of law. Still, these laws often worked in mysterious ways. Ordered to improve care by increasing their staff-patient ratios, some states simply released additional patients. This response was particularly common in states with tight budgets, strong public sector unions, and/or rural towns whose economic viability depended on continued employment in the local state mental hospital. That is one powerful reason why although the patient population decreased by 66 percent from 369,969 to 125,246 between 1969 and 1981, total hospital expenditures in constant dollars dropped just 3 percent, from $1.81 billion to $1.76 billion.[23]

The same incentives impelling the states to release patients also encouraged them to adopt more restrictive admission requirements. By combining tighter admission criteria with the existing policy of easier discharge, these new requirements broadened the meaning of deinstitutionalization and marked a new phase in its development. This change affected people with many different kinds of emotional difficulties. Those most severely affected, however, were the group now known as the young adult chronic patients. Never institutionalized, most "young chronics" would have been admitted to a state hospital under the old standards for admission.[24]

New York's tightening of admission criteria typifies its effect on the states' hospital census. First, in 1965, New York switched the burden for involuntary commitments from the individual to the hospital and established a special arm of the courts called the Mental Health Information Service, which was mandated to represent patients. Three years later, hospitals responded to this change with a stricter admission policy. Henceforth, patients would be rejected for admission "if care and treatment would more appropriately be given in another facility. Patients," the regulations said, "should not be admitted when their problems are primarily social, medical, or financial or for the convenience of some other facility."[25] Once the state reserved inpatient facilities for those who could not survive without ongoing care, deinstitutionalization was in full swing. New York State's inpatient population, which numbered 76,000 in 1968, plummeted 54 percent to 35,000 people by 1975.[26]

The combined effect of easier releases and more difficult admissions brought about similar declines in other states. The Ohio census dropped from 28,555 in 1962 to 4,709 twenty years later. Likewise, the 20,000 residents of Massachusetts mental hospitals in 1960 had, by 1985, been reduced to just 2,600 people. All told, during a thirty year period from 1955 to 1985, three states—Arkansas, Wisconsin, and Kentucky—closed more than than 90 percent of their beds, while another seven states including Massachusetts, Illinois, and California, closed between 85 and 89 percent.[27]

Yet the decline in the hospital census is perhaps the most misunderstood aspect of the whole controversy about deinstitutionalization. Appearances to the contrary, the numbers do not exhibit a simple downward trajectory. In fact, releases and admissions both grew until 1970, when, for the first time, releases began to exceed the admissions. Instead, what made the hospital census decline was deaths, shorter inpatient stays, and changes in the "locus of care." Mortality of elderly residents was particularly crucial in the early years of deinstitutionalization, accounting for 20 to 40 percent of the decline through the early 1960s. Later, however, shorter inpatient stays became the primary instrument for limiting the number of residents, so much so that by the late 1970s, 400,000 admissions a year—two-thirds of them readmissions—could move through the state hospitals, stay a few months, and have little impact on the census.[28]

Although shorter lengths of stay remain an important factor, the essence of deinstitutionalization was always supposed to be the replacement of hospitalization with care in the community. To some extent, this has happened, though not perhaps in the way that was originally intended. With the rate of inpatient care episodes remaining relatively stable, the single clearest shift in care has occurred among the elderly. For example, between 1971 and 1975, the admissions rate of the elderly to state mental hospitals fell by 46 percent.[29] As a result, in 1977, a little more than a decade after the enactment of Medicaid, half the 1.3 million nursing home residents in the country had a mental disorder, and nursing homes had become the single most commonly used psychiatric facility.[30]

This development does not really qualify as *deinstitutionalization*, because care was merely transferred from one kind of institution to another. The twelvefold growth in the rate of outpatient services might well be more to the point, except that there is a catch here as well. The legislation establishing community mental health centers authorized the provision of mental health services to the community, but never mandated aftercare for the deinstitutionalized patient. The growth in outpatient services therefore reflects an increase in services to less disturbed residents; it does not, nor was it intended to, include people who have been released from state mental hospitals.[31]

Deinstitutionalization failed. Its failure is a complex story, one that is complicated by a variety of different incentives including the economic. Although the coalition behind deinstitutionalization originally consisted of people with both humanitarian and financial goals, budgetary concerns dominated the actual process of implementation. Deinstitutionalization saved money. It saved money for the states because it reallocated some of the cost of caring for the mentally ill to the federal government; it saved money for the federal government because in the absence of a link to the state hospital system, it could implement deinstitutionalization on the cheap. Deinstitutionalization may well be able to trace one of its roots to a humane desire to reform the mental health system. Yet as with so many other reforms, in the end the humanitarian gave way to the economic.

Deinstitutionalization as a Cause of Homelessness

It has long been customary to assert that since the policy of deinstitutionalization failed the mentally ill, it must be a primary cause of homelessness. First heard when homelessness proliferated in the early 1980s, this argument got weaker with the passage of time. Sixty-five percent of the decline in the hospital census had already occurred before 1975. Deinstitutionalization therefore cannot explain very much about the spread of homelessness one decade later. Clearly, by the early 1990s, when 40 percent of the homeless consisted of families, and upwards of 100,000 children were without shelter, even federal agencies such as the National Institute of Mental Health were reporting to Congress that deinstitutionalization had played a comparatively small role.[32]

A Texas study attests to its limited impact. Between 1979 and 1984, the institutionalized population in the state declined by 10.5 percent, from 5,508 to 4,928 people. At the same time, however, the number of Salvation Army users jumped from 4,938 to 11,271 people, or 126 percent. Although mental hospitals did set stricter requirements for admission, it would still stretch anyone's powers of argumentation to explain how a five year decline of 580 people yielded a 6,333 person increase in the number of those who turned for help to the Salvation Army.[33]

The passage of time and better current behavior add to the doubts about the relationship between homelessness and previous institutionalization. Although 22 percent of the population had been institutionalized in one Berkeley study, slightly less than half had been released five or more years before. Deinstitutionalization may have made them vulnerable, but it was other events that made them homeless. Similarly, while 29.9 percent of an Ohio study had spent time in an institution, interviewers judged less than 5 percent to be currently in need of hospitalization. The coincidence of homelessness and deinstitutionalization is indisputable, but a causal relationship of real significance is hard to detect.[34]

What ultimately disproves the hypothesis of deinstitutionalization as an explanation of homelessness are the research data on psychiatric hospitalization. In thirteen studies of the previously institutionalized among the homeless conducted in cities throughout the United States, the proportion of the homeless population ranged from 11.2 to 33.2 percent. The low and high figures—both of which come from New York—encompass a relatively narrow set of results from other cities including Los Angeles, 14.8 percent (1986) and 20 percent (1985); Chicago, 23 percent in 1983 and 1986, and Detroit, 26 percent in 1985.[35] The implications of this data are unequivocal: deinstitutionalization has contributed to homelessness, but since the vast majority of homeless people have never been in a psychiatric institution, most explanations substantially overemphasize it as a cause.

Previous psychiatric hospitalization is, of course, a poor indicator of the prevalence of mental illness within the homeless population. Moreover, one could well argue that fewer people have histories of previous hospitalization precisely because deinstitutionalization has tightened the standards for admission. But this argument would miss the larger point. Even if fewer people carry with them the stigma of a former inpatient, the psychological and the social symptoms of homelessness are hopelessly intertwined. This is not to say that mental illness does not exist among the homeless population, or to deny that in some cases, psychosis has pushed some people toward homelessness. It is, however, to warn against an overly psychological interpretation of a social problem, especially when, despite numerous flaws, that interpretation has been repeatedly deployed to explain the problem away.

But if deinstitutionalization and, more generally, mental illness do not deserve the prominence they usually receive, the incidence of mental illness among the homeless does highlight the changes in their plight. Most mentally ill people are not homeless; neither, to be sure, are most poor people. In both groups, however, the growth of homelessness suggests that inadequate shelter is what has put them at risk. Though each confronts a shortage of affordable housing, a lack of affordable housing with adequate supportive services compounds this shortage for the mentally ill. A loss of SRO hotels affects both the poor and the mentally ill; the shortage of community residences leaves the mentally ill trapped in a still tougher game, the housing equivalent of musical chairs.[36]

This is a game for which the players are particularly ill-equipped. While a direct route from an institution to the street is not their usual path to homelessness, they are vulnerable to defeat by any crisis or personal catastrophe, from the public assistance check that fails to arrive to the medical emergency that they cannot handle. Although poor people with greater emotional resiliency might cope successfully with these events, the mentally ill cannot. Increasingly, in the United States, homelessness is the punishment for this failure.

Reinstitutionalization

Deinstitutionalization, then, is not a proximate cause of homelessness. While mental illness bears a closer relationship, it, too, is clouded by its interaction with the social consequences—the hunger, sleepnessness, and anxiety—of lacking a home. For those who believe in the prevalence of mental illness among the homeless, these conclusions create two problems. First, they dilute the power of mental illness to explain homelessness as a public issue, and second, they do not get the most conspicuously mentally ill off the streets. Only reinstitutionalization would do that, and it, according to its most enthusiastic advocates, would virtually sweep the streets clean.

Several well-publicized cases have been instrumental in broadening the appeal of reinstitutionalization. In 1978, Angus McFarlane, a resident of Pierce County, Washington, murdered an elderly couple in his neighborhood after he was denied voluntary admission to a state mental hospital. The resulting clamor brought about passage of the 1979 Involuntary Treatment Act, which eased commitment standards. A similar controversy arose in 1986, when Juan Gonzalez, a homeless man who had been staying in the shelter at New York City's Fort Washington Armory, was held briefly in the emergency room of Columbia Presbyterian Medical Center. Crying "Jesus wants me to kill," Gonzalez was so disturbed that four doses of an antipsychotic drug had to be administered to him in the space of ninety minutes. Although Gonzalez actually signed a voluntary commitment form, the hospital released him after forty-eight hours because its psychiatric service was overcrowded. Two days later, Gonzalez used a sword purchased in a Times Square souvenir shop to kill two passengers on the Staten Island ferry. Together with the widespread visibility of the homeless mentally ill, cases like these sensitized the public. As a result, by the time a debate erupted in 1988 about Joyce Brown's "right" to live on a New York City street, it was mental health, and not merely violence, that had crystallized popular feelings.[37]

Out of the sentiment that deinstitutionalization had gone too far came a campaign to recommit both the dangerous and the seriously disturbed. Acting on this change in public opinion, five states besides Washington—Alaska, North Carolina, Texas, Arizona, and Hawaii—have revised their commitment laws, and a number of other states have such revisions under active consideration.[38] As part of the vanguard to reinstitution-alize, the decision of these states suggests that the United States may well be beginning what can only be described as another period of reform.

In the United States, attitudes toward the mentally ill have always run in cycles. At one end of the cycle, we attribute the causes of mental illness to the society at large, as we did in the 1830s. At the other end of the cycle, we discharge patients because we see institutions as contributing to mental illness. There are really two issues here. One revolves around changes in public sentiment about who is more at fault—the society outside the institutions or the institutions themselves. But underpinning this issue is a second consideration. Chronic mental illness is an intractable problem for which there is no sure remedy. Imputing the failure to the locus of care, we have consistently oscil-lated between institutional and noninstitutional modes of treatment. Neither works very well. In the next cycle, we then hope that the other mode of treatment will be more successful, or at least substantially cheaper.

The issue, then, is the quality, rather than the locus, of care. Just a small minority of people are dangerous enough to necessitate com-mitment to an institution. For everyone else, a high quality of care does not depend on its delivery at a particular site. Good care could be given in a mental hospital; good care could be provided in the community. We might well prefer the latter for civil libertarian reasons, on the principle of the least restrictive environment. Yet a larger problem looms. The problem is that with some notable exceptions, adequate care in the United States has never really been provided at either site.

The commingling of the poor and the mentally ill has always been the most damning index of this failure. The mentally ill were thrown into almshouses with the poor throughout the nineteenth century. Al-though reformers periodically tried to separate them, the mentally ill rarely resided in an institution devoted solely to their own needs. When counties transferred aged senile people to the state mental asylums in the early 1900s, they exacerbated the problem. The centralization of power within the state government sanctioned a model of the mental hospital that maintained rather than cared for the patient. Containment of the most disruptive poor was a none too hidden advantage of this custodial arrangement.[39]

A history in which long periods of shabby treatment follow closely on the occasional cry of outrage comes equipped with its own warning. There was no magic in deinstitutionalization of mental patients, and there will be no magic in reinstitutionalizing the homeless mentally ill. When Washington enacted the first flexible commitment laws, involuntary commitments doubled within two years. The new patients nevertheless received very little treatment. In effect, a scarcity of resources replicated exactly those conditions that had initially prompted the movement to deinstitutionalize.[40]

Without new resources, the campaign to send the homeless mentally ill back to an institution implies the existence of a quality of care that has yet to be forthcoming. Since history is not very reassuring on this account, reinstitutionalization can be seen for what it is: misdiagnosing the causes of homelessness, it misprescribes the solution. The drive to reinstitutionalize the homeless therefore suffers from a very large credibility gap. Those in the movement with a short historical memory may genuinely believe that the homeless as a group would receive better care in an institution. But overall, it is hard to resist the conclusion that the main goal of the campaign to reinstitutionalize is simply to get the homeless off the streets and out of public view.

If quality of care is the true objective, reinstitutionalization and the current fragmented system cannot be serious alternatives. For this purpose, the homeless mentally ill need a multitiered approach like that recommended by the 1984 Task Force on the Homeless Mentally Ill of the American Psychiatric Association. Insisting first on the provision of adequate food, shelter, and clothing, the association argued for a comprehensive, integrated model of care. This model would include readily accessible psychiatric services along with a range of supervised community settings appropriate to each individual's needs. To avoid a major pitfall of deinstitutionalization, case managers would be responsible for ensuring that no one fell between the cracks.[41]

Ideally, this system would provide superior services to both the homeless mentally ill and to everyone else who needed help with their emotional problems. It would universalize mental health services and remove the stigma from those seeking assistance. True, in the short run, it would be more expensive. But a large part of these expenses derive from addressing social costs that were previously unacknowledged: the emotional difficulties visible on the street, as well as the emotional difficulties hidden at home. The homeless mentally ill are not the only people who need help. Both for them and for everyone else, a comprehensive multitiered approach would represent the best alternative.

The Causes of Homelessness

At first glance, the mentally ill belong in an entirely different category from those who are homeless for economic reasons. Whether it is one of the working poor or a public assistance recipient experiencing a grant cutback, "economic" homelessness is the result of inadequate resources relative to the availability of affordable housing. These homeless people are vulnerable, and their homelessness is something that happened to them.

Conversely, when homelessness happens to the mentally ill, it is supposed to be something that their illness caused. Although this argument has, at least in its tidiest form, been disputed here, even its temporary acceptance ultimately proves to be a distinction without a difference. For if mental illness did cause homelessness, then that would merely signify that more people were at risk. This argument is inadvertently damning. True, it does transfer the blame about the origins of homelessness to a personal defect. But if its intent is to exonerate the political and economic institutions of the United States, it fails dismally, because those same institutions have never cared very well for the mentally ill.

In this respect, deinstitutionalization and mental illness actually possess a lot in common with the other causes of homelessness. Mental illness shares the economic causes of homelessness—the insufficient income of working and poor people, bound together by the concept of less eligibility. It also shares the lack of a support system. What mental illness adds to this list is the element of emotional frailty. Everybody who is homeless lacks the resources to pay for housing. As a group, however, only the mentally ill are doubly burdened, because they possess neither the economic nor the emotional resources to keep them from a life on the street.

PART III

The Response

7

Social Movements, Advocates, and the Law

Every society shapes the demands made against it. In the United States, the two-party system, the absence of a socialist tradition, and the distinctive role of the judiciary in interpreting the Constitution encourage the dissatisfied to present their demands as claims under the Bill of Rights.
PAUL STARR

Absent constitutional mandate, the assurance of adequate housing ...[is a] legislative, not a judicial function.
The U.S. Supreme Court in *Lindsey* v. *Normet* [1972]

It is very hard to sustain a movement when everyone is hungry.
MIKE NEELY, homeless activist, Justiceville, Los Angeles, California

The sight of so many visibly homeless people has produced two major responses. The charitably-minded have established food banks, set up temporary shelters, and distributed old clothes. For some lawyers and social activists, however, this response was not enough. Seeking to go beyond the limits of private charity, they organized a movement to affirm housing as a human right. While they have not progressed very far in gaining recognition for this right, their lawsuits, demonstrations, and political campaigns have nonetheless gotten enough attention from the government to propel homelessness into the first rank of policy issues.

The government, social activists, and the charitably-minded: what is perhaps most surprising about this list is the absence of the homeless themselves. While the charitable help the homeless, and social activists advocate for them, homeless people have fought against considerable odds to carry on their own political struggles. Those who have succeeded are the exception. In New York, the leadership of Ruth Young and Jean Chappell was vital in obtaining permanent housing for the 235 residents

of the Brooklyn Arms, the city's second largest welfare hotel. In Philadelphia, Chris Sprowal organized the first union of the homeless; others
have followed suit in Chicago, Baltimore, Los Angeles, Boston, and San
Francisco. There have even been efforts to found a national union.[1]

Amid the comparative quiet, tent cities of homeless people have become centers of political activity. When these cities rose in places like
Portland, Maine, New York's Tompkins Square Park, and beneath the
freeways of San Jose, California, homeless people traded on their aggressive visibility and took an active role. The homeless have established
tent cities in front of the Illinois and California state capitols to lobby
for additional funding. In Phoenix, Arizona, they forced local officials
to provide service to a site at a local railroad yard; in Los Angeles, Ted
Hayes, a former minister, became the leader of Justiceville, a tent city
that publicized local conditions.[2]

These forays into politics are noteworthy, because for the most part,
they have been relatively unusual. In fact, the same reasons that make
the homeless population hard to count also make it hard to organize.
Both the census-taker and the organizer must cope with the population's
dispersion and transience. In addition, however, the organizer also confronts a whole series of other obstacles to political activity by the homeless. These obstacles demonstrate that the causes of homelessness have
not only made people homeless; to a large extent, they have disabled
them politically.

The political impairment of the homeless derives from the circumstances of homelessness itself. Political activity requires a certain minimal
self-confidence, a belief in one's power to bring about change. Yet loss
of this faith is one of the first psychological effects of homelessness.
Stigmatized and facing constant rejection, many homeless people gradually come to accept the world's own view of them, and this self-image
gradually destroys their feelings of political efficacy. The message is a
simple one: someone without a home is an inconsequential person, and
the actions of an inconsequential person cannot have political
consequences.

It would be far too conspiratorial to see any conscious plan in the
political disabling of the homeless. Nobody intended their political si-
lence, any more than anyone deliberately intended to make them homeless. Nevertheless, as with other poor people, their quiescence is
exceedingly useful. Imagine, for example, that instead of being politically
demobilized, the homeless population was militant, disruptive, and actively fought for decent housing. This kind of militance would transform
the political landscape; it would force the powers that be into spending
long hours figuring out just how they might induce the political quiescence they now have.

In political terms, at least, the response of private charity has been
equally noncombative. The spectacle of public homelessness invests private charity with new meaning. People do give more freely when they

know that their money is going for an immediately evident purpose, to provide a homeless person with a night's shelter. Perhaps that is why by 1987, a survey of 130 large corporations showed homelessness ranked sixth in donated funds.[3] On the local level, such donations may well instill stronger feelings of community among the charitable. A program to aid the poor in its midst can boost a church's lagging attendance; an auction to sell used furniture can reactivate the membership of many a civic group. The money that is raised will assist the homeless and make the donors feel better about themselves. But apart from its effects on the consciousness of individuals, these programs rarely challenge the notion that every person they help suffers from a discrete, private trouble.

Charitable organizations have produced several major media events to publicize the issue of homelessness, of which the Hands Across America in 1986 is probably the most famous. The magnitude of the event, however, did not really change the underlying philosophy. A line of people holding hands across the United States to make a statement about homelessness creates a tantalizing intimation of what a true community might be like. A few people on the line may commit themselves to do something more about homelessness. A keener awareness of the issue may penetrate the consciousness of some spectators. But when, after ten minutes, participants put their hands down at their sides and return to their own pursuits, the line disintegrates, and with it, its help for the homeless, both real and illusory.[4]

The Social Movement for the Homeless

The social movement to house the homeless sees homelessness as a social problem rather than as a private trouble. Politics replaces charity. Food, clothing, and shelter are no longer donations to the less fortunate. Instead, in this social movement, advocates see the necessities of life as a basic human right.

Social movements are an elusive phenomenon. For this reason, a substantial controversy exists about their character and definition. Even so, the recent history of homelessness probably conforms most closely to the theory of social movements known as resource mobilization.[5] Associated especially with the work of John McCarthy and Mayer Zald, this perspective argues that since grievances always exist, it is access to resources—defined broadly as people, money, and materials—that transform a grievance into a social movement. These resources are scarce, and the competition for them is intense. The social movement for the homeless burgeoned in the 1980s partly because the visibility of the homeless made such a compelling demand on these resources.

What McCarthy and Zald term *conscience constituencies* are crucial to responding to these demands. Unlike *beneficiary constituencies* who would themselves gain from achievement of the movement's goals, conscience constituencies support the movement without benefiting directly from it.[6] In the social movement that has been organized around homelessness, conscience constituencies have been by far the more powerful.

It is this comparatively greater power that has made the issue of housing for the homeless into the perfect social movement for the late twentieth century. As a movement for, rather than by, the poor, it demonstrates both the extent to which the poor have been demobilized and the degree to which other people, for reasons of both conscience and politics, rush to help.

The Advocates

Thousands of people have become active in the social movement for the homeless. They are the movement's troops. Angered by the spread of homelessness, they have both helped homeless people and performed the political tasks that enabled the movement to function. Distributing sandwiches, blankets, petitions, and press releases—whether it was services or politics, they have done whatever was needed.

As director of Project Domicile, the housing program of New York City's Partnership for the Homeless, Sister Georgette Lawton typifies the advocates' energy and commitment. The partnership, which is a coalition of the city's religious organizations, gets an allotment of city-owned apartments from the municipal government, and Sister Georgette allocates them, with sensitivity and care. Some organizations merely put homeless people in a van and take them to apartments, saying "the next one is yours." Sister Georgette is different. She shows them the unit and if they decide to move in, sees that they are visited at least once a week. "We don't just leave them at the door and say 'Good luck, now. Bye.' " she says. "We establish relationships with people."[7]

Within the social movement for the homeless, advocacy groups coordinate the work of activists and sympathetic service providers. The best known of all these advocacy groups is undoubtedly the Coalition for the Homeless. Founded in 1980 when police tried to remove the homeless from the vicinity of the Democratic National Convention at New York City's Madison Square Garden, the organization soon broadened into a national coalition with its headquarters in Washington, D.C., a ten region administrative structure, and affiliated groups in thirty-four states.[8] The coalition is loosely organized, with shared interests and concerns, but little attempt to achieve the ideological unity associated with other groups. For this very reason, it has been unusually successful in channeling the political energies of a diverse group of people.

The leadership of the movement as a whole reflects this diversity. In Portland, Oregon, Beverly "Ma" Curtis, who was once homeless herself, has been instrumental in the development of the Burnside Community Council and its efforts to provide services to the population. In St. Louis, Reverend Larry Rice, who operates the New Life Evangelistic Center, a downtown men's shelter, has worked with the homeless since the mid-1970s. His efforts, and especially his use of the media, have played a significant role in the enrichment of the city's services. And, of course, before his suicide in 1990, ex-Wall Street stockbroker and once homeless Mitch Snyder used a variety of protest tactics including his own fifty-one day hunger strike to force the federal government to renovate Washington's Second Street shelter.

When leaders like these speak of their work, it has the ring of a true calling. After several years of volunteering, Jane Haggstrom took a salary cut of 80 percent from her job as an administrator at a local hospital to assume her position as coordinator of the Santa Barbara Homeless Coalition. A psychiatric nurse by training, Haggstrom is totally immersed in her role. "I love the homeless," she says. "In many ways I was directed to this job. I have tried to get out and (eventually) I get back to it. It is not up to me to decide what is happening in my life any more. I feel like this is what I'm supposed to be doing. It has given me a real sense of spirituality." In her job as advocate, Haggstrom has argued with the police, represented the homeless before the Santa Barbara City Council, and been abused by those she tried to help. She also succeeded in increasing the operating budget of the coalition from $17,000 to $115,000 in just two years. Politicians in Santa Barbara used to ignore the homeless. Now, as a result of the coalition's growth, they have to treat it as a legitimate interest group.[9]

Louisa Stark's involvement with the homeless in Phoenix dates back to 1981. Arriving in Arizona after fourteen years as a professor of anthropology at the University of Wisconsin, Stark found that the city had already demolished thousands of low-income housing units to clear the way for a downtown urban renewal project. When homeless people began to appear on the streets, Stark conducted the first study of their demographic characteristics. The study contained a modest set of recommendations for transitional housing, but city officials ignored them until a tent city of 750 people rose on the avenue leading to the Capitol. Forming a consortium with a small group of other advocates, Stark persuaded the St. Vincent de Paul Society and the Salvation Army to open temporary shelters. This housing remained open for about one year. Then Phoenix officials, working with state and county agencies, agreed to establish Central Arizona Shelter Services, which provides nightly shelter for hundreds of homeless people.

Stark was elected chair of the National Coalition for the Homeless in 1984. At first viewed locally as somewhat of a troublemaker, she was comparatively conciliatory in her dealings with Congress and the White House. Her national lobbying, though, has not caused her to sever her ties with the local advocacy network. She still transports carloads of homeless people to small church shelters in the Phoenix area and administers the distribution of donated materials to needy families. Stark is, however, no longer on the advisory board of the Central Phoenix

Shelter. She resigned in 1987 after shelter administrators, in response to the arrest of a resident in the murder of a six-year-old boy, began to give a list of residents to the police for comparison against outstanding arrest-warrants. The policy, she argued, wrongly "[stereotyped] homeless people as criminals."[10]

Legal Advocacy for the Homeless

Lawyers represent a special kind of advocate for the homeless. With few exceptions, their names are not well known, but their cases have made new law and turned the courts into the branch of government that is most supportive of the homeless. In St. Louis, Kenneth Chackes of Washington University Law School led the fight for municipal shelter services. Likewise, David Sciarra of the State Public Advocates' Office won a right to shelter in New Jersey. The homeless gained voting rights through the efforts of Williard Hastings in Santa Barbara. And elsewhere, Gary Blasi of the Los Angeles Legal Aid Foundation and Steve Banks of the Homeless Family Rights Project in New York City have, respectively, overturned the identification requirements for shelter and secured a right to shelter for families.

Legal advocacy for the homeless began with Robert Hayes. Hayes grew up on Long Island, went to college at Georgetown, and spent a year as a reporter for the newspaper of the Long Island Catholic Diocese, where he was almost fired for writing an article about gay rights. After his second year at New York University Law School, Hayes was hired as a summer intern by Sullivan & Cromwell, one of the most prestigious Wall Street law firms whose roster of clients included Exxon, General Foods, and General Electric. Upon his graduation from New York University in 1977, he became a full-time employee of the firm.

By then, the homeless were becoming increasingly visible in New York City. Hayes first began to notice them on his daily commute to work. When he inquired about the reason for their presence on the street, they told him about the deplorable conditions in Bowery flophouses and at the East Third Street Men's Shelter, the city's processing center for the homeless. Hayes became curious. Visiting the places they described, he got the permission of a partner at Sullivan & Cromwell to do some *pro bono* work. He thought that "by talking to city officials about what was going on, they would be moved to do something." But when Hayes met the director of the Third Street Shelter, the administrator bluntly explained that conditions were kept "forbidding" in order to "encourage these people to make other arrangements." "It was then I got angry," Hayes said. "And when lawyers get angry, they can only think of one thing."

His anger, however, did not appear to have much support in the law. All Hayes could find was a clause in the 1938 New York State Constitution providing that "the aid, care, and support of the needy are public concerns and shall be provided by the state...as the legislature may from time to time determine." Treating this constitutional provision as a bit of decorative rhetoric, courts in the past had generally refused to enforce its terms on the state or any of its municipalities. The one hopeful sign was a speech by Edward Corsi, the chair of the social welfare committee who had introduced the passage at the 1938 convention. In justifying the rationale behind this provision, Corsi said:

> Here are words which set forth a definite policy of government, a concrete social obligation which no court may ever misread. By this section, the Committee hopes to achieve two purposes. First: to remove from the area of constitutional doubt the responsibility of the State to those who must look to society for the bare necessities of life.... [11]

Using this piece of legislative history and some applicable provisions of the municipal code, Hayes sued the city of New York.

The resulting class action suit, *Callahan* v. *Carey* became a legal landmark. Robert Callahan was an Irish short-order cook who had lost his job four years earlier, been evicted from his apartment, drunk too much, and ended up on the Bowery. Together with two other homeless men, Thomas Damian and Clayton Fox, he represented the category of all homeless men in this legal action. When Hayes filed his brief in October 1979, he estimated that there were 10,000 homeless men in New York City. Only 1,200 to 2,000 sought lodging every night in winter, mostly because after the Third Street Shelter provided 750 vouchers for Bowery hotels, the only available facility was the floor of the shelter's "Big Room." Several hundred men could be accommodated there, but everyone else was turned back into the streets.

The heart of the plaintiff's brief was a bare, legalistic description of Robert Callahan. In Hayes's words, Robert Callahan was "a 54 year-old resident of New York City residing at the Delevan Hotel located at 143 Bowery. He is dependent on the Men's Shelter for lodging. He has virtually no income or property and is unable to provide for himself." [12] In an ordinary case, this kind of identification would be just so much legal boilerplate. But here it was far more. Before, when the homeless were named in court proceedings, they were usually defendants in disorderly conduct actions. This description, however, formally recognized their visibility. While the outcome of this suit was dependent on Hayes's assertion that the homeless possess a legal right to shelter, no court grants rights to people whose invisibility prevents them from appearing before it. The function of the *Callahan* suit was to make this appearance possible.

In December 1979, the Supreme Court handed down a preliminary injunction in the *Callahan* case that recognized a right to shelter. Even though the jurist who issued this injunction also referred to homeless clients as "flotsam and jetsam," [13] the decision was nonetheless precedent-setting. It was the first time that an American court had recognized the existence of this right, and it generated a host of similar cases in many jurisdictions all over the United States.

What happened in New York, though, foreshadowed what would happen in other municipalities and dramatized the difficulties facing legal advocates. After two years of intense wrangling, the preliminary *Callahan* injunction was formalized in a 1981 consent decree. But despite its signature on this decree, New York City spent most of the next five years trying to modify the terms of its implementation. A right to shelter did not amount to much when 1,400 people slept in cots on the drill floor of the Fort Washington Armory, and the city commissioned a twenty page report entitled *An Observational Study of Toilet and Shower Utilization at Three Men's Shelters*—complete with twenty-three charts—to prove that there was an excess of plumbing.[14] The city's attitude toward implementation was begrudging. As a result, Hayes, in his official capacity as legal counsel to the Coalition for the Homeless, had to go to court some thirty times to enforce the terms of the decree.[15]

Legal advocates, then, have won some significant victories. Yet in many respects, the courts are not naturally hospitable to the homeless. The courts do not like to enter into the legislative arena, and getting them to do so is both costly and time-consuming. There are also, as the *Callahan* case illustrates, ongoing problems of implementation. Because judges would rather dispose of a case and be done with it, they generally resist making decisions that transform them into the de facto administrators of large social welfare agencies. Moreover, since even the most sympathetic courts usually redress individual rather than group grievances, few courts are going to authorize broad entitlements for jobs, housing, and guaranteed income. Without these programs, no advocate can be entirely proud of funding a multitude of temporary shelters, which is, odds-on, the "most favorable" possible outcome.

In law school, lawyers learn to see judges as philosopher-kings who will, under some circumstances, set a social agenda: make a good argument, and the litigator wins.[16] But the truth is more complex. The courts are, in their own depoliticized way, highly political. Driven into court by the absence of sympathetic political forces in other branches of government, advocates had to submit to a judicial decision-making process that was relatively insulated and depoliticized. It was this very depoliticization that enabled the judiciary to take the political step of granting rights to homeless people. At the same time, however, it is the judiciary's own freedom from political forces that compels the homeless to accept the limits placed on those rights as the courts define them.[17]

The Courts and the Homeless

Under the doctrine of separation of powers, the courts are not supposed to make law. Indeed, according to the classic statement of this doctrine, the role of the courts is restricted to interpreting laws that the executive and legislative branches enact. The response of the judiciary to the homeless is therefore perplexing. While developments dating back to *Brown* v. *The Board of Education* in 1954 have certainly blurred the boundaries among all three branches of government, few would have anticipated that in responding to the homeless, the judiciary would assume such a prominent role.

For those concerned about losing the uniqueness of the judiciary, the intervention of the courts in social problems is most worrisome. As one writer puts it, "augmenting judicial capacity may erode the distinctive contribution the courts make to the social order. The danger is that the courts, in developing a capacity to improve on the work of other institutions, may become altogether too much like them."[18] From this perspective, two separate questions are at issue. The first, legitimacy, relates to the question of whether the courts should intervene at all; the second, capacity, raises the question of whether they can intervene effectively.[19] With the failure of other institutions, both questions become more pressing.

In theory, when government is working properly, the executive and legislative branches pass laws to address social problems as they arise. Whether it is an issue of racial discrimination, equal pay for equal work, or access to decent housing, it is only possible for the judiciary to retain a circumscribed role if the other two branches demonstrate some political leadership and fashion an adequate response. When, however, that leadership is lacking, the problem festers, and those who suffer on account of it will seek remediation by defining their social needs as rights under the U.S. Constitution. The next, logical step is to assert those rights in court.

In the case of the homeless, as with other social problems, the courts therefore make law to fill a political vacuum. Thus, during the 1970s, the homeless began to appear on the street. Their numbers grew, and their visibility called into question some basic assumptions about U.S. society: the existence of poverty, the commitment to minimal standards of social welfare, the erosion of caring and community amidst the single-minded pursuit of wealth. In short, homelessness was an obvious social problem that nobody was doing anything about—not the cities where it first appeared, not the states, and certainly not the federal government. The judiciary's natural reluctance to intervene collapsed in the face of this political vacuum.

Paradoxically, it is the insulation of the judiciary from politics that gives it the power to act. Powerful conservative forces in business and the population at large buffet the other branches of government. While these forces may prevent the legislative and executive branches from responding to a social problem, they often do so at the price of letting political tensions build to the bursting point. Under these circumstances, the *depoliticization* of the judiciary is essential to overcoming the paralysis of politics. Judges hold office for a longer term and therefore possess somewhat greater autonomy from direct, conservatizing influences. For this reason, they are able to accommodate the demands of disenfranchised groups whose challenge, if ignored, might well transform a social problem into a larger political crisis.[20]

The intervention of the courts has had significant practical consequences upon the homeless. In the process of granting some measure of legitimacy to their demands, the courts have established some new laws and revised many more. There are, however, limits to what the courts can do. The courts can insist on procedural guarantees. They can even recognize a few rights. But they cannot go much farther, because as an expression of the society's dominant values, the law in the United States subordinates any general recognition of these rights to the rights of property.

The Law and the Homeless

Federal law is perhaps least hospitable to the homeless. The U.S. Supreme Court, for example, has never recognized the existence of a right to shelter. Dismissing the idea in *Lindsey* v. *Normet* (1972), it stated, "The Constitution does not provide judicial remedies for every social and economic ill. We are unable to perceive in that document any constitutional guarantee of access to dwellings of a particular quality." Nor has the Court acknowledged the existence of a minimum welfare grant, rejecting, in *Lavine* v. *Milne* (1976), the notion of any state or federal obligation to provide benefits. Demands for the adoption of an adequate standard of need on which to base AFDC benefits have also been turned down (*Rosado* v. *Wyman*, 1970), as have arguments about seemingly invidious distinctions in the treatment of AFDC recipients (*Dandridge* v. *Williams*, 1970). In the latter case, the Court upheld a Maryland rule restricting monthly family grants to a maximum of $250 regardless of family size after the fourth child. The ostensible goal of this regulation was to give the mother an incentive to work. Since, however, the state also acknowledged that "only a small percentage of the total universe of welfare recipients are employable," the Supreme Court accepted as "rational and free from invidious discrimination" a regulation whose primary outcome would be to increase the number of hungry children in large AFDC families.[21]

On the state level, the record is somewhat better. Although a few defeats have occurred when legal advocates made broad claims to decent, permanent housing, they have rolled back many other obstacles to the provision of shelter. It is just possible that history is repeating itself. When most states enacted mothers' pensions in the period from 1911 to 1919, they set a precedent for the inclusion of aid to dependent children in the 1935 federal Social Security Act. It took a generation then; it will probably take another generation now. But these newly acquired rights to shelter at the state level could percolate upward, until, like AFDC, they are embodied in federal law.

The legal docket of advocacy cases for the homeless encompasses an extraordinary range of disputes. There are cases about the right to beg, the right to vote, and the right to sleep in public places, among other issues.[22] Amid this explosion of lawsuits, however, there are basically three kinds of litigation involving the homeless. These are first, challenges to the adequacy or availability of relief; second, the right to raise children in one's own home, or at least to keep the family together; and third, the right to shelter.[23]

The first category includes several cases where the courts overturned eligibility criteria demanding a fixed address. In *Martin* v. *Milwaukee County* (1985), a Wisconsin circuit court ruled that such a requirement was illegal under state law. *Turner* v. *City of New Orleans* (1989), a similar suit in Louisiana filed under the state's Pauper Relief Act, was somewhat less successful. The settlement in this case authorized assistance despite the lack of a fixed address, but then made that assistance contingent upon the availability of funds.[24] Since the judiciary, unlike the legislature, does not have the power to tax, this contingency is often the single biggest obstacle to the success of the courts' interventions.

A cluster of Los Angeles cases also belongs in this category. There, Gary Blasi and a group of lawyers from eight Los Angeles public interest law firms (together with the *pro bono* contributions of several private law firms) put together a Homeless Litigation Team that won several important victories. First, in *Eisenheim* v. *Board of Supervisors* (1984), the advocates successfully challenged regulations requiring identification for the receipt of emergency housing benefits. As part of the ruling in this case, benefits that had previously taken weeks, even with identification, were now available on the same day. Los Angeles County used to have thousands of empty hotel rooms. After the court issued a temporary restraining order in *Eisenheim* on 24 December 1984, homeless people filled the hotels within two weeks.[25]

The success of *Eisenheim* soon led to two other hotel-related suits. In one, *Ross* v. *Board of Supervisors* (1984), legal advocates brought an action against the county for its policy of limiting each homeless person's hotel allowance to eight dollars a night. When *Eisenheim* caused the cheaper hotels to fill up, the Homeless Litigation Team got the county to increase the payment to sixteen dollars. Nevertheless, many homeless people understandably continued to prefer the streets: the county might be subsidizing the hotels, but its Board of Health was simultaneously prosecuting them for numerous health violations. The advocates sued again. In *Paris* v. *Board of Supervisors* (1984), they persuaded the court to prohibit the county from issuing vouchers for hotels that failed to comply with minimum health standards and maintain a winter temperature of sixty-eight degrees.[26]

Another issue also proved amenable to court intervention. As a matter of policy, the county of Los Angeles had withheld aid for sixty days to recipients of general assistance who failed to follow strict regulations for working off their grant. Some 2,500 people a month, or about 5,000 people altogether, experienced two months of enforced homelessness because they were late for their work project, did not turn in a form on time, or neglected to document their twenty required monthly job searches. In *Bannister* v. *Board of Supervisors of Los Angeles County*, the plaintiffs won a ruling that modified these practices. As a result, homeless people are now allowed to show good cause for their failure, and at least on paper, the county can no longer arbitrarily withhold their benefits.[27]

These cases illustrate the potential of an adroit legal strategy. Despite the absence of broad-based popular support, advocates in Los Angeles have altered the system that the county uses for delivering benefits to the homeless. If the shelter is not yet adequate, and homelessness remains an unenviable condition, it is no longer quite so desperate as before the courts intervened. By operating within the judiciary, professional advocates have brought about a distinct, yet carefully circumscribed, measure of reform.

The second category of cases exhibit a similar pattern. Their underlying premise is that since the Social Security Act conclusively ended the practice of forcing the poor into institutions to obtain relief, outdoor assistance—in the form of AFDC—has enabled them to raise their children in their own homes. States whose welfare grant does not provide enough money for this purpose are therefore in violation of their own regulations. This is the line of argument behind the landmark New York State decision, *Jiggetts* v. *Grinker*. In this 1990 case, Steve Banks of the Homeless Family Rights Project argued successfully before the New York Court of Appeals that courts had the authority to determine whether the local shelter grant—$312 a month for a family of four—was sufficient to obtain housing in New York City.[28]

The potential of *Jiggetts* v. *Grinker* is considerable, because it goes even farther than a parallel Massachusetts case that has already had considerable impact. In *Massachusetts Coalition for the Homeless* v. *Dukakis*, the plaintiffs asserted that by setting the AFDC grant for a three person family in Massachusetts at 46 percent below the poverty line, the state had failed to uphold the standard of a 1913 law entitling poor people to raise children in their own home. Throughout this trial, the state coalition complemented the legal advocacy of Barbara Sard from Greater Boston Legal Services with the grass-roots organizing of an "Up to the Poverty Level" campaign. Both inside and outside the courtroom, the plaintiffs argued that since the deficit was one of the fundamental causes of homelessness, it was incumbent upon the state to develop a more adequate standard of need and fund public assistance at the official poverty level.[29]

The coalition won its claim about an adequate standard in Superior

Court. As Judge Charles M. Grabau stated, "There is no more compelling statutory policy in need of enforcement than protecting families from homelessness—a phenomenon increasing in severity and frequency, largely due to inadequate public assistance." On appeal, the Supreme Judicial Court supported his interpretation of the law, but unlike *Jiggetts*, let the legislature, and not the court, determine the adequacy of the grant. The legislature took the hint. Eager to avoid any further judicial intrusions, it promptly voted AFDC increases for private housing of 14 and 12 percent in successive years.[30]

These decisions all relate to families who have been able to maintain a home in which to raise their children. When a family loses its home, however, welfare departments sometimes take children away. Then, and only then, do they make emergency assistance available. After legal advocates contested this policy in California, the appeals court declared in *Hansen* v. *McMahon* that the provision of assistance to homeless children was not contingent upon separation from their families. More generally, courts in Delaware, the District of Columbia, Illinois, Pennsylvania, and New York have looked with disfavor upon cases where homelessness was the primary reason for the placement of a child in foster care.[31]

Despite the impact of these cases, it is probably the third category of right-to-shelter advocacy on the state level that has aroused the most interest. Though this reaction may be understandable in the wake of *Callahan*, most state constitutions do not have language like New York's, and there is little reason to believe that equivalent rights could be won. In fact, twenty states lack any statutory basis for a right to shelter, and only seventeen state constitutions make any reference to aid for the poor. By the time the constitutional rhetoric is stripped away, legal advocates are left with just six that contain unambiguous language. From the perspective of existing law, it is simply not a very hospitable landscape.[32]

Some successful forays have nonetheless been made. One in St. Louis, *Graham* v. *Schoemehl*, produced a consent decree where the city promised to provide services to the homeless. From the results of *Maticka* v. *Atlantic City* and *Algor* v. *County of Ocean*, it is clear that a statutory, though not a constitutional right to shelter, exists in New Jersey. Similarly, in Connecticut, a class action suit by the homeless, *Lubetkin* v. *Hartford*, resulted in the issuance of regulations requiring the provision of aid. When legal advocates went looking for a right to shelter, they found it where one would most reasonably expect it to be found—in the older, and more traditionally liberal, Northeast.[33]

Besides New York, West Virginia is the only state that has located a right to shelter within its constitution. Even here, though, in *Hodge* v. *Ginsberg*, it located that right by identifying the homeless as "incapacitated adults" under the terms of the West Virginia Social Services for Adults Act, the legislation mandating adult protective services. While people who need shelter can hardly afford to be too particular about its

legal justification, the reasoning in this case illuminates one of the assumptions underlying most social welfare law. Adults have homes; only
a person who is somehow less than adult requires governmental intervention. Nowhere in this conception is there room for fully functioning
adults who just cannot afford a home.[34]

Although individual cities may declare the existence of a statutory
right, and a few states may make some legislative moves in that direction,
New York is still the place with the most fully developed right to shelter.
New York not only possesses a constitutional foundation for the right
to shelter movement, but it also has a sophisticated group of legal advocates. They have made some further inroads since *Callahan* v. *Carey*.
Still, as the cutting edge of legal developments in the advocacy movement, both their successes and failures may well anticipate what everybody else will one day confront.

The Legacy of *Callahan* and
The Limits of Judicial Intervention

While virtually every homeless case in New York can trace its legal
origins back to *Callahan*, *Eldredge* v. *Koch* and *McCain* v. *Koch* are its two
most closely related descendants. In *Eldredge* v. *Koch*, legal advocates
sought to apply the *Callahan* decree to women. New York City insisted
that conditions in the women's shelters were as good as the men's; the
Coalition for the Homeless sought to prove otherwise, first in the lower
court and then again, after the city appealed, in the appellate division.
The court ruled that since the precedent of *Callahan* applied, evidence
should be collected about conditions in the women's shelters to ensure
that they adhered to this standard.[35]

The application of *Callahan* to families proved to be a more complicated process. By the fall of 1984, New York City had exhausted its
supply of emergency shelter for families, and mothers with their children
were sleeping in welfare offices. Other families were living in hotels
where infants slept in bureau drawers, and rooms were little more than
a cubicle with exposed wires, crumbling plaster, and inoperable plumbing. In *McCain* v. *Koch*, lawyers for the homeless tried to remedy these
conditions by establishing that every family in New York had a right to
safe, adequate emergency shelter.[36]

Orders of the lower court to maintain minimum standards were reversed on appeal and then reinstated by New York's highest court. As
it moved up through the state's judicial system, the debate in *McCain*
clarified the single most important issue facing legal advocates, namely,
what are the limits on the courts' proper role? The issue was so pointed
in *McCain* because New York courts have struggled recently with several
important social welfare cases that address precisely this question.
McCain fell in their shadow.

The longest shadow was cast by *Tucker* v. *Toia*. In this 1977 case, the court required the state to provide support for needy persons. In New York, the court reasoned, such aid was not "a matter of legislative grace; rather, it is specifically mandated by our Constitution."[37] The court, however, then substantially diluted the impact of this statement by granting the legislature virtually total discretion in carrying it out. In essence, New York State had to do something for the poor, but what it did lay outside the purview of the courts.

Subsequent cases such as *Bernstein* v. *Toia* and *RAM* v. *Blum* amplified this principle. In the former, a suit against the state for fixing maximum shelter allowances, the court distinguished between "the impermissible exclusion of the needy from eligibility for benefits" and the "absolute sufficiency of the benefits distributed to each eligible recipient." In the latter, the court rebuffed the claim of a group of welfare recipients that 1974 grant levels were constitutionally inadequate by 1980.[38] The law was quite clear: while the state cannot totally deny benefits, it can give very little.

Although the decision in *Jiggetts* v. *Grinker* suggests that the court is now willing to insist on an adequate welfare grant, the judiciary is not going to overturn the principle of less eligibility which these cases embody. There is simply too much at stake. After *McCain*, New York City has to maintain minimum standards in the welfare hotels; after *Jiggetts*, the state has to provide "adequate" housing grants. The courts will try to hold both the city and the state to this standard. Nevertheless, whatever they do, housing for the homeless and housing for the poor is sure to be distinguishable from housing for the lowest paid worker.

That the courts have granted new rights to the homeless testifies to the crisis of belief that their visibility has caused. Yet the interaction of the legal system and the economy place distinct limits on the courts' intervention. Much of U.S. law is devoted to analyzing and protecting property rights. The homeless lack property. As a consequence, in this conflict between persons and things, there is only so far that the courts can go.

The Role of Legal Advocacy within the Social Movement

Legal advocacy has obviously made a substantial difference in the lives of the homeless. Still, as a number of advocates have emphasized, its greatest successes have occurred as part of a larger social movement.[39] The homeless certainly need lawyers who are willing to fight for their rights. These lawyers will be most successful, however, when the social movement for the homeless creates a political environment in which these rights can take root.

This is not an easy task, for the social movement on behalf of the homeless has been heavily skewed toward the professional advocate. Certainly, these advocates—whether lawyers, political activists, or the thousands of people of good conscience—have made a difference. Nonetheless, in the absence of a militant homeless population, the social movement for the homeless fights with just one hand. And given the political and economic obstacles it faces, this one hand has not been enough.

8

Municipal Responses

> Cities are actually caught in the crossfire of the business interests
> calling for restraint and the workers and consumers refusing to carry
> the burden of a crisis that is not theirs.
> MANUEL CASTELLS

> Redistributive demands, which create class conflicts in national pol-
> itics, have little place in local politics.
> PAUL PETERSON

     The social movement for the homeless has lobbied for assis-
tance at every level of government, but in practice, it is cities that deliver
most of the benefits and services. The federal and state governments
normally fund part of this aid. Yet by the time the homeless actually get
assistance, the money has generally been handed down to the local government, which may, or may not, add its own tax revenues. If a municipality relies entirely on the nonprofit sector, or spends no money from
other governmental sources, then services to the homeless will follow
broad state guidelines. These guidelines tighten considerably, however,
when there is state and federal funding. Under these circumstances, the
city still administers the program, but it does so more accountably, with
the other funding sources looking over its shoulder.
    Beyond these broad patterns, there have been obvious differences
in the response of each municipality to the growth of the homeless
population. Some municipalities have responded more completely than
others. Cities have also differed in their mix of programs from the public
and private sectors. The visibility of the homeless, their concentration
and dispersion, have played a role too, though the city's reaction has
always been filtered through the locality's traditional mechanism for aid
to the poor. Hence, while cities like Houston, which generally provide
little help to the poor, have carefully limited their assistance to the homeless population, other municipalities such as Boston, with a less restrictive
tradition, have relied on the public sector and developed a whole new
set of programs. Though public poverty in downtown urban areas has

109

been bad for business all over the country, what a specific city did about the homeless depended on political and economic conditions in that locality.

Two important policy issues shape any interpretation of the response of cities to a growing homeless population. One issue involves the question of the behavior of cities as economic and political units; a second issue relates to the constraints on that behavior. Together, these issues raise the question of the interaction between the freedom of cities to choose a response and the limits on their process of decision-making.

Cities, like individuals, are supposed to be economic maximizers. Consistently seeking to gain the greatest possible economic advantage, cities compete with each other as places to conduct business. For this reason, they cannot afford to enact policies that would give more money than their competitors to poor people. Unlike nations, cities cannot inflate currency, erect trade barriers, or prevent immigration. Without these options, it is argued, they have no choice but to pursue strictly developmental policies. Since any program that redistributed income to poorer people would represent an absolute loss to every city resident, business development must benefit everyone.[1]

These premises seem quite problematic after three decades of urban crisis. From homelessness to tax policy, the marketplace distributes its benefits unevenly. Moreover, high social costs often accompany the uneven distribution of these benefits.[2] When, for example, real estate investors construct a cooperative apartment in a gentrifying neighborhood, they create profit for themselves and housing for those residents who are prosperous enough to purchase units in the new building. The same apartment will undoubtedly have inflationary effects on the cost of housing in the neighborhood, and these inflationary effects may well push rents out of the reach of local residents. If some of these residents subsequently become homeless, the gulf between the promoter, the housed, and the homeless is sufficiently large to discredit any argument about the uniformly benign effects of business development.

Neither are the consequences for local government financing necessarily benign. As proponents of economic development frequently stress, it is true that the government will receive additional tax revenue from an increase in the valuation of its real property. But since the city government also assumes responsibility for sheltering the newly homeless, rising welfare costs can easily devour these new revenues. In addition, when the city grants a tax deferment to the developer to encourage this investment, it most likely exchanges a sharp, immediate upturn in the costs of welfare for the promise of greater tax revenues at some future time.

This example illustrates the causes of the urban fiscal crisis that has beset major U.S. cities since the 1970s. Cities do have to compete in order to bring in business investment, but business investment generates social costs in welfare, pollution, and the demand for expanded municipal services. Caught between taxing business at low rates to encourage investment and paying for the costs of that investment, local governments often face a balance sheet in which expenses exceed revenues. In these dire financial straits, the homeless who need shelter find that municipal funds are often quite scarce.

Yet there are powerful reasons for finding these funds. First, just by their presence, the homeless belie the minimum standards of treatment for the poor in U.S. society. Some money must therefore be spent on them, because like crime, mass transit, and the environment, they have attained the status of an urgent social problem. Second, since virtually every city is committed to a strategy of economic development, cities must eliminate the most conspicuous signs of public poverty if that strategy is to succeed. No one wants to conduct business in a central business district overrun with beggars. A city might have the most hospitable set of tax laws, but if its physical setting seems inhospitable, if its streets appear disordered, corporations are going to express doubts about the government's capacity to manage and invest their money elsewhere.

Cities, then, have their own institutional interests, and these interests commingle with, but are not always the same as, those of private capital. To the extent that they converge, cities share the goals of business for favorable economic conditions and long-term political stability. To the extent that they differ, cities possess a modicum of autonomy and independence to pursue their own goals. Thus, while localities are limited in the tax burden they can place on business, they must still collect public revenues if they wish to function. Cities want to enhance their own power; they want to augment their capacity to manage. The officials who run them derive both income and status from their positions in the municipal bureaucracy. For reasons of self-preservation, cities must therefore respond to anything that threatens these institutional interests.[3]

Homelessness is therefore both bad for business and bad for government. Homelessness is a sign of underlying social stresses; its presence indicates that the state is not doing its job. When homelessness proliferates, government appears less competent, and perceptions of diminished competence soon lead to perceptions of diminished legitimacy. By then, homelessness has undermined such an essential part of the basis for the government's existence that even cities which are starved for funds are likely to take some action.[4]

The Federal Response

When cities and states tried to establish programs for the homeless, they quickly discovered that the lack of federal funding was a major impediment to their plans. The squeeze they were feeling was real: from the late 1970s to 1990, the federal government cut local aid by one-third.[5] While Washington did gradually increase its assistance for the homeless, it shortchanged states and localities of both money and leadership. In fact, with little money and less leadership, its response was so haphazard that even the government's showcase legislation, the Stewart B. McKinney Act of 1987, could do little to rationalize the patchwork.

The slow evolution of the Reagan administration's policies began after the first congressional hearings about homelessness, held before the House Banking Subcomittee on Housing and Community Development in December 1982. The administration had previously denied the existence of homelessness as a national issue. But in the face of powerful testimony by a long list of advocates and providers, it had to modify its position.[6] Nevertheless, the administration did not concede much: homelessness, it said, was only a temporary problem requiring, at most, some emergency measures.

The first of these measures was enacted on 24 March 1983, when the passage of Public Law 98–8 gave the Federal Emergency Management Agency (FEMA) responsibility for administering an emergency food and shelter program. The act appropriated $100 million, divided equally between the states and a national board chaired by FEMA and comprised of representatives from some major charitable organizations. Congress also appropriated $70 million, $20 million, and $70 million in the next three fiscal years. FEMA normally aids the victims of hurricanes, floods, and other natural disasters. Even though the Reagan administration opposed the establishment of a separate FEMA program, using FEMA to assist the homeless had the fewest long-term policy implications. Hurricanes in summer, homelessness in winter—under the auspices of FEMA, it was easy to treat the homeless as just another natural disaster.[7]

Other federal agencies moved with equal caution. In 1983, the Department of Defense allocated money to renovate or repair military facilities. Over the next six years, however, it spent the modest total of $4 million transforming these buildings into shelters. The role of the military was limited because few bases have buildings suitable for renovation, and those that do are often inaccessible to the homeless population. Moreover, since the Defense Department cannot operate shelters, local governments must absorb the cost.[8] Like assistance from FEMA, Defense was not quite the right agency to provide housing to the homeless.

Of course, HUD, which was the right agency, got relatively little funding. By 1 October 1983, 119 local jurisdictions had used $34 million worth of their Community Development Block Grants for assistance to the homeless. But when Congress authorized $60 million so that HUD could make grants to localities for shelter rehabilitation, President Reagan threatened to veto the legislation because so much had already been done.[9] Money might trickle down to the homeless at the discretion of an individual state. In general, however, during the Reagan years, the administration did everything possible to prevent a coordinated set of policies and programs from taking hold within the federal government.

The Stewart B. McKinney Act epitomizes this aspect of the administration's response. Though President Reagan signed it at night to signal his lack of enthusiasm, the law did represent a partial breakthorough: nearly twenty different provisions addressing the needs of the homeless were combined in one act. Yet the McKinney Act hardly remedied the fragmentation of federal policy. With a variety of different methods to distribute funds—competitive grants, block grants, and formula allocations—the act allocated money to as many as seven different agencies in one state. And, since the McKinney Act does not pay for some needed services such as social supports in permanent housing, the delivery of social services by the states continues to reflect the patchwork of programs financed by the federal government.[10]

The McKinney Act has also been consistently underfunded. Overall, between fiscal years 1987 and 1991, Congress allocated just $2.3 billion of the $3.4 billion it authorized. Consistent with this trend, the Bush administration proposed a 1992 fiscal year expenditure of $776 million out of $1.13 billion in authorized funds. This amount sounds substantial, but by the time these funds had been distributed throughout the whole country, they had thinned out into a vital, but insufficient, resource.[11]

Not only was this money inadequate; it was also appropriated late. In 1987, shelter operators had only until September to spend funds that they had just received in March. When a study by the General Accounting Office criticized this practice, the 1988 deadline was extended until December 31. Although new disbursements were supposed to have been made by the first of the year, late appropriations have often meant that agencies did not get the money necessary to operate their shelters during the critical winter months.[12]

In addition, for legislation intended to provide emergency relief, the McKinney Act itself was, in its first few years at least, extraordinarily entangled in red tape. After Sanctuary for Children, a New York City organization that runs two battered women shelters, learned that it had been awarded $11,000 for a new boiler, Alisa Del Tufo, the agency's executive director, spent sixty hours of her time trying to obtain the money. The check eventually arrived, fifteen months, and one and half winters, later. Likewise, another director, Joseph Bucchieri, of the twelve bed Bensonhurst Homeless Residence in Brooklyn, was initially optimistic about expansion using funds from the McKinney Act. Then he saw the application. The preface was six pages long. The main document consisted of thirty-three pages divided into twenty-six subsections inquiring about issues like zoning, environmental impact, and employee assistance programs. This was followed by seventeen pages of "24 CFR Parts 840 and 841: Supportive Housing Demonstration Program: Rules and Notices," plus a ten page postscript entitled "Notice of Changes to

Final Rules." Hefting its sixty-six page bulk, Mr. Bucchieri decided not to apply.[13]

Another product of the McKinney Act, the Interagency Council on the Homeless, has been timid and ineffective in its role. Established to streamline the application process for thousands of community groups interested in information about the act, the council adopted a very low profile. In one of a dozen letters submitted to the 1989 congressional hearings, Grace Lewis of the Ohio Department of Mental Health wrote that "We have received no information, assistance, consultation or advice from them.... For all intents and purposes, the Interagency Council doesn't exist." Criticisms like these stirred the Bush administration to replace all nine members of the council's professional staff and prompted an investigation by the General Accounting Office. Among other findings, it was discovered that although two studies for which the council contracted had cited "lack of affordable housing" as the primary cause of homelessness, this conclusion was absent from its annual report. The General Accounting Office explained that

> the former Executive Director of the Council told us that the Council staff did not emphasize this finding in the annual report because they believed that the lack of affordable housing was just one element of the homelessness problem. The former Executive Director also said that the Council staff believed that an annual report that was critical of the former administration's federal housing policy probably would not be approved by the full Council.[14]

Hence the council's ineffectuality was not solely a matter of its staffing. It was, rather, a mandated ineffectuality, the perfect expression of the Reagan administration's policies toward the homeless.

Ever since the early 1980s, the federal government has contended that since localities deliver services, homelessness was fundamentally a local problem. This argument confuses financing with service delivery. Cities deliver services because that is where the homeless are. Yet they can only deliver these services when the national government makes adequate monies available through a well-coordinated system of policy and program. Thwarting the development of this system, the federal government has opposed the establishment of any program that implicitly acknowledges homelessness as a deeply rooted and intractable problem. It has, instead, handed the problem to the states. But without money, without planning, and without coordination, all the states have is the mystique of localism, and that, by itself, has never been enough to deliver effective social services.

The Role of the States

The states often blame the federal government for problems in domestic policy. This pattern is certainly no less evident with the homeless, where 89 percent of the governors believed the federal government was doing an inadequate job. The governors, however, were not much easier on themselves. Faced with a worsening social problem, a surprising 81 percent doubted the adequacy of their own services.[15]

These estimates help explain why the states have had to do much more than simply funnel federal monies to the localities. Most have created some form of advisory council, task force, or interagency group. While some of these committees merely served to deflect political pressure, others led to new policy initiatives. In fact, a total of twenty-four states implemented new policies for the homeless; in another eight, initiatives are planned. Amid all this activity, policies in just six states—Florida, Idaho, Louisiana, Montana, Nevada, and Vermont—have remained relatively unaffected by the growth of the homeless population.[16]

Hawaii's response was typical of the states that instituted some incremental changes. After appointing members from several important state agencies to a State Homeless Task Force, the governor gave them the responsibility of reviewing applications for McKinney Act funds and asked them to ensure statewide coordination of services for the homeless. In 1988, the governor also reorganized the Hawaii Housing Authority. Among other functions, the reorganization charged the authority with the development of services for individuals and families who, like the homeless, have special needs.

More elaborate policy initiatives have been put forth in New Hampshire. Following the recommendations of a 1987 Task Force, the governor's office submitted a $3 million package so that nonprofit groups could construct and operate shelters. The governor also proposed the establishment of a pilot program of interest free loans. Supplemented and leveraged by monies from the New Hampshire Housing Finance Authority, funds from this program are designed to help more people make their first housing downpayment.

Missouri and Connecticut have further diversified their service programs. Besides creating a State Coordinating Committee to improve services delivery, Missouri has a special program for the homeless mentally ill as well as a Homelessness Challenge Grant that used matching funds to generate a total of $4 million in fiscal year 1989. Another $1.3 million has also been allocated for an Emergency Shelter Grant program. Similarly, in Connecticut, where both advocates for the homeless and the courts have kept up pressure on the state government, state agencies have implemented a large number of new initiatives including programs for Security Deposit Assistance, ongoing rental assistance, and capital grants to eligible developers for low-income housing. Perhaps most remarkably, $2.9 million from a federal oil settlement has been targeted to subsidize homeless shelters and individuals in the payment of their utility bills.[17]

Because so many different programs affect the homeless, it is difficult to make a precise estimate about the cost of this increased funding. Still, it does appear as if state funding for programs specifically targeting the homeless rose by approximately 80 percent between 1987 and 1988. And since fifteen states with the best data reported that they spent $244 million in fiscal year 1987, total state spending on the homeless probably approaches close to $500 million.

As might be expected, the leaders in developing and implementing new policies are those states where both a statewide advocacy group and a state task force existed prior to the passage of the McKinney Act. These states—California, Connecticut, and Ohio, for example—had at least a skeletal organization within the state government that could quickly take advantage of McKinney Act funds. By contrast, in predominantly rural states such as Georgia, New Mexico, and Wisconsin, the perception that homelessness is only a problem in the one major urban center (Atlanta, Albuquerque, and Milwaukee) has impeded the establishment of statewide advocacy coalitions. These states lacked such coalitions either before or after the passage of the McKinney Act, and as a consequence, their development of policies for the homeless has lagged somewhat behind.[18]

Possessing neither the political and the economic leverage of the federal government nor the primary responsibility for the delivery of services, states nonetheless hold a pivotal position. Their decision to add, or not to add, their own funds to those of the federal government helps to determine the adequacy of the programs available to the homeless. These monies, in turn, pass down through them to the municipalities, where local tradition and the composition of the governing coalition steer the municipality toward a politically acceptable policy.

Types of Municipal Responses

There are three basic types of municipal responses. In the first type of municipal response exemplified by Miami and Houston, the private, nonprofit sector operates programs for the homeless with little or no assistance from the municipal government. Somewhat common in the early 1980s, this response has gradually been superseded by more interventionist policies.

The second kind of response represents the policy of the government in most big cities. In this response, the municipality contracts with the nonprofit sector to deliver services to the homeless, but it does not itself manage any programs. Within this category, there is obviously a wide variation in the behavior of different cities. Some cities make a token contribution to the efforts of the nonprofit sector, which must then seek additional funding. Other cities have established a genuine partnership with the nonprofit sector and actively seek to improve the delivery of services for the homeless.

Philadelphia, Boston, and New York represent responses of the third type. The municipal government in these cities both contracts with the nonprofit sector and operates its own shelters for the homeless. In Philadelphia and Boston, directly-operated shelters constitute an important but hardly dominant part of the whole service delivery system. In New York, however, publicly-operated shelters predominate.[19]

While the second and third types of responses have been consistently superior to the first, nothing in this categorization is intended to imply that a largely public response is inherently superior to a public/private partnership. There are, in fact, advantages to each. A public response usually possesses the advantages—and the disadvantages—of a large bureaucracy. A large bureaucracy routinizes the task of shelter provision. Though it provides shelter for everyone, its size intimidates people and creates obstacles to helping them. By contrast, a nonprofit agency funded with public monies may be better able to deliver services in the community. But unless there is strict public monitoring, the money may be wasted, and the lack of accountability can wipe out the advantages of its community roots.

In making these comparisons, several other guidelines are also in order. First, while data may not be strictly comparable, and a program operated in one locality by the municipal government may have county funding in another, it is generally necessary to go beyond the three basic categories of municipal responses to obtain a meaningful portrait. Usually, the best way to refine these distinctions is to examine the extent of development within each system. Some of the most pertinent factors for this purpose are information on the number of shelter beds, the amount of money spent, and the degree to which the system differentiates among various subgroups within the population—for example, family shelters for families or substance abuse counseling for the substance abusers. True, this information highlights emergency assistance delivered in shelters, which does not necessarily translate into quality of care. Very few localities, however, financed permanent housing. Information about the development of the emergency shelter system is, then, still the most accurate index of the help provided to the homeless in any city.

Second, no comparison would be complete without devoting special attention to the role of advocates for the homeless and their impact on local policies. While advocates—especially legal advocates—extracted a more elaborate response from some cities, other municipalities implemented programs for the homeless without being sued. Homelessness was bad for business and bad for poor people. Occasionally, these two reasons were by themselves sufficient to make a city act.

Municipal Responses

Miami

Miami has a service system of the first type. The city does not provide municipal funding, and as a result, there are only about 400 beds located in six shelters. Although another 500 beds are added during the winter months, a seasonal increase in the population keeps the number of turnaways fairly constant, and the total number is never adequate for a homeless population that is estimated at about 15,000 people.

Except for the higher proportion of immigrants from Central America, the demographics of this population resembles that of other localities. Approximately 40 percent are members of families. Single individuals make up the rest. Thirty to 40 percent of the population work full or part-time; another 40 percent are veterans. Racially, 55 percent of the population is African-American, and 12 percent is Hispanic. The latter figure doubled in one year, due to the influx, in 1989, of 100,000 Central American immigrants to Miami.[20]

In the absence of a municipal reponse, this population urgently needs services. To some extent, Dade County has tried to fill this vacuum. By the late 1980s, it was spending about $8 million annually on the homeless. This money contributed to the cost of shelters, health services, and residential programs. That still left the primary financial burden to private, nonprofit groups, because by comparison with other cities, Miami's policy toward the homeless was relatively underdeveloped.[21]

The importance of the tourist industry accounts for much of this underdevelopment. Homelessness is generally bad for business, but it is especially bad for tourism. Vacationers want pleasantness; they want to escape from work, ugliness, and the vicissitudes of daily life. Since the presence of the homeless conflicts with these plans, Miami has adopted openly repressive policies to get them out of sight. In 1986, for example, the city made a total of 6,893 arrests of homeless people—at an estimated cost of $2 million—for such offenses as drunkenness and sleeping in public. Although a successful 1988 suit brought by the American Civil Liberties Union sought to halt this practice, the city never really changed its policy. As a result, in 1991, a federal judge found it to be in contempt of his earlier ruling. Miami, he declared, could neither destroy the belongings of the homeless nor roust them from public parks in the daytime.[22]

Perhaps it is not very surprising that sweeps of downtown Miami should constitute such a significant part of the city's policies toward the homeless. Florida is loathe to commit public funds and always ranks near the bottom of all fifty states in its public expenditures. And since the city, like the state of Florida, shuns public expenditure, it has few social services with which to help the homeless. Yet the visibility of the population persists, and in Miami, this visibility creates some special difficulties. Miami is a city that beckons people with an implicit promise: come to Florida, and you will be free from care. The cares of the homeless are all too conspicuous; for this reason, Miami has no choice but to round them up.

Houston

Houston also depended on the private sector for its response to the homeless. Unusual among big cities, this policy is totally consistent with both the city's charter and state law, which bar it from spending any of its own money on welfare programs.[23] More generally, a policy dependent on the private sector reflects the power of the business community to insist on solutions that are most congenial to it.

Altogether, Houston probably has about 7,500 homeless people, though some estimates range as high as 15,000. By 1988, however, a strategy relying on private charities leavened with $4.75 million in McKinney Act funds had produced only 2,845 shelter beds in thirty-eight conventional shelters. These facilities included the Star of Hope Mission's family shelter (180 beds but housing 240 people each night), the mission's main building with more than 500 single men—the largest mission shelter in the United States, and the Salvation Army residence, also the largest of its kind. Most of these programs do not assess a fee, but without public monies, they cannot provide very elaborate services. Indeed, it was not until 1987 that Houston began to explore the possibility of differentiating among the population and targeting services to specific subgroups, such as the program at Baylor Medical College for the health needs of the homeless. Once again, McKinney Act funds keyed this change in strategy.[24]

Houston often presents itself as a capital of free enterprise, a place with no zoning and little planning. Yet throughout this century, the city's growth has been heavily subsidized, mostly by the federal government. In 1902, the U.S. Congress allocated $1 million for local port development. This allocation was followed in 1910 by another $1.25 million to deepen the Houston ship channel, probably the largest single grant of its kind up to that time. The port of Houston grew rapidly, through the export of cotton and lumber products, and later of oil. There was federal money for bridges and roads, federal money for the petrochemical companies during World War II, and the economic stimulus of the Johnson Space Center, constructed in south Houston during the 1960s. By the early 1980s, Houston was booming, and its federally subsidized private sector towered over its public counterpart.[25]

Then came recession. In its wake, the number of unemployed people in the state of Texas, which had averaged 5.2 percent in 1980, increased to 8.9 percent by 1986. Between 1980 and 1988, the state census increased 21 percent, but the number of poverty-level households jumped 42 percent. Although homelessness proliferated with the poverty, the city was typically cautious in its response. The United Way established two shelters in churches during the winter of 1982–83. The next winter, Mayor Kathy Whitmire created a Task Force on the Homeless, which evolved within one year into the Houston/Harris County Coalition for the Homeless. Tempered by its origins in the mayor's office, the coalition limited its responsibilities to matching individuals with needed services. As a result, it never adopted the broader advocacy role common to advocates in other cities.[26]

Though Houston's response was inadequate, it did follow a logical progression. As the problem of homelessness in Houston grew, and the limitation of a private sector strategy became apparent, the city moved very tentatively toward a larger public role. Consistent with its historic pattern, the funding for this new role was still largely federal: in 1985–86, when Houston derived just 8.8 percent of its municipal budget from intergovernmental revenues—less than virtually any other major city— it nonetheless received 64.6 percent of these funds (one of the highest shares) from the federal government.[27] The gradual escalation of Houston's commitment demonstrates the potency of homelessness as a social problem. In a city whose laws forbid it from dispensing its own funds, the government will eventually find other public money to spend on the homeless.

Chicago

With Chicago, policies for the homeless slip over into the second category. Not by much, though: Chicago spent its own monies—$3.57 million in fiscal year 1988, but McKinney Act funds of more than $10.2 million dwarfed this investment. The city also maintained its political distance from the issue of homelessness by relying on a strong public/ private task force. While the city's commissioner of Human Resources chaired this task force, no city official bore responsibility for program coordination and implemention. Instead, the task force advised the mayor and established joint priorities. Sharing responsibility for policymaking with this task force, the city has even gone so far as to pool its funds with those of The United Way.[28]

Chicago's policies toward the homeless therefore fall on the lowest rung of a public/private partnership. As the first city of the second type, its shelter capacity is actually about 84 percent of Houston's, with 2,578 beds in fifty-two facilities, even though its population is nearly 50 percent larger. Yet unlike Houston, it has invested its own money. The rate of growth in its shelter capacity has also been much faster, 109 percent as compared to 28 percent between 1984 and 1988. The dividing line is thin but clear: however tentatively and uneasily, Chicago's policies were more interventionist.[29]

This intervention has intensified since 1983. In February 1983, the city opened its first shelter on the West Side of Chicago in the John Philip Sousa Elementary School. Subsequently, in June of that year, Mayor Harold Washington established the first Homeless Task Force. Under the task force's guidance, the city's commitment grew. Between 1984 and 1988, the amount of money spent on homeless programs rose 900 percent, first on the strength of greater investment by both public and private interests and then, more recently, on a stream of funds from the McKinney Act. The size of Chicago's homeless population may be the subject of considerable dispute, with numbers ranging from Peter Rossi's 1985–86 census of some 2,700 people to a 1989 estimate of 40,000 by a local advocate. But the program itself has gradually evolved into a

skeletal system—inadequate to the demand and temporary in its orientation, but financed by a public/private partnership with most of the
parts in place.[30]

This system has two main elements: overnight shelters that house
individuals for one night at a time and transitional shelters for longer
periods. Often located in churches, overnight shelters have small budgets
and usually depend on volunteer staff. They constitute two-thirds of all
Chicago facilities. Transitional facilities make up the remaining one-
third, offer a greater variety of services, and cost three to five times as
much. When the temperature drops below eleven degrees, and these
facilities are filled, the city's "Warming Center Plan" goes into effect.
This plan draws on the resources of ten churches scattered throughout
the city to provide another 600 beds.[31]

Like many cities, the need for Chicago's public/private partnership
in social welfare derives partly from Chicago's public/private partnership
in economic development. Between 1972 and 1985, Chicago lost between
10,000 and 12,000 units of SRO housing, in some instances with the
municipality's active support. In May 1982, for example, the city displaced 350 men from the Starr and Major SRO hotels to make way for
the Presidential Towers, a luxury residential development. Although
many of the men were elderly pensioners who had lived in the hotels
for ten or fifteen years, Chicago set their relocation allowance at ten
dollars and restricted it to those who could submit receipts from their
new landlords. When half could not, it took a lawsuit, *Lacko* vs. *City of
Chicago*, to compensate the tenants.[32]

While cities of the first type also had a public/private partnership,
the relative power of the private sector tends to limit that power to
economic development. The public sector was stronger in Chicago,
strong enough to carve out a role for itself in social welfare. Funding
some programs with its own money and channeling federal funds into
others, the city consulted with the private sector but did not exercise
strong programmatic leadership. Chicago had a partnership with the
private sector, but having less power, it behaved very much like the
junior partner in this relationship.

San Francisco

San Francisco belongs more firmly to the second category of cities
for the homeless. Under the mayoralty of Dianne Feinstein, its policies
trailed behind the city's liberal reputation. But with Art Agnos's election
as mayor in 1988, the city began to catch up. The task became immeas-
urably more difficult, however, when the 1989 earthquake added those
who lost their homes in a natural disaster to the existing homeless
population.

Approximately 6,500 people are homeless in San Francisco. While
the total number requesting shelter increased by about 25 percent between 1988 and 1989, a new state program providing thirty dollars a

day for up to twenty-eight days of emergency housing assistance reduced homelessness among families. As a result, by 1990, single men and women constituted about 70 percent of the population, with 20 percent in families, and unaccompanied youth accounting for the rest.[33]

Under Mayor Agnos, shelter facilities for this population, which originally consisted of 2,900 beds, expanded to 4,395 in 1991. Religious organizations operate two shelters for homeless families. In addition, the city has also entered into a partnership with nonprofit agencies to run two multiservice sites that provide shelter and a wide array of social services. But the most distinctive feature of San Francisco's shelter system is its extensive use of vouchers. Begun during the 1984 Democratic National Convention, this policy puts people in one of thirty-two hotels for periods of three to five days. Five and half million dollars were spent on this program in the 1987–88 budget, or about 20 percent of the city's total costs of $27.4 million.[34]

The need for this shelter has grown, because San Francisco has a real shortage of affordable housing. The city lost 14,000 of its 33,000 residential hotel rooms between 1975 and 1988; its median rent of $898 for a two bedroom apartment is $110 more than the total monthly AFDC grant for a family of four.[35] Amidst this housing crunch, the most pertinent question is why was San Francisco, a city with a liberal reputation, so slow in responding?

The underdevelopment of policies for the homeless is largely the legacy of Dianne Feinstein, who was mayor from 1980 until 1988. While other cities with far less progressive traditions established task forces and allocated new funds, Feinstein was a business Democrat with close ties to the real estate industry. Committed to economic development, she treated homelessness as an unwelcome intrusion on her political agenda.[36]

Sometimes, when Feinstein did pay attention to the homeless, her concern was not necessarily welcome. In July 1987, the Social Service Commission sought to reduce the weekly workfare requirement for General Assistance—at $311 a month, one of the main sources of income for the homeless—from three to two days. Feinstein wrote them an indignant letter urging that it be increased to five days a week. Yet the mayor's dogged insistence on work standards for the poor contrasted with her indulgence of the residential hotel owners. Throughout Feinstein's second term, the city provided vouchers to the homeless, but never signed a written contract with any of the thirty-two hotels, and never insisted on competitive bidding. Without these controls, it was easy to make money: in 1985–86, five hotels charged the city $500,000 for rooms they never rented.[37] No work program was apparently necessary for those with such entrepreneurial instincts.

Feinstein's successor, Mayor Art Agnos, has paid much more attention to the development of a comprehensive policy. Appointing Robert Prentice, a city health care administrator and an activist with the local homeless coalition, as his homeless coordinator, the Agnos administration implemented a twelve point plan for the homeless. It also invested $3.7 million in the acquisition and renovation of five Tenderloin hotels containing 525 rooms, and got the city's Redevelopment Agency to commit another $892,000 to purchase a residential hotel for the mentally disabled. Advocates for the homeless have criticized the administration for its two major sweeps of the Civic Center Plaza, which removed camping equipment such as tents in 1989, and the homeless themselves in 1990. The administration did direct these homeless people to several newly opened facilities, but advocates were angry because these facilities were not completely ready and served only men.[38]

In 1989, the federal government recognized the Agnos administration's increased commitment to the homeless and awarded it five McKinney Act grants worth $6 million—every grant for which the city had applied. Indeed, had it not been shattered by the October 1989 earthquake, it could have devoted its full attention to judicious use of these funds. But the earthquake destroyed 800 hotel rooms and created a whole new population of homeless people. Given $12 million in relief assistance, San Francisco would have been expected to distinguish victims of the earthquake from those who ostensibly brought their homelessness upon themselves. The earthquake, though, made so many people homeless that in some shelters, homeless people of every kind slept side-by-side.[39]

Los Angeles

Los Angeles employs a somewhat different strategy for dealing with the homeless. Its public/private partnership is more developed than San Francisco, but its parts are not very well integrated. As a result, most programs for the homeless tend to get money from either the public *or* the private sector, without mixing the funds.[40]

The cost of housing is the primary reason for the growth of homelessness in Los Angeles. Nationally, homelessness is the product of insufficient money to obtain available housing. In some localities, however, homelessness may be attributed more to either an economic recession, with its trend toward depressed wages, or to greatly inflated housing costs. Los Angeles clearly exemplifies the latter phenomenon. Between 1974 and 1988, for instance, the median price of a home in the United States increased from $32,000 to $91,000; during the same period in California, prices jumped from $34,000 to $150,000. This increase was so rapid that by 1989, only 19 percent of the state's population could afford to buy a median-priced home, down from one-half just seven years earlier.

Renters did not fare any better. The average rent in Los Angeles doubled to $525 a month between 1980 and 1988; rentals in new buildings cost $908 monthly. Fourteen thousand units annually join the housing stock, but with 25,000 new households forming each year, the supply of rental housing continues to shrink. This shrinkage is especially evident in the supply of low-income housing, where families earning less than $10,000 spend, on average, 53 percent of their income on rent, and the California Department of Housing and Community Development estimates the statewide shortage at some 500,000 units.[41]

With housing statistics like these, both the working poor and those on welfare are at risk. Many, in fact, do become homeless: the homeless population of Los Angeles, estimated at 35,000, was second only to New York. To serve this population, the number of shelter beds grew by 231 percent between 1984 and 1988. Yet the total beds—6,930 beds in the city and 10,332 in the county—was still far from adequate to meet the demand.[42]

Two main obstacles have blocked the development of programs for the homeless. The first is the friction between the city and county of Los Angeles. The city is responsible for providing low-income housing; the county, for health, welfare, and social services. While the city has generally been more sympathetic to the homeless, the dispute has been filled with suits and countersuits. As a consequence, even when these suits produced new programs, the conflict between the county and city has hindered their operation.

Second, despite talk of a public/private partnership, the partnership is not truly integrated: 85 percent of the shelters received the vast majority of their funding from either public or private sources. In truth, the funding system consists of a hybrid collection of public and private institutions whose practices—short and irregular funding cycles, rigid reporting and reimbursement procedures—have kept community agencies on a very short leash. According to one study, for example, agencies must expend eighteen hours of staff time a week just to acquire public funding.[43] The system of services to the homeless needs to be flexible, and, of course, individual programs must be accountable to their sponsors. These truisms fade, however, before the sense that the system is designed to shrink as easily as it can grow. The lesson in this response for homeless people is that whatever problems they may have, they cannot count on help from permanent, well-functioning government programs.

The death of four homeless people from the cold in January 1987 revealed many of the contradictions in Los Angeles' response to the homeless. Although the city quickly opened shelters containing another 900 beds, they closed them again within two months. After receiving nothing more than four day vouchers at city-funded hotels, many homeless people established "cardboard condominiums" in the downtown area. The homeless carpeted these refrigerator boxes to cushion themselves against the hard sidewalk. Pressured by Center City East Association, a group of business owners in the skid row area, the Department of Public Works ordered these settlements destroyed. Only the protests of eight service providers, arrested for blocking the bulldozers, stopped the raids. Poignantly, the people loading the belongings of the homeless into the mouths of the bulldozers were General Relief recipients—some homeless themselves—doing their mandatory workfare. Had they refused the assignment, they would have lost their assistance for sixty days. Like trusties in a prison, they then would have joined the ranks of those whom they had been ordered to sweep from the streets.[44]

Los Angeles' policies for the homeless reflect its long-standing wariness about the role of the public sector. The city did build several thousand low-income housing units in the 1940s. But when it proposed the construction of 10,000 units on Bunker Hill, real estate interests launched a "red scare" that succeeded in stopping the project.[45] Yet even though the allies and supporters of the public sector have never really been able to challenge the dominance of private interests, accumulating social costs have strengthened their hand. Just as Los Angeles was the leader in implementing stricter regulations on automobile pollution and has constructed its first commuter train, so the city has begun to recognize that policies for homeless require a larger public role. The public sector still has not coalesced with the private: it does not have the power, nor does it have the tradition. But the outlines of a public/private partnership are discernible, and greater integration is only a matter of time.

St. Louis

Like the other cities in this category, St. Louis' policies for the homeless are the product of a public/private partnership. In the case of St. Louis, though, the partnership is better coordinated: the city has already gotten to where Los Angeles seems to be headed. Admittedly, the system lacks adequate financing and should not be held up as a model—something that would be hard to do in a city with only 950 shelter beds for a homeless population estimated at 12,000 to 15,000 people. Nevertheless, on a smaller scale for a smaller city, the system does represent a public/private partnership of greater sophistication.[46]

While the concept of a public/private partnership draws on the local tradition of dealing with social problems, the city of St. Louis did not freely choose this method of addressing the issue of homelessness. Rather, advocates imposed the policy upon the city as part of the *Graham* v. *Schoemehl* consent decree. It was this 1985 class action suit that mandated a high degree of coordination.

As in so many other cities, homelessness in St. Louis grew in step with the economic revitalization of its downtown area. When the Gateway Arch opened in 1968, the accompanying redevelopment of the downtown area forced the relocation of many single adults. These local actions combined with national economic trends to multiply the number of homeless people. In 1982, the governor's report to the National Governor's Task Force on Homelessness cited statewide figures that were double those of just two years before. By 1983 and 1984, in the city of St. Louis itself, the annual, unduplicated count of shelter users exceeded 10,000 people.[47]

That is when the legal advocates took action. In December 1984, Kenneth M. Chackes of Washington University Law School together with a team of lawyers from Legal Services of Eastern Missouri sent a letter to Mayor Vincent Schoemehl describing the extent of homelessness in St. Louis. The letter asserted that the provision of shelter was the city's duty under Missouri law. In reponse, the mayor's office acknowledged the extent of the problem, but expressed doubt about the city's responsibility. After the attorneys filed a lawsuit, one year of negotiations ensued. These negotiations were facilitated by the mayor's appointment of a task force that made very similar recommendations. Finally, on 15 November, 1985, three days before the suit was scheduled for trial, the city reached agreement with the advocates and signed a consent decree.

Going beyond the mere provision of food and shelter, this decree laid out the essential elements of St. Louis' service delivery system. During the first year, a minimum of 200 emergency beds had to be added to the local supply; another 100 units of permanent housing were reserved for the homeless. In addition, however, the city also promised to fund a crisis-oriented reception center, transportation, daycare, and transitional housing. The city subsequently contracted with a different social welfare agency to provide each of these services.[48]

Graham v. *Schoemehl* transformed St. Louis' treatment of the homeless. Prior to the suit, The Salvation Army Emergency Lodge was the only shelter receiving local government money, in this case, through block grant allocations. But by 1988, local government funding alone reached 41 percent of all St. Louis shelters. With the infusion of funds from the McKinney Act, total public support undoubtedly exceeds Chicago's level of about 50 percent.[49] The system is, moreover, better coordinated.

This coordination is in large part due to the mechanisms for monitoring and accountability that attorneys for the plaintiffs built into the consent decree. Under the agreement, the city must provide legal advocates with data from the agencies with which it contracts. Lawyers and researchers can also analyze computerized demographic data taken from calls to the local shelter hotline.

St. Louis has a housing crisis: 50,000 individuals live in substandard housing, and more than 43,000 pay at least 50 percent of their income in rent.[50] The city needs more beds; it requires more services. Still, to the extent that this public/private partnership succeeds for the homeless, it is not because the arrangement is inherently good; it is, rather, that the demands of the advocates have made it so, through their insistence on services and accountability.

Seattle

Seattle has the same institutional arrangements as St. Louis—a partnership with the nonprofit sector. But unlike St. Louis, where a lawsuit brought the partnership into being, Seattle's policies never required litigation. Instead, a close-knit social service community with ties to local government employed a cooperative strategy. This strategy was relatively successful: the city not only funded shelters for the homeless, but it also placed two tax levy propositions for low-income housing on the ballot. In 1982, Seattle authorized $50 million of housing for the elderly; five years later, voters approved another $50 million for unrestricted low-income housing. As a result of these expenditures, Seattle became one of the few municipalities that used their own tax funds to compensate for the decline in federal housing assistance. In 1991, under Mayor Norman Rice, it was also one of the few cities to experiment with a self-governing shelter.[51]

The Seattle-King County Emergency Housing Coalition deserves considerable credit for the progressive aspects of city policy. Founded in 1979, before virtually any other similar group in the country, the coalition was able to identify homelessness as a public problem three to five years sooner than groups in most other localities. Its strategy, too, was well-chosen. Since conflict would merely sow dissension within the small community of social service providers, the coalition adopted the posture of a reasonable, well-intentioned pressure group. This pressure group naturally considered it impolitic to sue their colleagues holding public office, even if those colleagues did not do what the group wanted on any given issue.[52]

Like other cities, Seattle has used Community Development Block Grants to pay for the cost of sheltering the homeless. In addition, during fiscal year 1988, it also spent $2.7 million of the city's own money. Yet despite these initiatives, the city's policies for the homeless have been neither completely adequate to the demand nor totally benign. Thus, while about 3,000 to 5,000 homeless people lived in Seattle, only about one-half of the single individuals and one-quarter of the families were sheltered on any night, and children—more than men or women—were the group most frequently turned away.[53]

Mayor Charles Royer's 1986 report, A Strategy for the Downtown Homeless, reflects the less benign side of the city's policies. Although the report recommended social services for the employable and those with substance abuse problems, it also enacted an ordinance against panhandling that the courts declared constitutional in 1991 after four years of legal wrangling.[54] In a moderately progressive city like Seattle, the local government may offer social services for the homeless in its downtown business district. If, however, these services do not succeed, the municipality is not averse to more repressive measures.

Seattle thrives on its reputation for pleasantness, and it relies on the appearance of civic benevolence to preserve that reputation. This reliance gives an important clue to its policies for the homeless. Seattle's public/private partnership may not be as well-coordinated as St. Louis, but it is more far-sighted, and it has demonstrated greater willingness to spend public money on a public problem. Nonetheless, an expectation understandably accompanies the expenditure of this money. To ensure the city's reputation for pleasantness, it is assumed that social issues can be minimized if they are addressed early. The money that is expended represents an investment in that reputation; the homeless who remain homeless in spite of the city's efforts demonstrate that this investment strategy is, at best, a partial success.

Philadelphia

As one of the few cities in the country that directly operates its own shelters, Philadelphia belongs in the third category of municipal responses. In fact, until its fiscal condition deteriorated in the late 1980s, its policies toward the homeless were among the most progressive in the country. Ninety-five percent of shelters in the city received some public support, and public monies financed 53 percent of the entire homeless budget.[55] Philadelphia depended on smaller shelters. Moreover, in its Center City Project, it had a model program linking services for the homeless mentally ill.

Then the city's fiscal condition worsened, and the backlash struck. From 1984 to 1988, Philadelphia had increased the number of shelter beds by 491 percent. But confronted with an $80 million deficit for the second consecutive year, the city began to shrink its support for homeless programs. In 1989, the city closed one dozen shelters for the homeless, reducing the number of beds from 5,500 to 2,650. It slashed the budget for its Office of Services to the Homeless and Adults from $30 million to $15 million, and reduced its assistance to the Office of Health Services for Homeless Persons from $7.8 million to $3.8 million.[56]

When advocates marched into the City Council Chambers to protest this 50 percent cutback in the city's support, they were trying to protect the integrity of a comprehensive shelter and service program that had been carefully developed during the preceding decade. Philadelphia originally guaranteed a right to shelter through a city ordinance, but then, in a posture that anticipated the backlash of the late 1980s, had to be sued in order to enforce compliance.

The system that evolved from this suit won respect throughout the country. Deemphasizing large facilities, Philadelphia helped to found Dignity Housing, a nonprofit organization run by the local Union of the Homeless. Dignity placed 300 homeless men, women, and children in former HUD buildings that were purchased with city aid. By directing a significant proportion of the homeless to personal care, foster care, and boarding homes, Philadelphia seemed to offer a more humane alternative to the widespread dependence of other cities on armories and welfare hotels. The system also had the capacity to shelter a bigger share of the local homeless population—an estimated 12,500 people—than other localities.

Yet the feature of Philadelphia's program that received the greatest acclaim was its Center City Project. Established in 1984 by the Office of Mental Health and Mental Retardation to address the special needs of the homeless mentally ill, the project consisted of a network of twenty-one service sites that provided aggressive outreach to the homeless. Careful planning linked services, so that an outreach team could bring someone they engaged on the street to an intake center. From there, the homeless could be referred to a "low-demand" facility to ease their way into the system, and then, as their capacity to tolerate rules increased, to a facility offering specialized care. While mental health professionals often advocate this kind of outreach and phased entry, the Center City Project was one of the few programs in the country where it was actually put into practice.[57]

A comprehensive system like Philadelphia's was expensive. Although the expense seemed justifiable when the city's finances were not quite so tight, a renewed budgetary crisis raised doubts about its cost effectiveness. As local officials themselves wrote about the Center City Project,

> the problems faced by homeless mentally ill persons are largely related to national trends that are beyond the purview of the local mental health system. Homelessness, first and foremost, comes about as a result of poverty and a shortage of affordable housing. Mental illness exacerbates these situations and increases the risk of homelessness, but is seldom the sole cause. Until the larger issues are addressed in a comprehensive manner, every year new faces will replace those who have been successfully served.[58]

Public support declined because when new people replaced the old, the signs of progress were faint, and it was easy to make the argument that the money could be better spent. In the 1989 cutbacks, the Greater Philadelphia First Corporation, the local business coalition, participated in the mayor's Task Force on the Budget and Taxation and pressed this view. As John P. Claypool, its executive director said, "Some people say if you spend less money on homeless programs you're doing people harm, but I'm not sure we were helping them before. . . . Our feeling was that the city's priorities should be cleanliness, public safety, and public education, and we're satisfied that there is now a significant effort to focus on these priorities."[59]

As the first city with a developed program to make significant cutbacks, Philadelphia demonstrated the political dilemma inherent in any attempt to implement a comprehensive response to the issue of homelessness. The dilemma is, quite simply, that while a less adequate approach helps too few people, a comprehensive response may not help enough to create a durable coalition. Philadelphia's public sector once possessed sufficient leverage to operate its own shelters. Homelessness, though, is an intractable problem. When the public's investment in comprehensive programs yields an inadequate return, public support can quickly fade.

Boston

Boston's response to the growth of the homeless population reflects its position as an archetypal public city. Public spending in the city of

Boston generates half of all personal income; in Houston, by comparison, the figure is 13 percent. Moreover, a higher share than virtually any other U.S. city—44 percent of the budget—comes from intergovernmental revenues (88 percent of which comes from the state). Since its residents are dependent on public spending, and the city itself is dependent on money from other governments, the public sector is going to be an important factor in developing a response to any social problem. Boston's policies for the homeless were no exception.[60]

By 1989, Boston's shelter system contained 2,754 beds, up from 972 in 1983. The city directly operated two shelters for the homeless and contracted out for the rest with a large number of nonprofit agencies. Emphasizing the diversity of needs, it tried to provide a fairly elaborate package of services, including employment counseling at its own 420 bed Long Island Shelter, and HealthLink, which offers comprehensive health care to the homeless in fourteen overnight facilities. Unlike other cities that sponsor similar programs, Boston made no attempt to keep them at arm's length. Instead, it embraced these policies without apology, as essential services that the homeless need.

Most of these programs owe their existence to the administration of Mayor Raymond Flynn. Elected in 1984, Flynn was one of the few big-city mayors to side openly with the homeless. Flynn served as chairman of the Task Force on Hunger and Homelessness of the U.S. Conference of Mayors and was an early advocate of the federal legislation that eventually became the McKinney Act. In addition to appearing frequently at Boston shelters to feed the homeless, he took the unusual step of appointing a homeless resident of the Long Island Shelter, Michael McGuire, to Boston's Emergency Shelter Commission, the city's liaison to the community of service providers. During his first term, the city spent a total of $44 million dollars on the homeless, including $21 million of its own money.

Boston also tried especially hard to prevent homelessness. It banned evictions from condominium conversions for those renters who do not wish to purchase their apartments and halted speculation in SRO hotels. For elderly, handicapped, and low-income residents, the city set the consumer price index as the maximum rent increase. And, through its linkage policy, it required downtown office developers to contribute money to a fund for low-income housing.[61]

While the Flynn administration enacted these measures, they represent more than just the policies of one progressive mayor. Boston used to be a city in decline, a northeastern urban center whose industrial base was decaying. Through intergovernmental funding and political entrepreneurship—the Boston-Washington, D.C. ties that extend from the Kennedys in 1960s to Tip O'Neil twenty years later—it made the transition to a service economy.[62] Like everywhere else, however, the transition to this service economy contributed to the spread of homelessness. By renovating the downtown, it drove up the cost of housing. By transforming the labor market, it made unskilled labor obsolete. Although these trends produced homelessness in other cities, only in Boston, and on a larger scale in New York, did the public sector's promotion of economic development also position it to develop a public sector response.

Obviously, there are still homeless people in Boston, just as there are homeless people in Miami and Houston. Municipal policies toward the homeless cannot "solve" the problem of homelessness, because they cannot compensate for powerful national trends. But municipal policies do make a difference. They can try to prevent homelessness. They can treat the homeless better or worse. In many cities, merely being homeless is cause for further mistreatment; in a few where the condition of homelessness is itself considered mistreatment, some measures have been taken to relieve the pain.

Why Did Municipal Responses Differ?

Since cities compete economically, the fear of capital flight is always present to influence what any city does about a social problem like homelessness. Yet the differences in municipal responses suggest that this fear does not affect every city equally. How, then, can these differences be explained?

Two major factors seem most compelling. They are, first, the form that homelessness takes in a particular city, and second, the composition of the political coalition that sits in judgment of it as a social problem.

Several key elements determine the form that homelessness takes in each locality. One is the absolute number of the homeless. Although homelessness is not a regional phenomenon, and there is no firm evidence that it is more significantly concentrated in one part of the country than another, its prevalence in some urban areas does create political pressures. These pressures intensify if the homeless are especially visible, and their visibility disrupts the normal functioning of a central business district. In addition, there is some indication that the spread of homelessness to the "worthy poor"—in Houston, for example, as part of a regional downturn—can arouse public sympathy and elicit a response.

Once again, though, since these phenomena occurred in many large cities, and these cities implemented very different policies for the homeless population, the phenomena alone do not explain the variations in the cities' responses. For that explanation, we must look instead to the second factor—the composition of the local political coalition. This is the ruling coalition that reviews the merit of existing policies for the homeless. Most particularly, it is the coalition that monitors the risk of capital flight and determines whether the comparative costs and benefits of the city's policy will make businesses want to leave.

All cities base their policies on the principle of less eligibility. Given the regional differences in the cost of labor and the cost of living, however, this principle means that the standard of living for homeless people will most likely be lower in one part of the country than it will in another. Moreover, regardless of the absolute standard of living, there are social costs to be considered. The social costs of an inadequate response can be quite extensive, ranging from the visibility of an unsheltered population and inflated charges for welfare hotels to violent crime and the long-term damage inflicted on homeless children. When these costs outweigh the benefits of a frugal policy, conditions have deteriorated to a point where they discourage rather than invite business investment. It is then that the local political coalition increases the benefits, so that costs and benefits are more closely aligned.

The composition of these coalitions differ considerably by locality. In some cities such as Miami and Houston, it consists largely of the business sector, without much organized opposition from nonbusiness groups. In other cities such as Boston where the coalition is more inclusive, labor unions and progressive community groups can often force the business community to rely on the public sector. A combination of costs and benefits that are acceptable in one community might therefore be unacceptable in another, depending on the makeup of the local political coalition.

The comparative political strength of the business community has been, then, the fundamental determinant of policies for the homeless. Where it was stronger, the local government usually left responsibility for the homeless to voluntary charitable organizations. Where business had to recognize the existence of contending political forces, it was likely to seek some kind of accommodation with them through a public/private partnership. This public/private partnership assumed many different forms, from those such as Chicago, where the private sector clearly dominated, to cities like Los Angeles and Seattle, where other political interests were better represented. Finally, there was a small third category of cities like Boston, where a powerful coalition of forces arrayed around the public sector tilted the response still more in its direction.

Of these responses, two have generally proven most adequate: cities with a strong public sector, and cities with highly developed and coordinated public/private partnerships. Neither, though, represents a panacea. A strong public sector may invest greater resources in its care of the homeless, but it cannot offset the effects of a skewed economic growth. And as long as no strong public sector exists in the United States without an even stronger private sector, the comparative weakness of the public sector restricts it to ministering to the homeless whom the private sector leaves in its wake.

9

New York City: Wealth, Poverty, and Homeless Individuals

While there are real limits to what city government can do to shape the economy, the city can make a significant difference in several areas by (1) becoming a less expensive place to conduct business...
From *New York Ascendant*, The Report of the Commission on the Year 2000

It seems like a continuous, perpetual thing. Evidently, it's part of some project to see what happens when you don't have any money in the City of New York.
A homeless woman on the occasion of her fourth stay in the women's shelter.

New York City made the most comprehensive response to the problem of homelessness. With the largest number of beds, 30,500, and the most money spent—some $757 million in 1988—the $375 million it allocated in local funds was sixteen times more than Philadelphia, at the time, its nearest rival.[1] Municipal officials were proud of these facts, which they recited whenever critics expressed doubts. As commissioner of the Human Resources Administration (HRA), the city's primary social welfare agency, William Grinker's stance was typical. When the Subcommittee on the Homeless of the New York City Council criticized the policies of the Koch administration, Grinker firmly defended its programs:

HRA provides decent and humane accommodations and extensive services for the homeless. In addition to operating and funding temporary shelter, in compliance with state regulations, HRA operates and funds programs providing social services, health care, counseling, employment training, day care, education, recreation, substance abuse prevention, and permanent housing. Simply put, the City of New York does more for its homeless population, and each individual homeless person, than any other city in the United States.[2]

133

Grinker was right. New York did try hard; it did make the best effort of any governmental unit in the nation. The city sheltered thousands of people and offered a wide-ranging array of services. But its public sector could never do enough, given the rate at which the local economy produced homelessness.

This effort and the failure of this effort were visible all over the city. There were 270 shelters, but 82 percent of New Yorkers saw homeless people in their neighborhood or on their way to work.[3] The city funded a half a dozen outreach projects, where staff in vans identified and sought to engage the homeless mentally ill. But with a shortage of permanent facilities, many New Yorkers became accustomed to their daily encounters with the emotionally disturbed: the man muttering to himself on the subway platform, the woman, urinating in the middle of the street. Together with the Department of Employment, HRA operated a large number of employment programs. Yet at many traffic lights throughout the city, drivers accelerated quickly to avoid the homeless men who wanted money for washing their windshields. All over New York City, the nation's biggest and most comprehensive program for the homeless both served the greatest number of people and left the greatest number of people on the street.

The problem was huge in New York, but size alone did not explain this apparent paradox. True, the city itself estimated its homeless population at as much as 90,000 people.[4] Perhaps with so daunting a task, New York could only hope for partial success. Indeed, this success was very likely to be little more than partial because the city, in the wake of its 1975 fiscal crisis, had tried hard to retain and attract business investment. This policy served as a model for other cities across the country as well as for the nation as a whole. Organized around the need to create a favorable climate for investment, the policy did trigger the economic expansion of the 1980s. At the same time, however, it also led to the growth of the largest homeless population since the Great Depression.

New York City's Fiscal Crisis

Fiscal crises have been a recurrent feature of New York City's political and economic life. Indeed, before 1975, there were five major New York City fiscal crises—in 1856, 1871, 1907, 1914, and 1932–33. Most of these upheavals followed a consistent pattern; each was set off by the city's inability to sell its bonds on the open market. Needing money to pay its creditors, suppliers, and civil servants, New York only regained access to the bond market by acceding to the demands of a local bank consortium. These demands were usually so stringent that they enabled a reform coalition to drive the incumbent administration from office. But this new coalition soon made its peace with the old, so that New York politics were modified but not transformed.[5]

From Mayor Abraham Beame in 1975 to Mayor Edward Koch in

1989, the politics of the city's most recent fiscal crisis hewed closely to this pattern. Elected in 1977 as an alternative to the machine politics that many thought responsible for bankrupting the city, Koch lost his bid for a fourth term in 1989, at least in part because of the accommodations he subsequently made with machine politicians like Queens Borough President Donald Manes and Brooklyn Democratic Leader Meade Esposito. In the interim, he presided over a New York City whose strategy for business investment restructured the local economy. This restructuring reduced the size of city government and heightened its reliance on the marketplace. By hastening the decline of manufacturing and reallocating urban space to the service sector, it reaffirmed New York's position as the world's financial center. Simultaneously. though, it also made the poor—especially the African-American and Latino poor—increasingly superfluous to the city's economy.[6]

There is an intimate relationship between the creation of this wealth and the creation of this poverty. New York City had few other options when it submitted to the demands of the marketplace that it reduce its workforce and tighten its fiscal policies: it needed money for taxes, and the relative power of the business community was simply too great. Yet tying the fortunes of the city ever more closely to the fortunes of business wrenched New York out of its historic role. Never the grand patron of the poor that some alleged, New York now treated the poor as a fixed social cost. As a moral issue, the city's political leaders might voice their regret about the existence of poor people. As a matter of policy, however, the poor warranted additional funding only when crime, high school dropouts, and the proliferation of homelessness threatened the success of their business-oriented strategy.

This business strategy had several key elements. One was its use of the municipal budget, which became, in Koch's first term, much more explicitly tied to business development. In fact, from 1977 to 1981, developmental spending—spending to promote the city's economic growth—rose 72 percent, while allocative funds (for all other agencies) grew 36 percent, and redistributive expenditures (public assistance, social services, and health) increased just 21 percent.[7]

Besides spending money differently, the Koch administration also appealed to business by granting generous tax abatements. In the late 1970s, major corporations such as IBM, AT & T, Philip Morris, and Irving Trust won several hundred million dollars worth of these abatements through the Industrial and Commercial Incentive Board (ICIB). The ICIB did become more selective during the early 1980s, turning down the Republic National Bank's application for a tax abatement on a Fifth Avenue tower. In total, however, during the period from 1977 to 1984, it handed out $750 million in tax savings.

At a time when essential services went begging, the ICIB's policies aroused considerable criticism. The city's own Department of Investigation claimed that the ICIB did not know the true value of the tax breaks it granted. Slipshod in distributing them, the ICIB failed to verify the number of jobs created or maintained and created a tax shortfall that other taxpayers had to offset. Finally, in 1984, the Koch administration reacted to political pressures by replacing the ICIB with the Industrial and Commercial Incentive Program (ICIP).

The new program was hardly an improvement. Instead of holding public hearings, it granted tax abatements in the area below Ninety-sixth Street as a matter of right. Successful corporate applicants included Macklowe Real Estate at 125 West Fixty-fifth Street for $8 million; Prudential Insurance/Hilton at 141–157 West Fifty-Seventh Street for $15 million; and the Zeckendorf World Wide Plaza at 825 Eighth Avenue for $18 million. Deputy Mayor Kenneth Lipper projected that altogether, the total revenue lost from 1984 to 1994 through the Industrial and Commercial Program would amount to some $358 million, or twice as much as the ICIB would have granted had it remained in existence. The case of Smith Barney's application for a tax abatement on the renovation of an old warehouse at 333 West Thirty-fourth Street suggests why the new program is so much more expensive. When the ICIB rejected their application, the investment firm went ahead anyway. The ICIP, by contrast, would automatically have granted the same tax abatement.[8]

Quite apart from ICIP, the largest single tax break granted during Mayor Koch's years in office was the $235 million package awarded in 1988 to the Chase Manhattan Bank. For its decision to move 5,000 workers to downtown Brooklyn instead of a site on the New Jersey waterfront, Chase received discounts on real estate and sales taxes worth $157 million. The bank also won $26 million to pay for lighting, roadwork, and other improvements at the Brooklyn complex; another $37 million city/state subsidy for utilities may be applied to costs at either its Brooklyn or Manhattan headquarters. The total value of the package was twice the previous record, awarded in 1986 to keep the National Broadcasting Company (NBC) in New York City.[9]

These tax subsidies demonstrate the city's eagerness to improve its business climate. By using government money to speed the transition to a service economy, they stimulated the development of a labor market in which some people could not find jobs. At the same time, however, they reduced the funds available to cushion the impact of this transition. These consequences were bad, but they had a less direct effect on the growth of the homeless population than such tax abatements for residential real estate as the J-51 tax law.

The J-51 tax law helped to finance the conversion of SRO hotels to coops and condomiums. Originally passed in 1955 as a way of inducing landlords to improve the living conditions of tenants in cold water flats, the law was gradually transformed into an all-purpose tax abatement for virtually every conversion in the city. All told, between 1978 and

1985, J-51 financed the upgrading of 535,272 units, or $860 million in construction. Consistent with other facets of the city's tax policy, the distribution of these benefits was heavily skewed toward richer communities. In 1982, for example, almost three-quarters of the benefits went to wealthy Manhattan neighborhoods, while the city lost almost $280 million in tax receipts. That is, of course, just the income foregone in one year. A 1982 New York City study indicated that 26.8 percent of those interviewed in the shelter system identified an SRO as their usual place of residence. For these displaced tenants, taxpayers may still be paying.[10]

New York City's investment strategy helped to bring about an economic transformation. By restoring business faith in its economic viability, New York kept some corporations in the city and generated new investment from others. All this economic activity revitalized the city's tax base and conferred political benefits on the Koch administration. As long as the city rationed its services to the poor, business prospered, and city government revived. The entire arrangement had just one problem; it depended on lowering the standard of living of the city's poorer people.

The economic restructuring proceeded according to this plan. From 1977 to 1987, the total number of jobs rose 12 percent. This increase was roughly equal to the difference between a 41 percent growth in the number of service jobs and a 30 percent decline of those in manufacturing. Led by a 123 percent gain (86,500 jobs) in the securities industry, employment in the FIRE sector—finance, insurance, and real estate—increased 32 percent. Salaries in this industry, which averaged $65,000, expanded the market for luxury coops and spurred the real estate boom of the 1980s. People of color were, of course, largely excluded from these positions.[11]

At the other end of the income scale, conditions were much less auspicious. As a result of the growing split in the labor market, 45 percent of all New Yorkers—compared with 34 percent nationally—were neither employed nor searching for work. Another 50,000 New York families remained in poverty even though their primary wage earner worked full-time all year.[12]

These statistics demonstrate both the extent of poverty in New York and, in addition, the remarkable shift of income upward. In 1986, the bottom tenth of New York City households earned an average of $3,698, or 1.5 percent of all city income. The second tenth received $6,081, or 2.4 percent of the total. By contrast, the top fifth received 47.3 percent of all income in the city and averaged $59,518.

Mayor Koch's investment strategy led to an ever-greater skewing of these income shares. From 1977 to 1986, the top fifth benefited from a 108 percent growth in income, while the bottom fifth gained 60 percent. Inflation rose about 80 percent in this period. That means the bottom fifth lost about 20 percent of its real income, while the share of the top fifth increased 28 percent. The growth of income among this top fifth was so large that even the middle 20 percent of households lost about 3 percent of their share of the city's income.[13]

These numbers go a long way toward explaining the proliferation of homelessness within New York City. For the city as a whole, 1.7 million people, or 23.2 percent of New York's population, were living below the 1988 official poverty line of $11,611. Sadly, this figure masks still higher percentages among particular subgroups: 33.8 percent of all African-Americans, 41.6 of all Latinos, and 37.5 percent of all children. In 1978, when some 18.8 percent of New Yorkers were officially poor, business was struggling to regain its competitiveness, and the city government was struggling to recover its financial credibility. To a large extent, both business and New York City succeeded in their struggles. Yet because their successes were based on greater poverty and income polarization, they unleashed some consequences that every New Yorker will be living with for many years to come.[14]

Homelessness and the Shortage of Affordable Housing in New York City

The formula for the production of homelessness in New York City was no different than for any other region: increase the number and variety of poor people, limit or reduce their housing assistance, and then leave them to find housing in a market with spiraling costs. Although this formula played itself out differently with families than it did with single individuals, two quick indicators suggest the overall acuteness of New York City's housing crisis. One is the 2.46 percent rate of vacant apartments; the other, more pertinent index, at 0.96 percent, reflects the number of vacant apartments renting for less than $300. Since five percent is generally considered the minimum necessary to balance supply and demand, the shortage of affordable housing for poor people matched in severity their shortage of income.[15]

This shortage had important implications for every New York household of modest means, but it had particularly significant consequences for individuals living alone, who constitute the only expanding portion of the New York City housing market. Between 1984 and 1987, their numbers increased by more than 8 percent. Because this rate was much faster than the 0.2 percent for households generally, it pushed the total proportion of such households to 33 percent, including a remarkable 53.4 percentage of all households in Manhattan.[16]

A housing market with a high percentage of single adult households presents some special problems. Single adults consume housing resources at a faster pace—one person for a one bedroom apartment that could easily house two. This fragmentation of the community not only puts an added strain on the housing market; it also implies a high proportion of individuals isolated from a supportive network of family and friends. Many families have the burden of supporting a large number of people on a restricted income, but the task for single adults is both simpler and more arduous. They do not have to support anyone else in the household, yet neither are there any other adults on whose income they can depend. A prolonged illness or the loss of their job jeopardizes their housing differently from those who live together.

For many years in New York City, the poorest segment of this population lived in SRO housing. SROs were a vital resource. They provided inexpensive shelter to the unemployed, casual laborers, and the recently deinstitutionalized, at prices that were not otherwise available. A 1979 survey of twelve Upper West Side SROs found that 85 percent of the 1,100 residents had incomes below $3,000. At the rents these tenants could afford, the only cheaper alternative would have been to move out onto the street.[17]

Many of them soon did. With conversions almost totally depleting the stock, it took until 1985 before the Koch administration belatedly acknowledged the value of SROs by imposing a partial moratorium on their further demolition. As part of this moratorium, the administration barred owners from warehousing units and required them to pay $45,000 into a low income housing fund for each unit they demolished. These restrictions quickly became the subject of a lawsuit, which the city lost in 1989 when the state's highest court decided against it. The U.S. Supreme Court refused to hear the city's appeal, most likely because it agreed with the reasoning of the state that the prohibition against warehousing represented a "physical taking" of property.[18]

Whether they were displaced from SROs or had become homeless for some other reason, the demographics of homeless individuals in New York City were somewhat different. Compared to the homeless from other cities, individuals from New York were more likely to be people of color (87 percent in New York versus 48 percent elsewhere) and less likely to have been married (75 versus 51 percent). Although there is little evidence that they have spent more time in mental hospitals, a larger proportion have been in prison (30 versus 23 percent), and they have been homeless longer (four versus three years). They also worked less often during the last month (10 versus 28 percent). In short, the data suggest that these single adults were already more damaged than their counterparts elsewhere, and that the experience of homelessness in New York City had significantly aggravated their plight.[19]

Single Adults in New York City:
The Municipality's Response

The contemporary upsurge of this population dates from the early 1970s. The *New York Times*, for example, first reported in 1971 that the homeless people who used to restrict themselves to the Bowery were now congregating near Grand Central Station. The public behavior of these homeless people disturbed many observers. In the past, homelessness had been linked to alcoholism, which had, in turn, been linked to begging. Now, however, the public behavior of the homeless suggested that mental illness might also be a factor. Indeed, allegations about the effects of deinstitutionalization soon began to appear in the media, only to be confirmed in 1976 by the HRA's own demographic study. By then, the homeless, who had originally been seen just in midtown, were evident all over the city, from Trinity Place to the Lower East Side, and all the way uptown along Broadway. Women with shopping bags, younger alcoholics, and people nodding out on drugs: when widespread homelessness returned to New York City for the first time since the Depression, it was visible on many new faces.[20]

For several years, the city ignored this new social phenomenon. Movements for the poor had lost momentum; the homeless were still poorer and even more politically isolated. The issue did not come alive until 1979, when Robert Hayes's encounters with recalcitrant city officials prompted him to file *Callahan* v. *Carey*. The *Callahan* case not only established a national movement by legal advocates; for much of the next decade, it defined the city's response. New York's official histories have often been tendentious on this point, describing the growth of the shelter system but omitting the decisive push the city received from the courts. In presenting this version of the city's response, these histories actually seek to perpetuate two distinct myths: first, that the city developed an elaborate shelter system of its own volition, and second, that the whole process of shelter openings was part of a previously determined and well-conceptualized policy.[21]

The truth was quite different. As a result of a complex interaction with advocates for the homeless, the city entered into a judicially enforceable agreement to provide emergency shelter. This agreement soon proved to be thick with unforeseen implications. Its purpose was to provide temporary shelter, but with the city's housing shortage making "temporary" into an ever more elastic concept, costs escalated rapidly. The city had seen the provision of temporary shelter as a way out of its policy dilemma: the city had to provide more help, but it could not provide too much. Too much help—large-scale permanent housing, for example—violated the principle of less eligibility; it ran counter to the rightward drift in national politics, the decline in federal housing assistance, and the need to recast the popular perception of New York as a place with overly generous social welfare programs. The decision to provide additional temporary shelter was therefore an obvious choice. More than a little, but not too much, it represented a natural, but badly flawed, compromise.

Handed down in December 1979, the preliminary injunction in the *Callahan* case ordered the city to provide shelter to any man who requested it. The city did not appeal this decision. Instead, it responded by opening the Keener Building on Ward's Island. Keener, which had been a deserted psychiatric hospital, was supposed to house 180 men, but by the spring of 1980, it sheltered 625. One of these residents was a homeless man who had been released from Manhattan State Hospital on Ward's Island to the Bowery, only to be returned to Keener. "A long way round to go nowhere," he said.[22]

Conditions at Keener soon became the basis for subsequent legal action. In April 1980, Hayes sued again for preliminary relief. This time the suit was predicated on the contract between New York State as owners of the Keener building and New York City as operators of the shelter. The city, it was alleged, had failed to limit the capacity of the shelter and provide the requisite psychiatric, medical, and social services. The court denied the plaintiffs emergency relief, but ordered an immediate trial. In August 1980, however, just prior to the beginning of this trial, the city agreed to provide the shelter with sufficient staff and tripled its funding. Without an agreement on overcrowding, though, the plaintiffs had to return to court in January 1981. Their attempt to hold the city to minimal standards of space utilization failed when Judge Richard Wallach ruled that although there was severe overcrowding, no standards for usage of space had been included in the original injunction.[23]

At the same time, in January 1981, the *Callahan* case went to trial. After two weeks of hearings, the parties agreed on a skeletal framework for an out-of-court settlement. The core of this agreement was Hayes's willingness to drop the demand for community-based shelter in exchange for the city's commitment to provide minimally decent quarters. It took six months of pressure to flesh out the details, but finally, on 26 August 1981, the parties signed the consent decree. In it, the city and the state agreed to

> provide shelter and board to each homeless man who applies for it; provided that a) the man meets the need standard for the homeless relief program in New York State; or b) the man by reason of physical, mental, or social dysfunction is in need of temporary shelter.[24]

In addition, the decree also established certain minimum requirements about living space, intake procedures, and compliance monitoring.

There is a striking parallelism in the factors that led both parties to sign this consent decree. The city agreed to a guarantee of temporary shelter as a compromise between giving too little and giving too much. Advocates for the homeless agreed to the compromise because the too little they got through the court was more than they could otherwise obtain. Nevertheless, within a very few years, the agreement would eventually come to burden both signatories. New York City did not realize that when it signed the consent decree, it had committed itself to a major social program. And the advocates could not foresee that the *Callahan* agreement would lead to the development of a shelter system that despite its basis in the law, did not take its residents much beyond the Victorian poorhouse.

The New York City Shelter System for Single Individuals

The heart of the system for single individuals consists of about twenty-six municipal shelters housing 10,400 people. New York City owns and operates these facilities, which mostly (88 percent) shelter men. The nonprofit sector further enhances the system's capacity. Its largest single component is the Partnership for the Homeless, which started in 1981 as a response to Mayor Koch's call for assistance from city's religious institutions. Beginning with three participating churches, the Partnership had blossomed by 1988 to include 132 religious institutions with a reported capacity of 1,577 beds. In these churches and synagogues, the city provides cots and bedding, the institutions offer space, and volunteers feed the homeless a decent meal. Finally, there are about seventy other voluntary agencies in New York City that house a mix of families and individuals. In 1988, the total capacity of these facilities was 864 beds.[25]

New York City therefore operates about 80 percent of the beds for homeless single adults. The growth of this system was very rapid, from three shelters housing 2,120 single individuals in 1978 to 6,500 people in eighteen shelters by 1984. Operating expenditures also skyrocketed, from $8 million in 1978 to $58.8 million in 1984, and $173 million in 1990.[26] Yet despite its rapid development, despite the assistance rendered, the policies underlying the operation of the municipal shelter system for homeless individuals have always prevented it from doing a satisfactory job.

Homelessness As a Transient Problem

The first obstacle to the effectiveness of the system was a long-standing belief in the temporary nature of homelessness as a social problem. From the late 1970s until the mid–1980s, the Koch administration refused to acknowledge that homelessness was likely to endure as a public issue for quite some time. While the administration did recognize that federal cutbacks contributed to a shortage of low-income housing, it tried diligently to keep this need separate from the demand for temporary shelter. For this reason, it was not until June 1986, when Mayor Koch first announced his plans to build and renovate some 252,000 apartments, that his administration frankly admitted the connection, and even then, the admission applied more to families than to individuals.

In the interim, virtually every policy for single adults treated their homelessness as if it were a temporary problem. The system itself was a product of crisis management, opening one shelter after another as each filled to capacity. Some of these facilities were relatively adequate, but others, like the Fort Washington Armory, with as many as 1,400 cots on its football field size drill floor, came to epitomize both the magnitude and the ineptness of New York City's response.

The proposals the city did not implement were drawn from the same policy bank. The city talked of housing the homeless in trailers and doubled up in apartments with public assistance clients, as well as on mothballed Liberty ships and old Staten Island ferries. It pushed plans to build shelters on Hart Island in Long Island Sound, the site of the municipal paupers' cemetery. Punitive, makeshift, and discomfiting, these plans, too, reflected an unwillingness to come to grips with homelessness as a social problem.[27]

Setting New York's permanent and temporary responses next to one another accentuates their apparent contradictions. With one hand, the city committed itself to a major housing construction program, while with the other, it lined up 1,400 cots on an armory floor. The contradictions, though, were more apparent than real. Although the Koch administration sometimes argued that it had fashioned different responses for different needs—emergency shelter for fires and other emergencies, permanent housing to compensate for the shortfall of federal housing assistance—it based its policies on the fear that these responses were, in fact, closely linked. Policies that deterred people from using temporary shelter were useful in their own right, as a means of keeping costs down. But disincentives in the city's policies also served to disabuse people of the notion that they could rely on the municipality for help. As Mayor Koch himself said,

> I can guarantee you if tomorrow by some stroke of luck, genius and magic, I was able to create 6,500 apartments to give to 6,500 homeless singles, the next day you'd have 65,000 homeless singles looking for apartments. Why not?[28]

There was, then, no real contradiction between the city's policies for temporary and permanent housing. It is not that the Koch administration knew about the need of the homeless for permanent housing, and acted otherwise. It is, rather, that the administration knew about the need of the homeless for permanent housing, and acted accordingly.

Large Rather Than Small Shelters

In its efforts to control costs, New York City adopted a second policy of housing the homeless in very large shelters. In 1988, for example, thirteen of the fourteen men's shelters and eight of eleven women's shelters had more than 100 beds.[29] Big shelters are cheaper in the short-term, but they arouse greater community opposition and are much more difficult to manage. It is also considerably harder to help homeless people in a large institutional setting.

New York City dismissed these arguments for ten years. Large shelters, the Koch administration asserted, benefited from economies of scale; they offered the most efficient method of delivering services to the whole adult population. Furthermore, while armories aroused neighborhood opposition, they relieved the city of the burden of conducting multiple negotiations with communities about the placement of many smaller facilities. For an entitlement program that could not pick and choose whom it helped, large shelters were the preferred setting.

From the Coalition for the Homeless to Mayor Koch's own commission on the reorganization of HRA, this insistence on large shelters persuaded few people outside local government. The coalition's opposition was to be expected. For them, large shelters meant warehousing the homeless, an adamant refusal to see that significant number of New Yorkers needed permanent housing. But many other people found their criticism persuasive. Soon, City Council President Carol Bellamy, the City Council's Subcommittee on the Homeless, and Governor Mario Cuomo were all echoing the commission's belief that "the City should re-examine its assumption that shelters must have at least 200 beds to be operated economically. Smaller shelters are certainly easier to operate and provoke less community opposition."[30]

Were smaller shelters cheaper? Probably they were, but not by as much as their advocates claimed. The definition of cost is obviously crucial in this debate. Cost can be defined narrowly as the dollar "cost" of the program; or as the amount spent by the local, state, or federal governments; or as either of the above *plus* what the resident spends; or as the total cost to society. For reasons that derive directly from its assumption that shelters serve a transitory population, New York City only used the first method.

The use of this method did close the gap between the large shelters and smaller community residences. In 1984, for example, one bed in the men's shelter cost an average of twenty-six dollars a night. This figure exceeded the national average of fourteen dollars for shelters housing more than fifty-one people, but it was consistent with the higher, thirty dollar average for the northeast region.

Yet even if it was not inordinately expensive, the cost of this shelter was high enough to foster comparisons with the facilities operated by the priests of the Franciscan Order. The Franciscans had renovated two SRO hotels, and many people praised them for the dignity and respect with which they treated their residents. Lest these SROs be held up as model community facilities, officials of the Koch administration launched a campaign in which they tried to rebut virtually every favorable reference to them.[31]

Some of their points were well-taken. When critics said that community residences like St. Francis could be operated for half the per diem rate, they were downplaying the donation, by the friars, of their administrative services; the contribution, by a variety of government agencies, of free on-site psychiatric services; and the awarding, by both the city and the state, of $685,000 in grants and loans. To some extent, then, the Koch administration was right: the St. Francis Residences would be significantly more expensive if the cost of both services and capital expenditures was included in the calculation.[32]

Yet these omissions pale beside the unacknowledged costs of New York City's own policy. The most expensive of these unacknowledged costs are the expenditure of capital funds on big temporary shelters, the rapidly increasing bill for security, and the determined community opposition to any major shelter facility.

From the outset, the city spent capital funds on large temporary shelters. In 1979 and 1982, the city constructed two dorms with a total of 850 beds in the Keener Shelter. The dorms cost $7 million, or about $17,500 a bed. By contrast, about $8,500 a bed was spent on the first St. Francis Residence.[33] The dorms were designed as temporary housing; the St. Francis Residence added permanent rooms. New York City obviously got less for more, unless the deterrent value of large, temporary shelters is factored in.

Shelter size is also partly responsible for the high cost of security. Security costs have risen rapidly, from $11.8 million in fiscal year 1987 to $30.8 million in fiscal year 1989.[34] And superficially, at least, the city's justification for this expense has a factual basis. It is true that the shelter system houses many people with criminal records, and that the incidence of emotional disturbance is high. It is also true that in dealing with such volatile populations, it does not take much—a casual word, an off-handed comment—to turn a verbal exchange into a physical one. It takes even less, however, if such groups are crowded together in large shelters and accorded indifferent, if not disrespectful treatment. Here is where the city's policies contributed to the dangers of a system in which 43 percent of all residents reported that they had been robbed.[35] Large shelters inflicted enough real assaults upon the dignity of their residents that a violent response to any perceived insult was all the more likely.

The city's shelter policy must also shoulder some of the blame for the vigorous community opposition. The Koch administration always claimed that communities resisted the establishment of shelters in their midst. This claim was true, but it was also self-fulfilling. In October 1981, for example, the East New York Community Board was entertaining the possibility of sponsoring two shelters. One was to have 75 beds; the other, 200. The board saw these shelters as a way of housing its indigenous homeless population. Yet pressed by the court to respond to a critical shortage of beds, the city abruptly opened the 400 bed Brooklyn Men's Shelter. The decision confirmed the neighborhood's worst fears about the city's intentions. It also effectively terminated negotiations about the community-sponsored facilities.[36]

Likewise, when a court order forced the city to act quickly, it converted the former Public School 156 at 2960 Frederick Douglass Boulevard into the Harlem Shelter. Picketing and noisy crowds greeted the conversion, with the shelter's strongest opposition coming from the 2,500 families living in the Polo Grounds housing project across the street. "Don't Bring the Bowery Uptown," said a number of picket signs. Speaking in the city's defense, Robert Trobe, deputy administrator of HRA, declared

> Believe me, we've looked all over. This should open people's eyes to the reality of opening shelters in the city. No one could tell me that if we announced it eight weeks ago, we would have had the people's blessing. The reality is, there is tremendous opposition in the communities.[37]

Some of these conflicts have surely resulted from the city's policy of responding solely to crises. But there were also occasions when the deceptive statements made by public officials added a further provocation. In a 19 February 1986 meeting with 150 Brooklyn residents, William Gould, another HRA administrator, stated that the new Park Slope shelter would be used to house homeless families. On 14 March, however, twenty-four single men filed past a picket line into the armory. As if this misrepresentation were not enough to arouse the community, the local community newspaper soon revealed that the state social service commissioner had made the armory available to the city for single men before Gould even spoke. The building, whose listed capacity was seventy, housed as many as eighty-seven men before HRA changed its population to homeless women over the age of thirty-five years. Although this switch pleased many local residents, the process angered them, because it was once again carried out without consulting the community.[38]

These three incidents illustrate the problem with New York City's characterization of community opposition: it is based on the city's own clumsy interactions. There is no denying that some people will fight to keep any facility serving a poor or disabled population out of their neighborhood. The city, though, through its policies, consistently managed to transform this bedrock opposition into a full-fledged community coalition. Frightened residents hear talk of the homeless and think of cavernous armories. They see one homeless man and think of hundreds flooding their neighborhood. In this respect, the Koch administration was right: do what the city did, and the opposition is sure to be galvanized.[39]

In the short term, on the narrowest of program criteria, large shelters may be cheaper than smaller facilities. This comparison, however, requires a certain mindset. It demands first, that homelessness be seen as temporary, and second, that government only recognize the program costs which are written in boldface. Clearly, advocates also ignored some program costs, but at least they based their arguments on the more realistic premise that the poorest segment of the single adult population needs affordable long-term housing.

Ultimately, perhaps the most remarkable feature of New York City's adherence to a policy of large shelters was its staying power. Although critics condemned the city's policy throughout the 1980s, it was not until the onset of Mayor Koch's 1989 mayoral campaign that he proposed a $500 million plan to replace the armories with smaller, more humane facilities.

Koch lost. His successor, former Manhattan Borough President David Dinkins, had shared the goals set out in the Koch plan. But the Dinkins administration was slow to put these goals into practice. The budget shortage explains some of this delay; so does the political momentum of the old policy. The conversion to small shelters is expensive, and the savings it promises will be realized only when the humane treatment of people reduces social costs over the long term. New York City cannot wait for the long term: it needs quick, if not instant, savings. Dinkins may have the best of intentions, but given the political and economic constraints under which he operates, it is quite likely that the costs of large shelters will accumulate until they burden the administration of a future mayor.[40]

Differentiating the Population

The gradual differentiation of the population has been the chief sign of evolution in New York City's response toward the homeless. Although its own research bureau documented the population's changing demographics, the Koch administration initially designated very few special shelters for subgroups among the population, and when it did designate them, the designation did not last long.[41] HRA reserved the Hanson Place Shelter in Brooklyn for young men in 1984, but closed it in 1985. Similarly, in 1983, the city reserved beds in the Park Avenue Shelter for older homeless males, but then reassigned the beds to homeless women two years later.[42]

Since assistance can most easily be provided when people with similar needs are housed together, the failure to make some distinctions among the homeless implied a reluctance to offer them appropriate services. While this policy was cheaper as long as the social costs of homelessness did not rise too sharply, there was a tipping point where the costs of homelessness exceeded the expense of new social welfare outlays. When the Koch administration reached this tipping point in 1986, it switched policies.

In the spring of that year, Mayor Koch proposed a four year, $82 million plan to provide separate housing for the elderly, employable adults, substance abusers, and the mentally ill. The plan, which was based on a study of client needs conducted by the New York State Psychiatric Institute, coupled the state's assistance for an increase of 4,382 beds with the use of existing facilities. Yet several problems arose. First, while the city/state's partnership is a delicate one that requires both governments to fulfill their commitments, the record of state sponsorship has been less than sterling. Second, tight city budgets have consistently hampered the implementation of the plan. In fiscal year 1987, for example, New York City cut funding for the homeless by $3.7 million. The cuts reduced shelter staff by 10 percent and deferred for six months a variety of new services.

By the early 1990s, then, New York City had implemented a policy of partial differentiation. Instead of a smaller number of large shelters, New York City had a somewhat larger number of smaller shelters, understaffed but grouped according to the population's needs. There were facilities for veterans, people with AIDs, and employable residents, as well as a city commitment to fund 5,000 SRO beds. Still, with budgetary considerations always looming in the background, New York could not provide adequate social services to each subgroup. Under these circumstances, it was of little consequence how many distinctions among the homeless the city made.[43]

Work Programs for the Homeless

Work programs were the fourth major ingredient of New York City's policies. Since the early 1980s, there have been two main types of work programs. One, exemplified by the Work Experience Program (WEP), seeks to prepare people for jobs; the other, typified by the Shelter Employment and Housing Program (SEHP), actually tries to find them paid positions in the competitive labor market. Essentially, WEP is a work-readiness program, and SEHP is an employment program. HRA studies carried out in the early 1980s were instrumental in their establishment.

The linchpin in the development of this policy was probably the publication, in 1982, of *Chronic and Situational Dependency: Long-Term Care in a Shelter for Men*. Although earlier HRA research had hinted at the altered demographics of the shelter population, these studies had primarily focused on the influx of ex-psychiatric patients. Not until *Chronic and Situational Dependency* appeared did it become apparent that the men's shelters housed an entirely new kind of resident, one who, even if he did not have much job experience, was nevertheless quite employable. With the population growing rapidly, and with Thomas Main using the data from *Chronic and Situational Dependency* for his influential neoconservative policy analysis "The Homeless of New York," there was a powerful incentive to place some conditions on the newly won right to shelter. The Koch administration responded by establishing WEP.[44]

First implemented in the Harlem Men's Shelter on 6 June 1983, WEP required all employable residents to work twenty hours a week for a $12.50 stipend. Residents who did not wish to participate were asked to leave the Harlem shelter for another facility where WEP had not yet been put into operation. The program's initial evaluation clearly states its overall purpose:

It provides clients with the opportunity to participate productively in the provision of shelter services for themselves and other clients. It is intended to build work skills and habits, prevent some of the potentially debilitating effects of dependency and lack of constructive activity, and provide clients with the opportunity to qualify for a supplementary personal expense allowance.[45]

Beginning with 110 men in the Harlem shelter, WEP expanded rapidly to include 3,140 men in twenty shelters.[46] During this expansion, the tasks diversified from shelter maintenance to the cleaning of nearby parks and subway stations. By assigning crews to clean some public areas in the neighborhood, New York City hoped to defuse local animosity toward the homeless.

From the outset, WEP has been engulfed in controversy. The Coalition for the Homeless greeted the announcement of its expansion in March 1984 with a broadside of unfavorable quotes from residents about inadequate pay and the time taken away from finding a real job. One resident said, "We need a real check to motivate us. We can't work on blind faith. We're like anyone else, you know."[47] Criticism also came from less expected sources. New York State derided programs like WEP as merely "the exchange of labor for services," and in its 1984 HUD report, even the Reagan administration expressed concern that the program was only acclimating residents to shelter life.[48] Yet, despite these disparaging comments, New York City has steadfastly defended WEP as one of the cornerstones of its shelter system.

The first of the city's arguments is that WEP keeps the residents busy and enhances their self-esteem. Without WEP, this argument goes, the shelter's employable population would languish in idleness and depression. Because the twenty hours a week residents devote to WEP helps to organize their day, it is certainly a far superior expenditure of their time than drinking, playing cards, or watching television. Keeping busy is, in this sense, a major psychological weapon against the gradual resignation to living in a shelter.[49]

The city also defends WEP as a means of preparing the residents for paying jobs. The premise behind this assertion has less to do with the erosion of skills than it does with the presumed decomposition of the work ethic. WEP participants use few marketable skills. But they must be punctual, respectful of their supervisors, and responsible in carrying out their assigned tasks. These traits are vital to the work ethic, which, the city fears, will quickly disappear unless it is continually refurbished by WEP.

Finally, there is the belief in reciprocity. Although the city has not made any explicit statement to this effect, the increasingly popular notion that assistance must be conditional on some evidence of the poor's "good works" permeates all of its assertions. Simultaneously, through its arguments in defense of WEP, New York City is making a demand on the homeless, subtlely declaring its right to make such a demand, and insisting that the demand is in their own interest. It is a politically attuned, but ultimately fallacious, argument.

WEP is, in essence, the modern version of a work test—cleaning shelters and subways instead of chopping wood, as many shelters demanded in the early 1900s. Seen in this historical light, WEP is punitive, does not enhance self-esteem, and prepares people better for life in the shelter than it does for adequately paying jobs. WEP punishes people for their homelessness by paying sixty-two cents an hour for the kind of menial labor that would hardly—at least at that salary—enhance anyone's feelings of self-esteem. Not surprisingly, even the city's own evaluation has shown, "long-term WEP participants have fewer potential barriers to employment than shorter-term clients but are less likely to be assessed as job-ready . . . they are less motivated towards independence . . . and WEP could be contributing to such habituation."[50] This is perhaps the decisive rebuttal to the city's arguments. New York City suspects WEP is not successful, but has kept it anyway.

Some WEP participants, however, are work-ready, and HRA often refers the most prepared of these to SEHP. SEHP makes job placements—a total of 727 during its first two years from 1985 to 1987. Most of these residents were placed in clerical, security, maintenance, messenger, and food service positions paying less than five dollars an hour, with about one-quarter of those enrolled moving out of the shelter system.[51]

By investing public funds in this program, New York City legitimates the right of the homeless to the job market: that is the program's true political import. Gaining this access is an important step because it gives the homeless rights that other groups of poor people already have. But the value of this right should not be overrated. Lacking any genuinely marketable skills, all the homeless get is access to the bottom rung of the labor market. The problem is, of course, that with the salaries they receive, it is virtually impossible to obtain housing in New York City.

In order to enable the homeless to pay for their own housing, New York would have to commit itself to a large-scale job training program. Even if it could only reach the one-quarter to one-half of the adult population who are employable, the cost of such a training program would be considerable. Moreover, from the city's perspective, there is little reason to finance a job training program that would flood an uncertain labor market with an excess of skilled people. At this level of commitment, then, WEP and SEHP combine to serve a very useful function.

New York City has retained WEP because a demand for menial work puts conditions on the entitlement to shelter. It likes SEHP because whenever critics attack WEP for its dead-end jobs, the city can point to SEHP as the outlet through which residents can find paid employment. WEP blends work as preparation and work as punishment; SEHP "creams" off the most employable segment of the homeless population without making a bigger investment in those who might be less readily employed. Between qualifying the receipt of shelter and getting the employable jobs, New York City has touched all the political bases. The only missing ingredient in this peculiar mix is the kind of large-scale job training program that could help a significant number of homeless people.

Policies for the Homeless Mentally Ill

The fifth, and final, policy for the homeless involves services for the mentally ill. More than with any of the other policies, the city is dependent on state funding for these services. This dependence both relieves the city of some responsibility for its mental health policies and gives it an excuse. The city would certainly prefer to have greater control over the funding of its mental health programs. In the absence of this control, however, it has gotten a good deal of mileage out of blaming the state for the condition of the homeless mentally ill.

The one decisive fact that dominates every aspect of New York City's mental health policy is a shortage of beds. There is a shortage of acute care hospital beds for psychiatric emergencies, and there is a shortage of long-term adult residences for those with chronic emotional problems. The whole system, in fact, suffers from shelter gridlock. Without satisfactory alternatives to discharge people, patients fill every bed, and emergency rooms overflow. As the directors of psychiatric emergency rooms in ten municipal hospitals wrote,

> The mental health system is moving toward a disastrous breakdown. The city's psychiatric services are in a state of unprecedented overcrowding; forty to seventy patients waiting for acute beds has been commonplace, turning our emergency rooms into holding wards... [Patients] eat, drink, sit, stand, lie on stretchers, and are restrained, all in the same small holding areas often for 2–3 days; in some cases for 7–10 days![52]

The origins of this crisis can be traced to a shortage of every other kind of housing. In the state mental hospitals, the census continued to drop, from 93,000 in 1955 to 14,000 in 1991. Further declines are projected. An alternative form of housing, adult residences for the chronically disturbed, are supposed to provide long-term supportive housing, but they too are in short supply. In 1985, state mental health commissioner Stephen Katz estimated that although New York needed a total of 10,000 beds in community residences, it had just a little more than one-third that amount. After the city and the state signed an agreement in 1989 to provide housing for another 5,225 homeless mentally ill people, a state court did order the municipality to fund 10,000 beds. The city, though, immediately promised to appeal this decision because there was no money to finance it. Hence, twenty years after the first emotionally disturbed people began to appear on the streets of New York City, neither the city nor the state had implemented an effective plan for housing the homeless mentally ill.[53]

This shortage of facilities for long-term care clogs up the entire mental health system. In New York City, the eleven municipal hospitals have a total of 1,450 psychiatric beds. Yet because these hospitals have no place to send their patients, the average length of stay rose by 40 percent between 1982 and 1988, from 18.6 to 26.1 days. By then, the occupancy rate had reached 99.2 percent, and psychiatric wards were functioning at the brink of their capacity, with three facilities—Kings County, North Central Bronx, and Woodhull—averaging over 100 percent for the entire year.[54]

This overcrowding spilled over into emergency rooms and turned them into temporary living quarters. Patients with any illness would have found them obviously unsuited. But keeping psychiatric patients in these conditions for days at a time was particularly questionable, since it often required that they be drugged or restrained.

Despite these conditions, emergency rooms sometimes became the primary site for the delivery of psychiatric services. Psychiatrists were reluctant to admit patients when there was little prospect of a vacant bed, and they repeatedly discharged people who needed ongoing care. The New York State Commission on the Quality of Care for the Mentally Ill Disabled prepared a study of one of these cases, a thirty-seven-year-old Greek immigrant who had allegedly murdered his elderly parents. Brought by the police to Kings County Hospital after his arrest, the accused said, "I'm crazy, damn it. I know I killed my parents. Nurse, are you going to keep me? Please don't let me go this time."[55]

Overloaded, backlogged, and on the verge of collapse, this is the mental health system to which the homeless are referred. Some referrals come from the Shelter Assessment and Referral Program (SHARP), state-funded mental health teams that are located in six city shelters. Two other shelters are served by HRA's own psychiatric unit, which screens, assists, and refers clients to suitable long-term facilities. Finally, the New York City Department of Mental Health uses state funds to administer the Community Support System Program. Staff from this program work in nine shelters to provide psychiatric evaluations and day programs for residents who are emotionally disturbed.[56]

Although the problems of the larger mental health system vitiate the effectiveness of these programs, shelter-based outreach has not, by itself, been the subject of any major public controversy. Instead, controversy has focused on the six street outreach programs, with their mandate to pick up the conspicuously poor and the conspicuously ill. Not-for-profit organizations manage five, including the Midtown Outreach Project in the Times Square area and, on the Upper West Side, Project Reach Out. The New York City Health and Hospitals Corporation runs Project HELP (Homeless Emergency Liaison Project), which operates out of

Gouverneur Hospital on the Lower East Side. In fiscal year 1988, New York City spent a total of $2,398,000 on these programs.[57]

Mental health staff in these projects use vans to drive around their catchment areas in search of homeless people who need some assistance. As the staff of Project HELP noted, this population

> is readily identifiable and tends to stand out even amidst Manhattan crowds. Primary visual indicators include an extremely dirty and disheveled appearance; torn, dirty, or layered clothing; clothing inappropriate to the weather (layers of heavy coats and woolen hats in midsummer and no coats in midwinter); and a collection of belongings in bags, boxes, or shopping carts. Primary behavioral indicators include walking in traffic, urinating or defecating in public, lying on a crowded sidewalk, and remaining mute and withdrawn.[58]

In 1987, as the numbers of such people grew, the Koch administration set aside twenty-eight beds for the homeless mentally ill in Bellevue Hospital and embarked on a program of involuntary commitment. One of the first people committed under this program was Joyce Brown, who had lived for one year on the corner of Sixty-fifth Street and Second Avenue. The Koch administration claimed that Brown's residence on the corner endangered her health and therefore met the state standard for involuntary commitment. Robert Levy and Norman Siegel of The New York Civil Liberties Union (NYCLU) filed for her release. They won in the lower court, but lost on appeal. The hospital subsequently discharged Brown when, in another court hearing, the judge ruled that the hospital could not medicate her against her will.[59]

In making their arguments for involuntary commitment, the Koch administration often cast itself as the protector of emotionally disturbed homeless people. However genuine and well-intentioned, this argument was disingenuous. As the NYCLU pointed out, the issue was not about the abstract "right" of homeless people to live on the street; it was rather about their preferring to live on the street in the absence of other, more satisfactory choices. From this perspective, the choice of one bed among twenty-eight in the Bellevue Psychiatric Ward was no choice at all.

Setting aside a mere twenty-eight beds for this program raises a host of other questions. Emotionally disturbed people are so common on the streets of New York that twenty-eight beds could not make a noticeable dent in the population. The original contract for the outreach programs puts this number in a still more questionable light, because until the NYCLU brought it to the attention of the local media, vans were only supposed to pick up homeless people south of 110th Street on the West Side and 96th Street on the East—in other words, only in the wealthier, and mostly white, parts of Manhattan. Even after the city revised the contract, just 1 of the 123 people committed during the program's first five months came from outside this district.[60]

From this evidence, it would appear that New York City's outreach policy was largely a political strategem to ease public concern about the visibility of the homeless mentally ill. Amid the acute needs of thousands of emotionally disturbed street people, the program might not amount to much. Its political utility, however, was considerable. By conveying the impression that the city's government was addressing the problem of the homeless mentally ill, the policy of involuntary commitment helped the Koch administration to combat perceptions of its ineffectuality.

More generally, outreach programs suffer from the same gridlock as the rest of the mental health system. In the Bellevue program, for example, patients were supposed to remain for twenty-one days. But stays have actually averaged forty-seven days, in part, because other facilities cannot be found. When beds are particularly scarce, the city has even referred some psychiatric patients directly to the shelter system. Of course, this policy does not merely shuffle people back and forth between the psychiatric emergency room and the shelter. A return to the streets is also an option for those who are lost in transit.[61]

Emergency assistance does save lives. In this respect, New York City's outreach programs doubtlessly constitute an important new tool for engaging one of the most difficult groups among the homeless. But without a corresponding investment in the capacity of the mental health system to provide care over the longer term, their current prominence acquires a different meaning. Outreach programs are the most cost-effective method of removing conspicuously homeless people. The help they provide may be short-lived, but they do get some homeless people off the street, and they do create the impression that the city government is actually doing something about the problem.

Conclusion

These five policies for homeless adults share a common approach. Beneath the surface of the most elaborate response to the homeless of any city in the country, New York still practices crisis management and still resists permanent solutions to the problem of homelessness. Its response is, admittedly, more dependent on the public sector than other cities. But the business constraints on that sector are severe, and New York, in its effort to compete with other cities, does not have much room to maneuver. New York can provide big temporary shelters, but not housing; work programs, but little genuine work; and emergency psychiatric assistance, but not long-term care. In short, New York can spend large sums of money on single homeless adults, as long as that money does not disrupt the political and economic arrangements that made them homeless in the first place. This is sad, but only part of the story, because there is considerable evidence that in New York City's policies for homeless families, the same principle holds.

10

New York City: Wealth, Poverty, and Homeless Families

It is the grimness of poverty that troubles us more than any other problem, a grimness that spreads its tragedy not just to adults but to children as well.
From *New York Ascendant*, The Report of the Commission on the Year 2000

Hellholes.
Congressman Ed Koch's description of welfare hotels (1970)

        The transformation of New York's economy affected families as well as individuals. To create a favorable business environment, the city government granted tax abatements for major real estate projects and tried to restrict increases in municipal salaries. Tightening its grip on welfare spending, it used the discretionary part of the municipal budget for business development instead of social programs. The effect of these policies rippled throughout the city, bringing about both an economic renaissance and a decline in municipal services. The economic renaissance greatly enriched the leaders of the business community and spread some new wealth among the professional classes. At the same time, however, it made life among poor families that much tougher.
    The effect on families demonstrates that this renaissance manifested itself in a full-scale retrenchment of social welfare. Sometimes, when governments restrict social welfare benefits, they limit the cutbacks to single individuals. Adults living alone do not support anyone else, and a decline in their standard of living has fewer unpleasant consequences. The political appeal of this policy, though, exceeds the financial benefits: not much money can be saved. To save real money, to reorder the uses and priorities of the municipal budget, social welfare retrenchments must cut deeper. To save real money, they have to affect families.

The Scarcity of Low-Income Housing

A low rental allowance for welfare clients is one of the most certain methods of saving government money. For eight years, from 1975 to 1983, the maximum rental allowance for four people in New York City stayed at $218 a month. New York State raised the grant to $270 in 1984, and then to $312 in 1988. Not surprisingly, the fastest growth in both the family and adult male shelter population occurred in 1983, when the real value of the average public assistance grant was at its lowest point.[1]

The decline in value of the rental allowance is part of a more general decline in the total value of the New York City welfare grant. From 1970 to 1987, the value of the maximum welfare grant fell by 39 percent to 65.7 percent of the federal poverty level. In New York, like the rest of the country, inflation during this period was particularly steep, and housing was one of the main factors pushing prices upward. From 1970 to 1985, the New York City/Northern New Jersey Consumer Price Index rose by 164 percent, but the average public assistance grant per case increased 88 percent, or a little more than half the rate of inflation.[2]

Strapped for resources, welfare families searching for housing in New York had very few choices. In 1987, the median rent of all New York City apartments was $395 a month. Households receiving public assistance, however, paid a median rent of $304, 23 percent less than the city median. Since fewer than 5,000 apartments renting at the below maximum public assistance grant became available during 1986, 63 percent of all welfare families who did not live in New York City public housing were paying a rent in excess of their shelter allowance. In fact, on average, the typical welfare family was sixty dollars short of the money needed to pay their monthly rent.[3]

This housing squeeze has greatly enhanced the appeal of public housing. Even though drugs and crime have tainted many of the buildings the New York City Housing Authority (NYCHA) operates, affordable shelter in New York City is such a scarce commodity that families must wait twenty years for these units. Another 100,000 people could not afford to wait and doubled up in the NYCHA's 178,000 apartments. This extra population meant more elevator trips, greater water use, and heavier demands on every aspect of the physical plant. As a result, NYCHA experienced an increase in operating and maintenance costs that contributed to a $62 million deficit over three years.[4]

The problem of doubling up is hardly confined to the NYCHA. It has also spilled over into the broader housing market, where the 1987 housing survey counted almost 150,000 "relative" households. This group is quite diverse; it consists of more than 46,000 two person households made up of a reference person who is neither a spouse nor a child, and another 103,000 households of larger size. Three generation households constitute some of this latter group. All told, however, 45 percent of these households had incomes below $15,000. Since a number of studies have shown that doubling up is among the characteristics most conducive to homelessness, these families are at especially high risk.[5]

Current housing construction in New York will not reduce this risk, because most of it is far too expensive for poorer people. Between 1984 and 1987, for example, the city's total housing stock increased by 37,000 units. But with construction costs reaching $200 a square foot, rents of $2,000 a month are necessary to make a development profitable.[6] These costs, coupled with the cost of land, serve to dramatize a fundamental fact about local housing policy: in New York City, perhaps more than any place else in the United States, housing for the poor requires some form of public subsidy.

Greatly inflaming the whole issue of the housing shortage has been the controversy about warehousing. Ever since the 1987 housing survey showed a rise from 56,000 to 72,000 in the number of apartments that have been kept off the market, laws have been introduced in the City Council to limit this practice. None of these bills have been enacted. Successfully blocked by real estate interests and, within the council, by Democratic Majority Leader Peter Vallone, the bills have suffered from a debate about the true extent of warehousing. The categories in the 1987 survey do not readily lend themselves to resolution of this issue: 18,807 apartments "undergoing renovation," 6,301 awaiting conversion to cooperative or condominium status, and 17,692 held off the market "for other reasons." Since information about how long an apartment has been "undergoing renovation" is open to multiple interpretations, the estimates have ranged widely, from a 5,000 apartment figure put forth by the Council for Owner-Occupied Housing, to the 12,000 cited by the state attorney general, and the 35,000 suggested by Peter Marcuse of Columbia University. For some, the notion that landlords were warehousing apartments in the midst of a housing shortage epitomized the speculative fever that plagued the New York City housing market. But the absence of generally accepted data has always defused this outrage and prevented enough people from mobilizing in support of a more restrictive law.[7]

The Growth in the Number of Homeless Families

During the 1980s, the growth in the number of homeless families quickly became the best single indicator of the housing crisis. New York City provided temporary shelter to about 800 families in 1979. By 1983, however, the HRA served 2,500 families. This figure peaked at more than 5,200 in 1988. Public criticism and the threat of federal sanctions then brought about a gradual decline to 3364 in 1990, but within a year, the recession and a shortage of apartments for homeless families had raised the number again to 4566.[8]

Several attributes distinguished the families who used emergency housing. Consistent with the other findings on doubling up, 44 percent of the families using the emergency housing system have never been long-term (for more than one year) primary tenants. Having never acquired a stake in the housing market, they depend on the good will of others: 71 percent were living with family or friends the evening before they sought shelter. Families applying for emergency shelter are also more likely to be African-American (54 percent) than are housed public assistance families (31.9 percent), and younger (44 percent, rather than 18 percent, under twenty-five years old). But perhaps most poignantly of all, there was a strong relationship between homelessness and pregnancy or recent birth. Thirty-five percent of the homeless were pregnant at the time they applied for housing, as compared with 6 percent of the housed. Likewise, for recent births, the 26 percent of the homeless who had a child within the last year was more than double the 11 percent figure among those who were housed.[9]

Four different kinds of facilities provided emergency shelter for this population: welfare hotels, congregate shelters without private rooms for each family (Tier I), shelters offering private sleeping quarters but with shared bathrooms and dining areas (Tier II), and family centers, with their private apartments. Although barrack-style facilities were more expensive, welfare hotels were the most controversial. Along with the number of homeless people on the street, there was no more powerful condemnation of New York City's policies than the idea that wretched hotels like the Martinique should be paid sixty-three dollars a night to house a family of four.[10]

Controversies about welfare hotels are not new. In fact, they have occurred periodically since World War II. The first of these scandals occurred on 9 May 1947, when the *New York World Telegram* published an article entitled "Family's Ritzy Relief Cost $500 in Month," about one family's stay in a West Side Hotel. Mayor William O'Dwyer immediately directed Welfare Commissioner Edward Rhatigan to rehouse the thirty-seven affected hotel families "as quickly and humanely as possible." But both the city council and the New York State Department of Welfare also ordered an investigation. Under considerable political pressure, the city initially sent the families to dilapidated and rat-infested apartments, then relented and returned them to the hotels, and finally directed them to a family shelter that was so well-kept no one wanted to leave. Commissioner Rhatigan had to resign later that year, and in large measure it was the hotel controversy that cost him his job.

Twenty-three years later, in 1970, another newspaper article—on this occasion in the *New York Times*—ignited a similar controversy. Eleven hundred families resided in welfare hotels under conditions that Mayor John Lindsay called "notorious sore spots," and Congressman Edward Koch described as "hellholes." In January 1971, three caseworkers in HRA decided to demonstrate that at the price HRA was paying, clients could just as easily be referred to the Waldorf-Astoria. And that is exactly what they did. Bypassing HRA's list of approved hotels, they sent Cleola Hainsworth and her four children to the Waldorf, at $76.32 a night. When the local media fumed, Mayor Lindsay accused the caseworkers of "malicious intent" and suspended them. He then instructed municipal agencies to place clients in the welfare hotels solely as a result of fires, evacuations, or other similar emergencies.[11]

These periodic outbursts about the use of welfare hotels occur because on the surface at least, it is plainly wasteful to spend so much money on such miserable, temporary housing. Every once in a while, some situation or event refocuses media attention on the welfare hotels, and when people are reminded of their cost, they get angry. Yet welfare hotels persist as a feature of New York's housing policy because except in times of great dependence on them, they actually save the state money.

It sounds paradoxical. When a family could be housed for slightly more than the maximum allowance—say, $400 a month—how can the expenditure of several thousand dollars a month for two small rooms in a welfare hotel save the government money? The answer is that families in welfare hotels usually represent the exception, and it is generally cheaper to pay outrageous rents for a few exceptions than it is to raise the maximum housing allowance for the entire state caseload. Clearly, however, if the exceptions mount, and many people must be referred to the welfare hotels, the policy no longer offers any savings. When that happens, it is a sure sign to government policymakers to increase the maximum housing allowance, because the welfare grant is too low.

This explanation, though, only partly explains why the periodic uproars about welfare hotels have failed to remove them from the list of housing resources. Welfare hotels not only save the government money, but they also make considerable sums for some well-connected people. In the mid-1980s, one-third of New York City's welfare hotel business went to two separate business partnerships that together grossed $25 million in rents. A partnership run by Bernard and Roberts Sillins housed 514 families in three hotels. But the largest hotel syndicate belonged to Morris Horn and partners, who owned seven hotels with 565 rooms in three boroughs. Between 1980 and 1986, this partnership donated $104,800 in campaign contributions, including $46,800 to Mayor Koch. By appearance, at least, the money was well-targeted. The partnership did not contribute to the campaigns for borough president in the Bronx and Staten Island, where it did not own hotels.[12]

New York City's willingness to enrich the hotel owners sometimes went to extraordinary lengths. In 1982, New York took title to the Jamaica Arms Hotel for nonpayment of taxes. Several months later, it sold the building to a corporation for $75,000. This corporation, in turn, resold the hotel to the Horn syndicate for $200,000. The deal soon turned into the most profitable kind of public/private partnership, because by 1986, New York City was paying them $1.2 million a year to house families in a hotel that it had owned outright just four years earlier.[13]

It is this determination to shed the responsibilities of public ownership that makes the city's budget so vulnerable to scavenging. Since the ownership of real estate is assumed to be a responsibility of the private sector, New York City is always the owner of last resort. This assumption dictates the policy that whenever New York acquires housing, it is supposed to return that housing to the tax rolls. The return of housing to the tax rolls means that New York often exchanges the power and benefits of ownership for the weakness and expenses of a tenant. At a time when New York City was the primary source of profits for many hotels, and annual profits in some hotels approached 25 percent, this exchange did not represent a good bargain.[14]

Children in Emergency Shelter

Critics have consistently upbraided the city for its reliance on the welfare hotels as an emergency housing resource. The hotels were costly, and conditions in them were deplorable. The typical hotel crowded a family with several children into one or two small rooms. It did not provide cribs, and children of all ages slept in the same bed. There were few amenities: no sheets, towels, pillows, or blankets, and in many hotels, the plumbing did not work either. Vermin-infested and overrun with drugs, conditions in the hotels animated popular exposés such as Jonathan Kozol's *Rachel and Her Children* as well as a host of other studies.[15]

Although the hotels aroused widespread public opposition, it was the prospect of raising children in such places that probably aroused the most sympathy. At its height in 1988, the 5,218 families who were living in temporary shelter represented a total of 17,746 people. Including single adults, New York City was therefore providing shelter to about 28,000 individuals. The image of the homeless most emphatically fixed in the popular mind was an adult single person, mentally ill and/or on drugs. Yet of all people sheltered by New York City, the 10,764 children were actually the most common type.[16]

Some very disquieting testimony came from these children. In the *McCain* v. *Koch* brief about the right of homeless families to shelter, Janet May Patterson described conditions in the Carter Hotel, where she stayed with her family for six weeks. In her affidavit, she says

1. I am seven years old.
2. I know the difference between right and wrong. I know that telling a lie is wrong. I am telling the truth in this paper.
3. This paper is being read to me. I read a little bit, but not well.
4. The Carter Hotel is a bad place.
5. Last week or so I saw three men on the eighth floor. Each of the men stuck a needle in his arm. Then the men put the needless in their pockets.
6. I was scared and took the elevator back to my floor.[17]

In addition to testimony that children were growing up amid scenes like these, other data accumulated rapidly about the effects of homelessness on the young. Homeless children had poorer nutrition, delayed immunization, and higher levels of lead in their blood. Moreover, in one study of 1,028 children at sixteen Robert Wood Johnson health centers throughout the country, the incidence of virtually every kind of physical disorder—from anemia to upper respiratory infections—occurred at about twice the rate of similar ambulatory patients. Unquestionably, homelessness had adversely affected their health.[18]

It also undermined their education. On 1 October 1988, 6,156 New York children of school age were living in temporary residences. According to a Board of Education survey, 3,809 of these children were registered in the school system, for a registration rate of only 62 percent.[19] But getting these children to school is only part of the problem. Anxious, depressed and deficient in self-control, homeless school children often exhibit a number of cognitive and emotional deficits. In New York City, homeless school children scored lower than other students on both the reading (42 percent compared to 68 percent at or above grade level) and achievement tests (28 percent compared to 57 percent). As a consequence, teachers held them back more than twice as frequently.[20]

Emptying the Welfare Hotels

Although critics amassed considerable evidence about the damage that conditions in the hotels inflicted on families, New York City did not commit itself to removing families from welfare hotels until the federal government declared its intention to change the reimbursement rate for the Emergency Assistance Program. The Department of Health and Human Services used to reimburse half of the cost of emergency housing up to and beyond a thirty-day period. Under this policy, the federal government was shouldering half the rental charges of a New York City welfare hotel, which could easily amount to $1,500 a month. In 1987, however, the department proposed limiting its reimbursement to half the city's welfare grant, or $156 of the $312 rate for a family of four. Several congressional actions including the 1988 refunding of the Mckinney Act delayed the quick implementation of this rule until the fall of 1991. Criticism from many sources may have laid the groundwork, but nevertheless, in the end, it was the prospect of losing federal money that prompted the city to act.[21]

At first, the city promised to empty the welfare hotels by 1992. It subsequently moved up this deadline to 31 July 1990. New York did not meet this goal, though initially, it made significant progress. As the deadline passed, there were 147 families living in the hotels. This figure was down from 3,600 three years earlier, but with more families becoming homeless, the number shot up to 650 again within several months. Most of the progress came from giving almost every vacant apartment in the public housing projects to a homeless family—a total of nearly 4,000 apartments in two years. Yet the city's policy of rationing scarcity angered many residents who were living doubled-up. When the Dinkins administration set aside 1,000 units for them, it created a shortage of available apartments that increased the number of hotel families.[22]

New York City may eventually fulfill its commitment to empty the welfare hotels. It is, however, far more likely that New York has simply entered one of those periods of less reliance upon them. On several occasions in the post-World War II era, financial considerations have combined with moral outrage to limit the number of families in the hotels. Invariably, though, the number has risen again, because welfare hotels are an exceedingly resilient institution that play an important role within the emergency housing system. Surely, New York deserves credit for its efforts to empty the welfare hotels. Yet just as surely, at some time in the not-so-impossibly distant future, there will be another hotel crisis.

Where Will the Families Go?

Although many homeless families have been referred to public housing, New York City has also developed a number of other policies to address the problem of family homelessness. Some of these policies are preventive measures to stop people from becoming homeless in the first place. But for those people who do become homeless, New York City has sought to improve its transitional facilities. Most significantly of all, it has committed itself to the largest municipal housing program ever launched in the United States.

One important preventive measure is the HRA's Eviction Prevention Program. This program includes initiatives like Housing Alert, which seeks to identify families who are at risk of homelessness and provide them with services to retain their current housing. HRA has also reorganized its intake procedures for families who need emergency shelter. By trying to resolve family and/or landlord conflicts and exploring the availability of other options, the agency hopes to divert people from use of the family shelter system. In the same vein, HRA has outstationed staff from the income maintenance centers in the city's four housing courts. They work at these sites to assist families who have received dispossess or eviction notices.[23]

Since most people who apply for emergency housing have exhausted all their resources, these efforts are not likely to yield significant results. New York has therefore focused a second part of its response on an effort to improve its transitional facilities. The key to this effort was a 1987 political compromise between Mayor Koch and members of the Board of Estimate.

In October 1986, Mayor Koch proposed that the city construct twenty new shelters—four in each borough—to house the rapidly expanding homeless population. Originally, each of the family shelters had congregate dining rooms and bathrooms. But gradually, the proposal changed. Kitchens and bathrooms would now be private, and the size of the apartments would be enlarged. Eager to avoid the presence of the homeless on Staten Island, Borough President Ralph Lamberti agreed to exchange the construction of a jail for cancellation of four shelters. Eventually, after weeks of negotiations, fifteen shelter sites came before the board.

It soon became apparent, however, that not all of the fifteen sites would gain approval. Some members of the Board of Estimate did not want additional shelters in their boroughs, while others were concerned about the quality of life that the facilities provided. The final compromise resulted in agreement on eleven sites—four shelters for single adults and seven for families. The latter are to be phased in as a substitute for the barracks-style (Tier I) facilities.[24]

The transitional family shelters constitute a definite improvement. All have 100 rooms: 70 single rooms of 275 square feet for a single adult and one or two children, and 30 apartments of 550 square feet for larger families. The complexes also have offices, consulting space, four day-care rooms, several common living rooms on each floor, and one 1,600 square foot meeting area. To avoid the appearance of an institution, there is even a landscaped area in the front.[25]

Unfortunately, these improvements cannot overcome the basic problem of housing scarcity. Between the shortage of permanent housing and the growing perception about the inadequacy of emergency shelter, transitional facilities are caught in a bind. Residents may stay longer as the private housing market shrivels up, and preferred access to government-assisted housing becomes the only route out. But while transitional shelter provides better living quarters from which to search for permanent housing, it can never substitute for it. From emergency to transitional to permanent housing, the effect is to create shelter gridlock all up and down the line.

As an example of the relationship between these kinds of housing, consider the efforts to replace the barracks shelter with transitional facilities. Critics have long indicted barrack shelters for their cost and lack of privacy—indeed, for all the worse aspects of institutional living. As a matter of fact, before he became mayor, Manhattan Borough President David Dinkins actually condemned them as "even more disturbing than the use of hotels."[26] But when a subcommittee of the New York City Council set a 1992 deadline to stop housing families in these shelters, Mayor Dinkins warned that too few transitional facilities might force homeless families back into the welfare hotels. The one exception to the bill specified that in the event the HRA commissioner declared an emergency, New York could reopen the barrack shelters for forty-five days, or longer with the consent of the City Council.[27]

The interaction between the emergency and transitional shelters may all be sorted out. Conceivably, New York could construct sufficient transitional facilities to permit the closing of both the welfare hotels and the barrack shelters. But this outcome is not likely. New York City has, and is probably going to continue to have, too many homeless families and too little affordable housing. This is the shortage that time and again, has returned homeless New Yorkers to the welfare hotels, and it is the same shortage that suggests New Yorkers have not yet seen the last of the barrack shelters.

The Construction of Permanent Housing

Ever since the early 1980s, when homelessness in New York first became a prominent local problem, it has been evident that construction of affordable housing was the first step toward addressing the issue. Housing is expensive, however, and in the absence of a federal commitment, the Koch administration was understandably reluctant to have New York City embark on such a large-scale municipal project. The spread of homelessness and the strong opposition of the Reagan administration changed municipal policy; plainly, the only way to add to the supply of housing would be for New York, as a municipality, to finance its construction.

On 30 April 1986, Mayor Koch announced a $4.2 billion, ten year program to construct and rehabilitate 252,000 units of city housing. This plan has since gone through several modifications. First, Koch expanded it to $5.1 billion to be spent in twelve years. Then, when David Dinkins became mayor in 1989, he returned to the $4.2 billion budget, but ordered production of this housing within eight years.[28]

Since almost 90 percent of this budget consists of city funds, the plan is by far the most ambitious housing program ever undertaken by any municipality. Its primary goal is to create or renovate 118,000 units of housing by 1994. In addition, New York will also upgrade and preserve another 168,000 units that are currently occupied. On its face, it sounds as if the city is moving forcefully to address the problem of affordable housing. Yet the size and cost of the plan are deceptive. Not only is the plan biased toward upper income families, but it is creating new ghettos among the poor and homeless people whom it does help.

The first major controversy about the plan is its income categories. When Mayor Koch announced the plan in 1986, its low, moderate, and middle-income groupings assumed a 1986 median income in New York City of $20,000. This standard was realistic, but it did not give New York much flexibility in allocating units. So, two years later, the Koch administration engaged in a statistical sleight-of-hand: it used a HUD regional index that included the suburban counties of Putnam, Rockland, and Westchester as part of its calculations and inflated the median to $32,000. By defining low income as less than $19,000, moderate income as $19,000 to $32,000, and middle income as $32,000 to $53,000, it made nearly 90 percent of New York renters eligible for city-subsidized housing.[29]

A program that makes so few distinctions about housing needs, and consequently subsidizes some New Yorkers in the top fifth of the city's income scale, inevitably raises questions about its allocation of scarce resources. It is true that for a family with several children, an annual income of $53,000 in New York City is not a lot of money. This is particularly true if the family is looking for new housing, because real estate developers find it hard to make a profit from families at this income. No wonder, then, that when Mayor Koch asked thirty-three of the largest local developers in 1985 what they could do to build housing for households earning $15,000 to $48,000, the developers offered a deal. In exchange for streamlining the regulatory process and changing some building codes, they would construct 3,000 homeowner units on donated city land. The housing was to be nonprofit; presumably, to make money, the developers would need either more assistance, or still wealthier families.[30]

This offer must be kept in perspective. It certainly discredits the housing market, which cannot build housing without subsidy for the vast majority of people. Nevertheless, as a matter of policy, it is debatable how much public funds should accompany the sympathy accorded families earning $53,000, when so much of New York City's population lives in far more acute need.

In theory, at least, the New York City housing plan does target low-income households. According to the city, 61 percent of the units will go to low-income families, 26 percent to moderate income, and 13 percent to middle income. Yet several factors distort the meaning of these percentages. First, since the Koch administration set the ceiling for the low-income category at $19,000, New York City could conceivably fill a major portion of its quota with families earning $18,000. While there is no doubt that a family earning $18,000 needs a housing subsidy, this family actually placed in about the fortieth percentile of the city's 1987 household income.[31] Subsidizing them may fill the low-income housing quota, but it still does not assist those who earn even less money.

Second, a large part of the low-income units comes not from new construction but from the city's stated intention to preserve and upgrade 168,000 units of occupied housing. In fact, looking at just the first 33,000 new units produced by the Koch administration, there was a pronounced upward bias to the program's benefits: 50 percent went to the middle-income category, 26 percent to moderate income, 16 percent to the homeless, and only 8 percent to other low-income families.[32] Once again, the program offered the least assistance to people who are poor but not homeless.

Gentrification and segregation constitute the two complementary consequences of this policy. New York is gentrifying twenty-two of the city's poorest neighborhoods because its average rents of $488 a month in new buildings are 48 percent higher than existing rents. The rent differential is even greater at the borough and community level: 60 percent higher for six neighborhoods in the Bronx, and 57 percent higher for Manhattan, including 113 percent for central Harlem. Altogether, rents will appreciate more than 50 percent in twelve of the twenty-two communities. In each of these twelve districts, people of color outnumber whites.[33]

Segregation accompanies this process of gentrification. Separated from the rest of the city by race and class, and by some physical barrier— a highway, avenue, or deserted lot—from the gentrification occurring in their own community, these neighborhoods have become the new ghetto for hundreds of homeless families. In the South Bronx, for example, one strip seven miles long and six blocks wide will contain six large shelters and half of all the apartments being rebuilt for the homeless in New York City. There is little mixed-income housing here, and less community stability. Instead, there are drugs, violence, and a few overwhelmed social agencies. The Koch administration may have designed a multi–billion plan to address the New York housing crisis, but as with urban renewal in the 1950s and 1960s, it seriously underestimated some of the more deleterious side effects.[34]

In Rem Housing

The heart of the city's plan is housing that it owns. Numbering more than 110,000 units in 1988, this in rem stock consists mostly of apartments that the municipality seized when their landlords stopped paying taxes. Until 1977, landlords had been permitted to fall as many as three years behind in their tax payments. But then New York City enacted Local Law 45, which set a one year limit. Officials hoped that a shorter deadline would bring scarce funds into the city's treasury. What they got instead was an avalanche of abandoned buildings, transforming the government of New York into the city's largest single landlord.[35]

For both political and administrative reasons, the municipality did not welcome this role. Politically, assuming responsibility for this housing gives the wrong impression: take over too many buildings, and the real estate industry begins to worry that the city is entering the housing business. New York itself was hardly enthralled with this prospect because nothing in its previous experience had prepared it for the task. The closest comparable responsibility, public housing as it is administered by the New York City Public Housing Authority, relies on a centralized system to oversee 3,000 buildings on 300 sites. By contrast, in rem consisted of more than 4,000 sites, scattered all over the city. To manage this housing stock, New York City would need another administrative model.[36]

Burdened with this new responsibility, New York has adopted two, seemingly conflicting approaches: manage the buildings, and get rid of them as fast as possible. The Department of Housing Preservation and Development runs some occupied buildings through its Division of Alternative Management Program (DAMP), which stresses tenant and non-profit community management. Costly and limited in the rent that it could obtain from poor tenants, this program has been eclipsed in recent years by the city's desire to return in rem housing to the tax rolls. For New York, the best, and perhaps the only, method of returning these buildings to the tax rolls is to subsidize developers.[37]

The Community Preservation Corporation (CPC) is one of the main organizations that helps to arrange these subsidies. In reality a consortium of the biggest local banks, the CPC lends money at market rates for development in marginal neighborhoods, often in conjunction with 1 percent city loans. The CPC tries to cultivate the image of your friendly local bank providing financing to a troubled community. But in its brochure to developers entitled "Financing for Multifamily Property Owners," the CPC assumes a different tone. The developer, it states, will get rent increases—subsidized for the elderly—and as many as thirty-two years of tax breaks. By buying an empty building from the Department of Housing Preservation and Development for one dollar, putting 10 percent down, and borrowing the rest from the city and CPC, developers can make an adequate return over the short-term and reap a real windfall on their investment when the property appreciates in subsequent years.[38]

In rem buildings represent a limited resource. When New York City exhausts its supply in 1993, it may well cost as much as $100,000 per unit for new construction, instead of $60,000 per unit to renovate a shell. Conscious of the decline in the number of in rem units, and responsive to criticism of the original Koch plan, Mayor David Dinkins moved to remedy some of its most prominent flaws. In addition to reaching the original goal of $4.2 billion in eight rather than ten years, he committed the city to building mixed-income housing—$50 million for 500 units, with 30 percent of those units set aside for homeless families. Larger city subsidies in its vacant building program will also reduce rents for two-bedroom apartments from $575 to $525 a month.[39]

Since New York City has serious fiscal problems, and the business community closely monitors its budget, such changes probably fall near the outer range of current possibilities. But while these reforms are the kind that Dinkins was elected to implement, they will have, at best, a modest impact on the housing shortage. In 1987, a housing study prepared for the New York Commission on the Year 2000 calculated the shortage at 678,000 units: 231,000 units needing construction and 447,000 units requiring upgrading. The same study projected that by the year 2000, the shortfall of new units would expand to 372,000, including 60 percent that are low income. New York City's plan for permanent housing involves a major commitment of resources, but it still will not produce numbers like these.[40]

The Limits on Housing Production

Why can't New York City produce sufficient new housing? Why, indeed, has New York City spent so much money on temporary rather than permanent solutions to homelessness—on outreach vans instead of psychiatric facilities, on armories and welfare hotels rather than adequate housing for the homeless? The most honest and straightforward answer is that it needs to maintain business confidence.

This need to maintain business confidence is very powerful, but it has the disadvantage of exacerbating some expensive social problems. New York City organized its own recovery around a real estate boom and the transition to a service economy. The real estate boom used tax abatements and other subsidies to set off an inflationary spiral that put housing for profit out of the reach of an ever-larger proportion of New Yorkers. The transition to a service economy made unskilled labor increasingly obsolete and detached a whole segment of the working population from the labor market. With housing costs up, and income for both unskilled laborers and welfare recipients down, the retention of business confidence created social needs that intensified the demand for greater expenditures on social programs.

Of course, the business sector is hardly an undifferentiated community, and what is popular with one sector may not be popular with another. Many New York corporations want a labor force that can obtain affordable, local housing, so that they can keep wages down; by contrast, the real estate industry's pursuit of profit drives up the cost of housing and makes that housing unaffordable. The government must choose between these different business interests, by deciding, among other considerations, when it might be prudent to enact a social reform.

This tension between social programs and a favorable business environment pervades New York City politics. It explains why even relatively progressive mayors such as David Dinkins do not strike fear in the business community. Listen, for example, to the words of Felix Rohatyn, investment banker and chairman of the Municipal Assistance Corporation, about the prospect of Dinkins becoming mayor:

> . . . you can be a philosophical liberal and a financial conservative. Dave is an extremely careful man. Careful people don't go about throwing money away. And he is as conscious of the need to maintain fiscal balance and a vibrant economy as much as we in the business community are of maintaining a stable social base.[41]

When a social problem arises, the government of New York City must handle it in a manner that is consistent with its need to maintain business confidence. At the same time, however, the business community recognizes that long-term stability demands a minimal degree of fairness and social harmony. In a New York City torn by crime, class, and racial tensions, the standard of what constitutes "fairness and social harmony" is steadily decreasing. New York City as a local government may need the approval of business to ensure its economic viability, but all business needs from the local government is a society that functions well enough to allow money to be made.

In the case of homelessness, this principle readily translates into a specific set of policies. New York City originally stressed large, temporary shelters and welfare hotels, but by the mid–1980s, these policies were clearly inadequate. There were homeless people everywhere, and the costs of homelessness—in visibility, damaged families, and wasteful temporary solutions—had risen to unacceptable levels. So New York upped its investment in social welfare. It began to differentiate among the population, enriched its shelters with social services and some piecemeal employment programs, and embarked on a plan to provide permanent housing. Although these policies relied on a larger public sector than in other cities, the municipality never overstepped the boundary defining proper government behavior. More to the point, even as its development policies contributed to the growth of the homeless population, it re mained, above all, respectful of the needs of the business community.

There may be irony in this statement, but there is no moralizing. It is simply the way the economy works. New York City outdid every other municipality in its elaboration of social policies for the homeless, and those policies undoubtedly helped many homeless people. Nevertheless, this is social policy as a palliative. For the most part, once politics and economics have combined in their usual way, the damage has already been done.

PART IV

Social Policy,
Social Needs

11

Homelessness and
Social Policy

To expect saintliness of the ordinary citizen is bad social policy. Further, to expose him hourly to a wretchedness far beyond his power to remedy is to make moral insensitivity a requirement of daily living.
CHARLES KRAUTHAMMER

   Poverty is useful. Poverty is not useful. These are the fundamental principles that guide U.S. social policy.
   Only 8 percent of the population is self-employed.[1] For the vast majority of people, then, there are only two ways of getting money— from a private pension or salary working for somebody else, or from a government social program. When workers in private industry get a bigger salary, the extra money either comes out of potential increases in managerial salaries, or from the profits of owners and stockholders. Similarly, when the government raises the salaries of public sector employees or increases social benefits to recipients, taxpayers must pay more to finance the additional cost. In both instances, the money that poor people do not get is money that someone else can get or keep. In both instances, some people benefit because they receive a larger share of the society's total income. The first premise in any analysis of U.S. social policy is, therefore, that for the well-to-do at least, poverty is quite useful.
   There is nothing very startling about this premise. It is merely intended to demonstrate that the existence of each poor person is not a random event. The alternative view of poverty as a random event is deeply embedded in the American ethos. It assumes that people are poor either because poverty is the hand that life dealt them, or because they badly misplayed the hand they got. Under no circumstances are they ever poor so that others can be rich.
   Yet such an analysis is incomplete without its opposite. Hence the premise that poverty *is not useful* is equally important in analyzing social

policy. Of course, this view is more conventional: poverty is expensive, wastes the society's human and financial resources, and sparks outbreaks of political instability. It follows from this list of destructive consequences, that poverty should just be wiped out. Put another way, if, in the first premise, poverty is a pure social benefit, in the second premise, poverty is a pure social cost.

In practice, it is hard to reconcile two such contradictory premises. Nevertheless, that is the role of social policy in most Western industrialized societies. Social policy must, at one and the same time, respect the dynamics of a market economy that makes people poor and try to assuage poverty's political and economic costs. In the United States, social policy is less interventionist than in Western European countries, because the coalition put together by business and its allies has usually defeated the opposing coalition put together by labor unions and other progressive groups. From public housing to national health insurance, from a minimum income grant to universal day care and generous parental leave, this business coalition has contested activist social policies and insulated the marketplace from social programs whose existence is largely assumed in other countries.

Once again, though, this is only half the story. The United States may be, in the classic phrase, a "reluctant welfare state." Its social policies may not cut as wide a swathe as those of the Netherlands, France, Germany, and Scandanavia.[2] But that does not mean American social policy—with fewer tools and in its own restricted way—does not try to carry out the tasks assigned to it.

What are these tasks? Foremost among them is the maintenance of the poor population in poverty, at a level which is, in keeping with the principle of less eligibility, below that of the lowest paid worker. Several different factors frame this task. In the most basic sense, the purpose of maintaining poor people in poverty is simply to ensure their survival. This is a good investment, for both political and economic reasons. It is a good political investment first, because poor people whose survival was at stake could turn rebellious, and second, because their suffering might induce other potentially sympathetic groups to demand some social reforms. It is a good economic investment because even a population of poor people constitutes a source of possible labor, either in the present, if they have the appropriate skills and economic conditions improve, or in the future, when their children make up the labor force of the next generation. The United States may not do as much as the countries of Europe, but for all these reasons, it does allocate some money for social welfare.[3]

Still, a second, conflicting task vastly complicates the responsibility for this allocation. This task is to maintain poor people in poverty by giving them money for food and housing without undermining the fundamental principle that these are commodities for which people should pay. Fearful that this principle could be easily compromised, and afraid of setting a precedent, social policy in the United States resolved this conflict in the most straightforward way: it gave less to fewer people. Rather than grant benefits and services to everybody and tax income at progressive rates, social programs served categories of people such as the poor, the old, and the medically needy. It then ranked the people within these categories on a finely calibrated yardstick extending from the worthy to the unworthy poor. For the worthy poor, social welfare could be passably adequate. For the unworthy poor, social welfare was usually stigmatized, less, and even under the best of circumstances, much harder to come by.

Social Costs, Social Investments

Up until the proliferation of homelessness in the 1980s, homeless people were indisputably the unworthy poor. The old terminology gave their status away. Before they were homeless, they were "drunks" and "bums" who made few demands on the social welfare system. With the exception of cities like New York that had several publicly-operated facilities, most municipalities relied on voluntary-sector agencies like the Salvation Army to provide food and shelter. Given to the homeless as the unworthy poor, this aid was clearly marked as charity, and the only issue it raised in the public's mind was whether they should receive it at all.

The growth of the homeless population swamped the social welfare system and changed the public's viewpoint. While the local, voluntary tradition underlay the historic model of helping the poor, it was hardly sufficient for a problem that had crossed the geographic boundaries of skid row and spread into the downtown business district as well as into other parts of most cities. In essence, homelessness signified that something was fundamentally wrong. By making every homeless person a messenger and every passer-by a witness, homelessness triggered a crisis of visibility that scratched the psychological armor of even those citizens who insisted that all those people on the street were still the unworthy poor.

The response to this crisis escalated steadily. In most cases, those cities where the voluntary sector had provided services gravitated toward various forms of public/private partnership, and those cities with public/private partnerships moved to develop them further. Starting from a higher level of development, the service delivery systems of public sector cities such as Boston and New York grew the most. In every instance, homelessness overwhelmed the resources that were available locally, forcing both the states and the federal government to become involved.

Two important principles shaped the nature of this involvement. The first principle is that the greater the social costs associated with homelessness, the greater the social welfare investment. The second principle is that even though social costs soared and social welfare investments

mounted, political and economic institutions in the United States con-
figured these policies into forms that usually prevented them from having too significant an impact.

The social costs of homelessness are extensive. They include the
political questions that the visibility of the homeless raise, as well as the
sometimes considerable cost of temporary shelter. Crime, drugs, begging—to whatever extent these phenomenon are associated with homelessness, they are social costs, also. Finally, there can be little doubt that
since the experience of homelessness wounds people, the total sum of
social costs will stretch out over many years. For adults, homelessness
loosens ties to the labor market, making it harder to get and keep a job.
For children, the incidence of physical ailments, serious psychological
problems, and a high rate of school absenteeism diminishes their future
prospects. If, in thirty years, they need welfare, if, in thirty years, they
are imprisoned, the homelessness they experienced as a child will deserve
at least some of the blame.

Faced with rising social costs, state and local governments intervened
with successively higher levels of funding. The presence of homeless
people on the street intensified demands for temporary shelter; the
recognition that many different kinds of people had become homeless
led to the establishment of targeted social services. Of course, not every
municipality took each of these steps. In virtually every city, though, the
spread of homelessness pushed the local social welfare system to a new
level of development.

A similar pattern occurred within the federal government. Early in
the 1980s, the initial reaction of the federal government was to downplay
the issue. In general, federal officials argued that the homeless were a
transient phenomenon, a local problem that deserved a local response.
The visibility of the homeless mentally ill gave credence to this view,
because it suggested that deinstitutionalization by the states, rather than
national economic policy, was primarily at fault.

The 1982–83 recession discredited this position and forced the federal government to make greater investments in social welfare. True,
these expenditures were limited, and they defined the problem as a
temporary emergency. But whether it was money for food or shelter
rehabilitation, the expenditures did represent an acknowledgement that
homelessness was a national phenomenon. The culmination of this approach was the 1987 Stewart B. McKinney Act, which added funding
for other temporary programs and then consolidated all this legislation
into one national bill.

This list of interventions is hardly inconsequential. The local, state,
and federal governments have spent billions of dollars on the homeless,
and those expenditures have undoubtedly saved lives. Still, the key question in analyzing these social policies is why, proportionately, so much
more money was spent on emergency measures.

To illuminate what was done, we can compare it with an alternative set of policies. Suppose that instead of emphasizing food, emergency shelter, and some social services, people at risk were offered permanent, affordable housing with social supports, if necessary. With these provisions, fewer people would become homeless, and those who did would not be homeless for long. There is, obviously, a major gap between this set of policies and the policies governments in the United States actually enacted. Government resources are supposed to be limited. Why, then, has every level of government persisted in carrying out wasteful short-term policies, when the cumulative social costs of these policies undoubtedly exceed the expense of providing permanent, affordable housing?

The answer is that a more adequate solution to homelessness would conflict with the underlying principles of the U.S. economy. Private profit, self-sufficiency through work, and the commodification of basic human needs such as food, housing, and medical care: social policies designed to eliminate homelessness violate these principles and hence cannot be granted serious consideration. Instead, billions of dollars are wasted in short-term solutions. As a result, even though the U.S. economy has produced homelessness, the social policies that offer assistance will, as much as possible, leave its basic institutions untouched.

If these policies can only do just so much for the homeless, the ethic of self-reliance is partly responsible. Although this ethic recognizes that people may need help in a crisis, it also assumes that after the crisis has passed, they are once again on their own. Someone who becomes homeless should therefore receive shelter. While living in the shelter, though, they must find their own permanent housing regardless of its availability.

This ethic, then, does more than merely attribute self-reliance to people. On some level, it also implies that the political and economic resources available really are sufficient to satisfy their needs. This is a very traditional notion. In the Old West, to be sure, there was land to be tamed, but nowadays, whether there is housing to be gotten by the homeless is much more open to question.

The principle of self-reliance is closely intertwined with the principle of less eligibility. Poor people cannot be given too much of what they need because altogether, this assistance might yield a standard of living higher than that of the lowest salaried worker. Thus, the impact of free food and shelter affects not merely the homeless, but has a ripple effect on the poor who are housed, and on every other working person.

While the principle of less eligibility has been around for a long time, it was the drive to reduce the wages of lower-paid employees that gave it new power to make people homeless. Working together, business and government fought to weaken unions, break strikes, and hold down the value of the minimum wage. To a large extent, they succeeded, and their success meant that social welfare benefits had to be decreased by an equivalent amount. The steady depreciation of these benefits pushed many employable people into the workforce, where their numbers heightened the competition for jobs and helped to control wages. As always, the principle of less eligibility maintained the comparative value of paid labor. This time, however, with wages low and benefits lower, less eligibility required a significant increase in the risk of homelessness among poor and working people.

These actions mark a striking departure from the stated role of modern social policy. Collectively, social policies are supposed to maintain the poor, to keep alive the possibility that they could be part of the current and future labor force. The failure to allow poor people to retain their homes does not meet this standard. It suggests that as the U.S. economy tries to place itself on a more competitive footing, some significant part of the population is being written off.

Many other urban ills also reflect this willingness to write off poor people. Inadequate education, deficient job skills and 37 million individuals without any health insurance demonstrate that current social policy has become increasingly short-sighted. The government is no longer willing to maintain most poor people in a condition that would enable them or their children to become productive. The Bush administration's rejection of any new antipoverty initiatives epitomizes this thinking. After acknowledging that an "investment in children" would yield significant long-term benefits, it nonetheless rejected the investment because it was "not likely to show an immediate reward."[4]

Interestingly, this focus on a quick return closely parallels one of the most frequent criticisms made about U.S. business. Many attribute the diminished competitiveness of American business to its excessive focus on short-term profits.[5] Writing off the poor reflects this growing indifference to the issues of human resources and the future workforce. Instead of trying to ensure that the vast majority of poor people have a minimally adequate standard of living, it has reduced social welfare funding and encouraged a form of national triage. And operating on a short-term perspective, this national triage is quite willing to accept the fact that many poor people are just not going to make it.[6]

Homelessness is, in this sense, one of the clearest examples of the new willingness to write off the poor. Homeless people need affordable housing, decent wages and/or an adequate welfare benefit; some undoubtedly require supportive social services. Since, however, each of these policies threatens important private interests, any government response must thread its way between them. It must preserve the political and economic institutions of the United States even when they are themselves the leading cause of homelessness.

The construction of affordable housing would be the most straightforward solution to homelessness. But the government cannot build more affordable housing because such a policy usurps the traditional prerogatives of the real estate industry. Similarly, if poor people do not have enough money to obtain the available housing, welfare and wages must be increased accordingly. But higher welfare benefits drive up wages, and higher wages cut into the profits of every employer. Finally, social services, too, set a bad example because the government usually offers them for free. Since a free service improves the recipient's standard of living, it undermines the relationship between work and economic well-being, which is, along with the concept of private profit, perhaps the underlying principle of a market economy.

This respect for private interests extends even to those governments that have relied most heavily on the public sector. Although the public sector may establish a domain where market incentives do not apply, it is not a world apart. Cities such as Boston and New York have a large public sector that impinges somewhat on the private. But nowhere in the United States is there a public sector powerful enough to set the terms of its relationship with the business community. The result is that when government raises the welfare grant, landlords make more money; when the government develops housing, it is likely to give private developers a decisive role. Hence, although social policy originates in the public sector, the size of the public sector is itself a product of the outcome of previous political conflicts between business and its opponents. In this sense, the limited nature of its response to homelessness is as much an effect of past political struggles as it is a cause of those in the present and future.

What form will these struggles take? Plainly, the short-term outlook is not very good. Government needs the approval of business; without it, it faces the constant threat of a capital flight that would throw the economy into a recession and the government out of office. Yet politics can subdue economics; it can bend the economy to its will. The development of this politics will be a difficult, but by no means, impossible task. Galvanized by the growing inequities of wealth and power, and predicated on the fulfillment of basic human needs, this political coalition not only has the potential to house the homeless, but also to emerge victorious over the politics of the last twenty years.

12

Homelessness and Common Human Needs

All concrete proposals for the expansion of economic benefits, for the implementation of new social policies, and for the extension of political rights must be framed within an evocative moral vision that "enlivens" these proposals with a sense of social connection and purpose.
PETER GABEL

There is no great mystery about the steps necessary to eliminate the problem of homelessness in the United States. Homeless people need what everyone else needs: affordable housing, wages and benefits sufficient to support themselves, and accessible social services. Meeting these needs is necessary for a minimum, though hardly extravagant, standard of living. It is also basic to meaningful political participation as well as to human dignity. For all these reasons, ensuring that people have sufficient income, a permanent home, and help when they need it hardly sounds like an extraordinary goal. It is only the increasing inability of the U.S. economy to meet this goal that has transformed it into what mainstream politics would describe as a "radical" proposal.

Yet what is it exactly that the economy cannot do which makes this standard so hard to attain? The answer is quite damning: it cannot provide everybody with sufficient permanent housing; it cannot pay everyone a wage large enough to support a family; and it cannot fund enough services—from drug counseling to job training and child protection—for people who need help. This list should give us pause. Conservatives argue that the United States "won" the Cold War; it triumphed over communism in Eastern Europe and the Soviet Union. But the economy that won this victory cannot house its own people and condemns a significant percentage of the population to a life of poverty and struggle. If this is victory, it is a hollow victory indeed.

The U.S. economy is organized for the pursuit of profit, and it turns virtually everything, including the most basic human needs such as food, housing, and medical care, into commodities from which a profit can be made. Since the economy rations the provision of these commodities for those who cannot provide profit, it leaves many human needs unsatisfied. The conservative politics of the last twenty years has exacerbated these needs and spread them more widely among the population. Yet this trend is not immutable: it can be reversed. If, together, poor and middle-income people organize around these needs, they have the potential to assemble the next great progressive political coalition.

Organizing a Coalition Around Common Human Needs

Several fundamental principles must guide the organization of this coalition. First, and perhaps most central, is the definition of its potential constituency, which extends far beyond poor people to include the vast majority of the population. Both politics and substance dictate this definition of the constituency. By itself, a coalition of poor people lacks political durability. Poor people do not make up a majority of the electorate, and they are also politically isolated. If they are the prime beneficiaries of a coalition, that coalition will fail. The coalition must therefore forge an alliance with middle-income voters who have gradually come to share the perception that the market also fails them.

This is becoming an easier argument to make, because as our analysis of homelessness suggests, the failure of the market is affecting an ever-larger number of people. In a society where absolute scarcity is no issue, everyone should be housed. Why, then, does the threat of homelessness creep steadily up the income ladder? The market may demand its due, but when poor and, increasingly, middle-income people must risk their homes to enrich others, they, too, may question the dominance of the market in the provision of housing.

Similar arguments can be advanced on behalf of a variety of other economic rights. Those with the most political potential over the next ten to twenty years probably involve rights to a decent paying job, day care, and a national health service. Each of these issues speaks to a common human need—for self-sufficiency, the well-being of children when the parent(s) work, or a right to health care—that has an inherent appeal to a large segment of the electorate. Each also has controversial issues associated with it. For jobs, there is the proliferation of low-wage employment and the danger of pricing the cost of U.S. labor out of the international labor market. For day care, debates about quality and affordability will always be contentious. And, of course, while a large majority of citizens support national health insurance, one should never underestimate the power of the medical lobby—doctors, hospitals, and insurance companies—that has made the United States the only major industrialized country besides South Africa without such a program.[1]

Yet beyond the details of a policy analysis, beyond the question of how each issue might best be formulated for a political campaign, all of these issues share the two common themes of economic rights and the failure of the unchallenged marketplace. These are the themes that demand emphasis in the years ahead.

The matter of a common theme is especially important because this set of issues is not simply a shopping list of the most "saleable" products on the political market over the next generation. One sign of the recent disarray of liberalism in the United States has been its tendency to push for single-issue proposals, including milder versions of all the reforms listed above, without linking them to a clear, unifying message. The proposals may be well-drafted, but politically, they are cast adrift, because proponents have not informed them with a persuasive alternative vision.[2] Yet this vision is just begging to be articulated. It is a vision of a society where, quite apart from an individual's relationship to the market, the satisfaction of common human needs for housing, health, and an adequate income makes it possible to nurture genuine feelings of worth and social connectedness. It is, quite simply, a vision of a caring human community.

Homelessness and Common Human Needs

The rise of homelessness in the United States is a reflection of these intersecting, and unaddressed, human needs. Since homelessness cannot be solved alone, it would be short-sighted to put forth single-issue proposals on housing without tying them, for example, to campaigns for higher wages and national health care, all united through the theme of common economic—read human—rights. Then, and only then, will it be possible to make some real progress.

Fundamentally, people are homeless because they get too little income to afford the housing that is available. This basic reality is then overlaid with every possible social ill: crime, drugs, alcoholism, mental illness, poor health care, and inadequate job skills are just the beginning of the list. People need more money. They need more housing. In conjunction with social services, national health care, and readily available job training, programs for greater income security and more affordable housing could have a truly significant impact.

An effective full employment policy must be part of this effort. The intent here is not to increase the number of low-salaried jobs, but rather to pay decent wages for those engaged in socially useful work. There is certainly plenty of work to do—in housing, education, health care, mass transportation, and the environment—indeed, in virtually every part of our social infrastructure. The decline of this infrastructure offers an opportunity. It means that this full employment policy will have no make-work. After a generation of neglect by the private sector, there is simply too much to do.[3]

Genuine income security also demands the enactment of a guaranteed national income. Such a program is consistent with universalistic principles of social welfare, which, by treating everyone similarly, avoids stigmatization of the poor and builds an alliance with other income groups.

As our ostensibly universalistic policy of public education shows, universalism is not a magic wand that will instantly obliterate differences of race, class, and gender. Moreover, though a guaranteed national income—set very low—was on the agenda of both political parties from 1969 to 1972, no branch of the U.S. government is going to enact such legislation in the near future.[4] In the meantime, the basic premise is still worth keeping in mind: give a liveable minimum to everybody and tax total income at progressive rates. Some may object that this proposal is inefficient because it sends money to everyone in order to help a smaller number of people. This process, however, is easily automated; the biggest inefficiency is actually the burden of administering millions of eligibility tests. The final, and ultimately decisive argument is that in a policy where everybody gets and everybody gives, the electorate is much less likely to make invidious distinctions between the poor and nonpoor, and social programs gain the support of a stable political coalition.[5]

In the shorter term, policymakers should consider three other options for getting money into the hands of poorer people. They are a national welfare standard equal to the poverty line, earned income tax credits, and an increase in the minimum wage. If each seems in its own way politically problematic, it is important to remember that since the rise of the homeless population is in large part a product of a lack of income among poor people, *any policy* that channels more money to poor people is going to raise wages, inflate welfare costs, and otherwise disrupt economic relations. The reforms are major, and their immediate prospects clouded, precisely because any policy recommendation worthy of the name must redistribute income.

There are two primary rationales for a national welfare grant equal to the official poverty line. First, while the official poverty line is set at the barest minimum ($12,675 for four people in 1990), it does present a standard higher than any state provides through its welfare program. And second, while there are differences in the labor market between the states, there is absolutely no justification for a system in which Alaska pays a family of three people more than seven times as much a month as Mississippi ($891 to $120). With all due respect for states' rights, there should be a uniform standard, and it should not be asking too much to set this standard at an amount which still leaves people, by the federal government's own calculations, officially poor.[6]

Since conservatives are right that the real solution for welfare is work, the working poor merit special attention. The clear dividing line here is not whether people should work; it is, rather, the salary they are paid, and the supports with which they are provided. In addition to day care and medical assistance, one of the most useful forms of support is the earned income tax credit (EITC). Under the EITC, 6 million families with low wages get a tax credit for each dollar they earn. The EITC therefore functions as a wage subsidy for low-income workers. In 1990, the federal government changed the existing EITC program from a 14 percent rate on the first $6,810, or $953, to 23 percent of the first $8,100 in 1994 for families with one child (25 percent for two or more children). A family with one child would therefore gain $1,861 in net income. While the increase is a step forward, the rate could go still higher, to as much as 30 percent. Even more importantly, to get more money into the hands of poor workers, the ceiling should be raised.[7]

Lastly, the minimum wage needs to be increased again, and pegged to inflation. Although the Bush administration raised the minimum wage to $4.25 in 1991, this increase only partly compensates for the effects of inflation, which would have yielded an equivalent in excess of five dollars. The minimum wage used to maintain a family of three people above the poverty line. At $4.25 an hour, however, this family's income has sunk to about 80 percent of the poverty line. Once again, there is no secret to the problem of why poor people do not have enough money. Since the value of the minimum wage has declined, another increase is necessary if poor people are to have any chance of obtaining housing.[8]

In addition to measures for augmenting the income of poor people, significant progress against homelessness also depends on the creation of enough affordable housing. The key here is the establishment of a social housing sector, where housing could not be resold at a profit. Instead of using government funds to sustain the private housing market, the government would grant money to a variety of public nonprofit developers, especially those that were community-based. These developers would then rehabilitate and construct housing. This housing would be publicly financed, so that debt costs would not be factored into the rents that tenants pay. If their income still limited their ability to afford the rent, the government would provide subsidies to make up the difference. The goal would be to promote social ownership for all publicly financed housing, new and existing.

In a system of social ownership, residents would not only acquire rights to their housing; they would also actively participate in its management, whether that management be nonprofit, direct tenant, or through a mutual mangement association. The alternative system of financing—direct government spending—would reduce dependence on private mortgage credit, one of the main factors that restrict the supply of housing and keep it expensive. The government already employs this method to finance military housing. By utilizing it for nonmilitary purposes, it could quickly expand the social housing sector.

This proposal obviously entails a major shift in the use of government power. The government now employs its resources on behalf of the private real estate market. Under this proposal, it would deploy its funds at every opportunity to create socially owned housing. When, for example, homeowners faced foreclosure, they could also convert to social ownership by giving up their right to resell in exchange for a sum equal to their equity and an end to their future mortgage payments. Over time, interventions like these would gradually shrink the space available to the private housing market; private developers could build new housing, but their projects would not be eligible for outright grants, tax benefits, welfare clients as tenants, or any other form of public assistance.

Although it is difficult to project the exact amount for this proposal, it is reasonable to assume that total expenditures might equal 5 percent of the federal budget, or approximately twice the current rate of direct outlays and tax deductions. This may seem like a lot, but think of what many Americans would get in return: security in their homes and a considerable reduction in their housing costs. Most importantly, with a progressive tax system and some changed budgetary priorities, the vast majority of citizens would get these benefits without paying any new taxes.

Housing is a human need. This proposal aligns the government on behalf of the largest possible number of people, but it does so by using government monies for local, nonprofit community development. In modern U.S. politics, antipathy to the policies of the federal government is often confused with antipathy to its size. Proponents of this view take the understandable position that if government is not going to do anything on their behalf, at least it should be smaller and therefore less inimical to their interests. A proposal for the establishment of a social housing sector clears up this confusion. By mobilizing federal power and money on behalf of local communities and neighborhoods, it demonstrates that decentralized public nonprofit ownership could go a long way towards resolving the problem of housing affordability in the United States.[9]

Who Pays?

A coalition built around the satisfaction of common human needs is going to propose initiatives that cost money. Years of neglect have driven up these costs, and the bill rises steadily, whether or not the costs actually appear on some government ledger. Any coalition that takes political notice of these needs must therefore explain who is going to pay for new social programs.

The question of who pays for new social programs is both legitimate and, over the last twenty years, increasingly tendentious. It is entirely legitimate that discussions of funding accompany every proposal for a new public policy. Over the last twenty years, though, the question of who pays has been carefully intertwined with the assumption that the government did not have any money. The $500 billion cost of the savings and loan bailout has not only given the lie to this assumption, but has created a new one: since the United States has to spend $500 billion on the saving and loan bailout, *now it really is true* that the government does not have any money. In the past and in the present, the argument is self-serving. There is no absolute limit on the availability of government funds. Any limit could be set, and all limits are political.

Fearful that human needs are insatiable, many conservatives worry that adding social programs will set the government off on a journey without end. This fear is quite overwrought. The United States has one of the smallest public sectors of any major capitalist nation, and there is a long way to go before we need to concern ourselves with the issue of whether the satisfaction of some needs necessarily implies the satisfaction of all. In both cases, politics rules. A political decision should be made now to fund these new social programs, and a political decision can be made then to choose among less pressing needs and allocate finite resources.

From medical care to housing, from day care to a welfare grant set at the poverty level, reductions in military spending and higher taxes on the wealthy should pay for these new social programs. In Grenada, Libya, Panama, and the Persian Gulf, military interventions produce a brief resurgence of patriotism which dissipates quickly amid the paralysis of domestic policy. Plainly, relative to Japan and the European Economic Community, the United States has entered a period of gradual economic decline. The history of other great powers has clear implications for us: military spending cannot prevent this decline and, in fact, tends to speed it up.[10]

The United States wants to remain economically competitive. But it cannot achieve this goal as long as it stints on the development of its human resources and its social infrastructure. While a 50 percent reduction in military spending is probably necessary, it would be a major step in the right direction for the federal government to implement cuts in the range of 25 percent over the next five years. These savings could then be used for civilian conversion of defense plants, as well to fund the social welfare and housing programs proposed here.

The other major source of revenue is changes in the tax structure. During his eight years in office, Reagan cut the top income tax rate from 70 to 28 percent. While Bush bowed to political pressure in 1990 and raised the top rate to 31 percent, the combination of lower taxes on income and capital gains with higher taxes on social security brought about an enormous shift of income upward. Deprived of these tax revenues, it is no wonder that the federal government seems poor.

Restoration of a truly progressive income tax would remedy this shortage. Moreover, as an international comparison shows, it would do so without weakening the economy. In 1989, the average top marginal rate of the eight-six countries with an income tax was 47 percent. Established welfare states with sound economies such as Denmark, the Netherlands, and Sweden had rates of 72 percent; the West Germans set theirs at 56 percent. But the rate was also quite high in many nations whose social policies were less developed: Taiwan, 50 percent; Japan, 50 percent; and South Korea, 63 percent. Only fast-growing exporters like Singapore and Hong Kong had taxes at or below the U.S. level. The worries of conservatives about the effect of higher income taxes on the economy are therefore unwarranted, because there is no relationship between the economic performance of these countries and their marginal tax rates.[11]

Neither can we continue to ignore considerations of fairness and equity. When a sales clerk in a major department store earning $25,000 a year is taxed at 15 percent and the president of the same store earning $250,000 is taxed at 33 percent, some changes are in order. Since President Carter came into office, the bottom half of the taxpaying public has paid more taxes: its resistance to tax increases is well-founded. The same cannot be said for the upper reaches of the income scale. If the effective tax rate were raised 20 percent on the wealthiest 5 percent, and 10 percent on the next 15 percent (the average 1988 income of this quintile was $81,400), the federal government would collect another $225 billion. Some of this money could be used to reduce the taxes of lower income wage earners. The rest would go a long way toward financing the social reforms outlined in this chapter.[12]

Since progressives often recommend cutbacks in the military budget and higher taxes on the wealthy, these proposals risk becoming a political cliché. They are not, but they do need to be reconnected to some larger vision. This vision is social, in that it speaks to the satisfaction of common human needs and the creation of a true community. But it is also economic, because it will improve efficiency, productivity, and the overall functioning of the economy.

People work best when they are secure in their homes and confident in their well-being. People may work hard when they are scared, but they do not work well. Despite this truth, fear has been one of the main operative principles of the U.S. economy since the late 1960s: workers have been afraid of speed-ups, layoffs, pay reductions, and homelessness. This fear succeeds for a while, but the constant apprehensiveness makes them angry. Even as they labor, one part of them is always fighting back. Instead of cooperation at work, there is bitterness and resistance. Instead of openness to new technologies, there is always the fear that a new technology might cost them their jobs. The result is a brittle and inflexible economy whose declining productivity gradually saps its international competitiveness. There can be no comparison: in the rapidly changing economic environment of the next generation, a skilled, housed, and satisfied workforce would win hands down.

The Triumph of Politics

This analysis of homelessness has repeatedly emphasized the obstacles to effective social policies. It has repeatedly stressed that the consequences of these policies—higher wages and less housing for profit—

would necessarily conflict with important business interests. Business confidence, after all, stimulates the economy; business investment generates the taxes that finance government. Under these circumstances, the effect of social policies will always be limited, unless politics intervenes.

An organized political opposition is, in fact, the only way to reconcile the apparent conflict between this analysis and the subsequent policy recommendations. On the one hand, the analysis stresses the power of the business community to veto social policies that harm its interests; on the other, it advocates changes that go well beyond the reforms that business is willing to entertain. This contradiction raises an obvious question: if business is so powerful, how will these reforms ever come to pass?

Within U.S. politics, the tensions are building for the next great period of social reform. Unless a profit can be made, social needs accumulate in a market economy. When that economy experiences a period of deregulation, these social needs are spread among an ever-expanding group of people. People need housing, and they cannot get it. They need day care, and it is not accessible. They need a universally available health program, and while some partial reforms may be enacted, no such federal program is in sight. Resourceful organizing could link these needs and forge a coalition powerful enough to redefine the terms under which business operates. The Progressive Era, the New Deal, the Great Society: it has happened before, and in the next generation, it will happen again.

The involvement of poor and homeless people is crucial to the success of this coalition. Obviously, the coalition needs everyone, but it must work particularly hard to engage the poor. The absence of poor and homeless people would not only deprive the coalition of an important group; it would also unbalance it, leaving others to take up their fight. To maintain their dignity and self-respect, poor people need to fight for themselves. And, as the history of social policy shows, once they do fight for themselves, they will transform the possibilities for political change in the United States.

This may seem all very dewey-eyed. It may not even happen. Yet the boundaries of conventional politics are misleading, because history sometimes takes inexplicably large steps. Who, in the mid–1980s, could have anticipated a reunified Germany and the changes in the Soviet Union? Who could have imagined the dramatic movement toward a nonracial South Africa? When the time is right, the unlikely does happen. When the time is right, we can, and will, house the homeless.

Notes

Chapter 1

1. Compare the 12–14 December 1990 national survey of 1,028 adults described in Jason deParle, "Suffering in the Cities Persists as U.S. Fights Other Battles," *New York Times*, 27 January 1991, with Robin Toner, "Homeless Gaining Wider Visibility," *New York Times*, 22 January 1989.

2. See Sharman Stein, "Bypass Beggars, Koch Urges," *New York Newsday*, 10 August 1988. For the national media's treatment of this issue, see "Begging: To Give or Not To Give," *Time*, 5 September 1988, pp. 68–74.

The following sources describe the pertinent laws in these cities: Santa Barbara: see Russ Spencer, "The Paradise Paradox," *The Independent*, 14 January 1988, pp. 19, 21; and Peter Marin, "The World of the Homeless in the City of Santa Barbara," *The Center Magazine*, September/October 1986, pp. 19–35 (since 1985, the Santa Barbara law has been restricted to camping). New Orleans: see the U.S. Conference of Mayors, *Responding to Homelessness in America's Cities* (Washington, D.C., 1986), p. 46. Clearwater, Florida: see Jeffrey Schmalz, "Miami Police Want to Control the Homeless by Arresting Them," *New York Times*, 4 November 1988. (Miami also considered a ban, but rejected it after bad publicity and the Clearwater law was declared unconstitutionally broad.) Fort Lauderdale: Majorie Hope and James Young, *The Faces of Homelessness* (Lexington, Mass.: D. C. Health and Company, 1986), p. 28. Burlington, Vermont: Sally Johnson, "Homeless Get Ticket to Leave," *New York Times*, 20 November 1988. New York City: John Kifner "New York Closes Park to the Homeless," *New York Times*, 4 June 1991; Council of the City of New York, Select Committee on the Homeless, *Report on the Homeless Crisis*, 22 January 1987, p. 19.

3. Jeffrey Schmalz, "Miami Is Accused of Chasing Homeless Out of Parade's Way," *New York Times*, 31 December 1988.

4. This passage draws on Mark J. Stearns, "The Emergence of Homelessness as a Public Problem," *Social Service Review* 58 (2): 291–301 (June 1984).

5. For some social welfare histories about this tradition, see Michael Katz, *In the Shadow of the Poorhouse* (New York: Basic Books, 1986); or his *Policy and Poverty in American History* (New York: Academic Press, 1983); James Patterson, *America's Struggle Against Poverty: 1900–1980* (Cambridge: Harvard University Press, 1981); John Ehrenreich, *The Altruistic Imagination* (Ithaca, N.Y.: Cornell University Press, 1985); Mimi Abramovitz, *Regulating the Lives of Women* (Boston:

South End Press, 1988); and Walter Trattner, *From Poor Law to Welfare State* (New York: The Free Press, 1984).

6. David Wechsler, *Wechsler Intelligence Scale for Children* (New York: The Psychological Corporation, 1949), pp. 63, 93. I am indebted to Sandra Baron-Blau for pointing out this question to me.

7. For the omission of health insurance from the Social Security Act, see Ann Shola Orloff, "The Origins of America's Welfare State," in *The Politics of Social Policy in the United States*, ed. Margaret Weir, Ann Shola Orloff, and Theda Skocpol, (Princeton, N.J.: Princeton University Press, 1988), pp. 40–41; Abramovitz, *Regulating the Lives of Women*, p. 232; and Walter Trattner, *From Poor Law to Welfare State* (New York: The Free Press, 1984), pp. 235–36. Stephen Kemp Bailey's *Congress Makes A Law* (New York: Vintage, 1964) is a study of the 1946 Full Employment Act. For discussion of both Full Employment Bills (1946 and the 1978 Humphrey-Hawkins) and the constraints on policy development, see Alan Wolfe, *America's Impasse* (Boston: South End Press, 1981), pp. 52–53 and p. 207, respectively.

8. Mayor Tom Bradley, *Housing the Future: 1988 Blue Ribbon Committee for Affordable Housing* (Los Angeles: Office of the Mayor, 1988) p. 24.

9. Institute of Medicine, *Homelessness, Health, and Human Needs* (Washington, D. C.: National Academy Press, 1988), p. 137, quoting the definition used in the Stewart B. McKinney Act.

10. U.S., Department of Housing and Urban Development, *Report to the Secretary on the Homeless and Emergency Shelter* (Washington, D.C., 1984), pp. 6–7.

11. See Richard B. Freeman and Brian Hall, *Permanent Homelessness in America?* (Cambridge, Mass.: National Bureau of Economic Research, 1986), pp. 28–29.

12. Ibid., p. 5

13. For the historical phases, see Peter Marcuse, "Neutralizing Homelessness," *Socialist Review* 18(1): 69–96, esp. pp. 71–72; for the concept of capitalist heydays, see Kevin Phillips, *The Politics of Rich and Poor* (New York: Random House, 1990).

14. Ellen Bassuk and Lynn Rosenberg, "Why Does Family Homelessness Occur? A Case Control Study," *American Journal of Public Health* 78 (7): 783–88.

15. For discussions of the effects on the loss of community, see, for city and suburb, Kenneth T. Jackson, *Crabgrass Frontier* (New York: Oxford University Press, 1985); for ghettos, William J. Wilson, *The Truly Disadvantaged* (Chicago: University of Chicago Press, 1987); and for the homeless specifically, Michael B. Katz, *The Undeserving Poor* (New York: Pantheon Books, 1989), pp. 190–91.

16. See, especially, the work of sociologists associated with the Columbia University Bureau of Applied Social Research such as Howard Bahr, *Skid Row: An Introduction to Disaffiliation* (New York: Oxford University Press, 1973), and Howard Bahr and Theodore Caplow, *Old Men Drunk and Sober* (New York: New York University Press, 1973).

17. U.S., General Accounting Office, *Homeless Mentally Ill: Problems and Options in Estimating Numbers and Trends* (Washington, D.C., 1988), p. 33.

18. Alice Solenberger, *One Thousand Homeless Men* (New York: Russell Sage, 1911), p. 36.

19. U.S., Department of Housing and Urban Development, *The 1988 Na-*

tional Survey of Shelters for the Homeless (Washington, D.C., 1989), p. 9; Institute of Medicine, *Homelessness, Health, and Human Needs*, p. 11.

20. Larry Paton, "The Rural Homeless," in Institute of Medicine, *Homelessness, Health, and Human Needs*, p. 183–217; Scott Kilman and Robert Johnson, "Homelessness Spreads to the Countryside, Straining Resources," *Wall Street Journal*, 5 March 1991.

21. Two standard works on this subject are J. L. and Barbara Hammond, *The Town Laborer* (New York: Doubleday Anchor Books, 1968), and E. P. Thompson, *The Making of the English Working Class* (London: Penguin Books, 1980).

22. Otto Lightner, *The History of Business Depressions* (New York: Northeastern Press, 1922), p. 169 in Frank Leonard, "Helping the Unemployed in the Nineteenth Century: The Case of the American Tramp," *Social Service Review* 40 (4): 429–34 (December 1966). More generally, see Kenneth Kusmer, "The Underclass in Historical Perspective: Tramps and Vagrants in Urban America, 1870–1930," in *On Being Homeless: Historical Perspectives*, ed. Rick Beard (New York: Museum of the City of New York), pp. 21–31.

23. Quoted in Katz, *In the Shadow of the Poorhouse*, pp. 50–51.

24. See Anne O. Hughes, Joseph S. Drew, and Emanuel Chatman, *The Third Washington: Homelessness in the District of Columbia* (Washington, D.C.: University of the District of Columbia, 1989), p. 22; David M. Schneider and Albert Deutsch, *The History of Public Welfare in New York State 1867–1940* (Chicago: University of Chicago Press, 1941), 2:50; and *A Year of Social Service*, the 32nd Annual Report of the Charity Organization Society, Indianapolis, Indiana, 1911.

Chapter 2

1. See the review of twenty-seven studies in U.S., General Accounting Office, *Homeless Mentally Ill: Problems and Options in Estimating Numbers and Trends* (Washington, D.C., 1988) and Institute of Medicine, *Homelessness, Health, and Human Needs* (Washington, D.C.: National Academy Press, 1988).

2. Peter Rossi et al., *The Condition of the Homeless in Chicago* (Amherst, Mass.: Social and Demographic Research Institute, University of Massachusetts at Amherst, 1986). Peter Rossi, *Down and Out in America* (Chicago: University of Chicago Press, 1989) is his book-length treatment of the data. Readers who wish to pursue some of the methodological issues the book raises should see Michael Fabricant's critical review in *Readings: A Journal of Reviews and Commentary in Mental Health* 5 (1): 16–20 (March 1990). For the reactions of local critics to the original study, see "Agencies Rally Around the Homeless, Hit Study," *Chicago Tribune*, 30 August 1986; for Rossi's response, see his "No Good Applied Social Research Goes Unpunished," *Society* 25 (1): 73–79 (November–December 1987).

3. Richard B. Freeman and Brian Hall, *Permanent Homelessness in America?* (Cambridge, Mass.: National Bureau of Economic Research, 1986).

4. Thomas Main, "What We Know About the Homeless," *Commentary* 85 (5): 27–31 (May 1988).

5. Institute of Medicine, *Homelessness, Health, and Human Needs*, p. 176.

6. See Michael B. Katz, *The Undeserving Poor* (New York: Pantheon Books, 1989) for a discussion of this tendency to analyze the attributes of the poor and classify them accordingly.

7. See, for example, Robert J. Barro, *Macroeconomics* (New York: John Wiley & Sons, 1984), p. 206; Rudiger Dornbusch and Stanley Fischer, *Macroeconomics*, 3d ed. (New York: McGraw-Hill, 1984), p. 466; William J. Baumol and Alan S. Blinder, *Economics* (New York: Harcourt Brace Jovanovich, 1988), p. 356.

8. Baumol and Blinder, *Economics*, pp. 96–97.

9. U.S. Conference of Mayors, *The Continuing Growth of Hunger, Homelessness, and Poverty in America's Cities* (Washington, D.C., 1987), p. 22.

10. See Michael Sosin and Irving Piliavin, "Tracking the Homeless," *Focus*, newsletter of the University of Wisconsin at Madison Institute for Research on Poverty, 10 (4): 20–24 (Winter 1987–1988).

11. Freeman and Hall, *Permanent Homelessness in America?*, p. 11.

12. For a discussion of the problems facing researchers on the homeless, see, for example, Norweeta Milburne, Roderick Watts, and Susan Anderson, *Current Research Methods for Studying the Homeless* (Washington, D.C.: Howard University Institute for Urban Affairs and Research, 1984); Paul Koegel and Audrey Burnam, "A Design for Drawing a Probability Sample of Homeless Individuals," The National Institute of Mental Health Conference on Mental Health Statistics, San Francisco, California, 28–31 May 1985; and Thomas Hirschl, "Homelessness: A Sociological Research Agenda," *Sociological Spectrum* 10: 443–67 (1990).

13. Edward Sutherland and Harvey J. Locke, *Twenty Thousand Homeless Men* (Chicago: J. B. Lippincott Company, 1936), p. 21.

14. Some typical examples of the functionalist approach to homelessness include Robert Merton's influential *Social Theory and Social Structure* (Glencoe, Ill.: The Free Press, 1957); as well as James F. Rooney, "Societal Force and the Unattached Male: An Historical Review," in *Disaffiliated Man*, ed. Howard Bahr (Toronto: University of Toronto Press, 1970); Donald Bogue, *Skid Row in American Cities* (Chicago: University of Chicago Press, 1963); and Samuel Wallace, *Skid Row as a Way of Life* (Totowa, N.J.: The Bedminister Press, 1965). For a review of this literature, see Joel Blau, "On the Uses of Homelessness: A Literature Review," *Catalyst* 6 (2): 5–25 (1988).

15. Howard Bahr and Kathleen Fouts, "Can You Trust a Homeless Man? A Comparison of Official Records and Interview Responses by Bowery Men," *Public Opinion Quarterly* 35 (3): 374–82 (1971).

16. U.S., Department of Housing and Urban Development, *Report to the Secretary on the Homeless and Emergency Housing* (Washington, D.C., 1984).

17. Mitch Snyder and Mary Ellen Hombs, *Homelessness in America: The Forced March to Nowhere* (Washington, D.C.: The Community for Creative Nonviolence, 1983).

18. U.S. Congress, Joint Hearing before the Subcommittee on Housing and Urban Development of the Committee on Banking, Finance, and Urban Affairs and the Subcommittee on Manpower and Housing of the Committee of Government Operations, *HUD Report on Homelessness*, 98th Cong. 2d sess. 24 May 1984.

19. The literature on the HUD report is extensive. Some of the major critiques include Chester Hartman and Richard Appelbaum's testimony at the congressional hearings, both of which have been reprinted in Jon Erickson and Charles Wilhelm, eds., *Housing the Homeless* (New Brunswick, N.J.: Center for Urban Policy, Rutgers, The State University of New Jersey, 1986), pp. 150–64; Richard Appelbaum's Preface to Richard H. Ropers, *The Invisible Homeless: A New Urban Ecology* (New York: Human Sciences Press, 1988), pp. 19–26; U.S.,

General Accounting Office, *Homelessness: A Complex Problem and the Federal Response* (Washington, D.C., 1985), p. 9; and Institute of Medicine, *Homelessness, Health, and Human Needs* (Washington, D.C.: National Academy of Science, 1988), pp. 171–72.

The report is not without its defenders. They include S. Anna Kondratas, "A Strategy for Helping America's Homeless," The Heritage Foundation Backgrounder, no. 431, 6 May 1985, pp. 3–6, reprinted in Erickson and Wilhelm, eds., *Housing the Homeless*, pp. 144–49; Karen Perloff, "Who are the Homeless and How Many are There?" in *The Homeless in Contemporary Society*, ed. Richard D. Bingham, Roy E. Green, and Sammis B. White (Newbury Park, Calif.: Sage Publications, 1987), pp. 33–45; as well as Freeman and Hall, *Permanent Homelessness in America?*; and the qualified endorsement of F. Stevens Redburn and Terry F. Buss, *Responding to America's Homeless: Public Policy Alternatives* (New York: Praeger, 1986).

20. See Institute of Medicine, *Homelessness, Health, and Human Needs*, p. 171.

21. Testimony of Ronald D. Pogue, U.S., Joint Hearing, *HUD Report on Homelessness*, pp. 137–44.

22. For Boston, see the statement of Valerie Dionne-Lanier, pp. 89–91 of the Joint Hearings report; for Hartford, see the congressional testimony of Maria DePinto, especially p. 57 of the Joint Hearings report; for Phoenix, see the statement of Louisa Stark, Joint Hearings report, pp. 53–56.

23. Richard P. Appelbaum's Preface to Roper, *The Invisible Homeless*, pp. 23–24.

24. Ibid., p. 24.

25. See the response of HUD to critics of the report's methodology in U.S., Joint Hearings report, pp. 281–87, esp. p. 283.

26. See the U.S., General Accounting Office, *Homeless Mentally Ill*, pp. 47–52, which contains a summary of methods for counting the whole population.

27. Ibid., p. 30.

28. See pp. 18 and 114 for reference to L. Darcy and P. L. Jones, "The Size of the Homeless Men Population of Sydney," *Australian Journal of Social Sciences* 10 (3): 208ff.

29. See, for Freeman and Hall, *Permanent Homelessness in America?*, p. 4; for Joint Hearings report, p. 17; for *Homelessness in New York State* (Albany: New York State Department of Social Services, 1984), p. 29; and, for Fairfax, Virginia, E. Goplerud, "Homelessness in Fairfax County: Needs Assessment of Homeless Persons and Implications for Programs and Policies," Department of Psychology, George Mason University, August 1987. See the U.S., General Accounting Office, *Homeless Mentally Ill*, p. 28, for a chart summarizing the street-shelter ratio of nine studies.

30. Interview with Alice Hasler, 25 July 1988.

31. See Mireya Navarro, "Census Peers into Corners to Count Homeless," *New York Times*, 21 March 1990; Felicity Barringer, "Despite Problems, the Census Bureau Hails Its First Count of the Homeless," *New York Times*, 22 March 1990; and Kim Hopper, "Good Reasons for Participating in a Flawed Endeavor: The National Coalition and The Census," *Safety Network* 9(3): 1, 4 (March 1990); Felicity Barringer, "U.S. Homeless Count Is Far Below Estimates," *New York Times*, 12 April 1991; and Dennis Hevesi, "Census Count of Homeless Is Disputed," *New York Times*, 13 April 1991, from which the quotation comes.

32. Capture-recapture techniques perform two counts in an attempt to match data on the same individuals at different points in time. Probability statistics are then used to estimate the unseen part of the population. Seymour Sudman, Monroe G. Sirken, and Charles Cowan, "Sampling Rare and Elusive Populations," *Science* 240: 991–96 (May 1988) contains a technical description of the methodology. For a positive view of its potential, see Institute of Medicine, *Homelessness, Health, and Human Needs*, pp. 176–80. For criticism of its applicability, see Peroff, "Who are the Homeless, and How Many Are There?" p. 41.

33. Pierce's revised total appears in Robert Pear, "Data Are Elusive on the Homeless," *New York Times*, 1 March 1988; Kondratas is quoted in Leslie Maitland, "Plan for the Homeless Is Called Modest," *New York Times*, 26 November 1989. It should be noted that an Urban Institute study, *America's Homeless*, authored by Martha Burt and Barbara Cohen, also places the 1987 population at from 496,000 to 600,000 people.

34. Institute of Medicine, *Homelessness, Health, and Human Needs*, pp. 3–4.

35. The New York studies, all authored by the Human Resources Administration, are *Chronic and Situational Dependency* (1982), *The Homeless in New York City Shelters* (1984), and *One Day Study* (1984). For Ohio, see the Ohio Department of Mental Health, *Homeless in Ohio: A Study of People in Need* (Columbus, Ohio, 1985). The St. Louis data comes from Gary Morse, *A Contemporary Assessment of Urban Homelessness* (St. Louis: Center for Metropolitan Studies, University of Missouri at St. Louis, 1986). For Minneapolis, see Irving Piliavin, Michael Sosin, and Herb Westerfelt, *Conditions Contributing to Long-Term Homelessness: An Exploratory Study*, (University of Wisconsin Institute for Research on Poverty Discussion Paper #853–87 Madison, Wis. 1988), and for Los Angeles, Albert Greenstein, *Report of the Countywide Task Force on the Homeless* (Los Angeles County: Community and Senior Citizens Department, 1985).

36. See, Rossi et al., *The Condition of the Homeless in Chicago*. For the estimates of the women's mean age, see the Institute of Medicine, *Homeless, Health and Human Needs*.

37. See The Bureau of the Census, Special Census of the Bowery, reported in *Literary Digest*, 107: 20–21 (29 November 1930) and cited in Kenneth Lovald, "From Hobohemia to Skid Row: The Changing Community of the Homeless Man" (Ph.D diss., University of Minnesota, 1960), p. 170.

38. U.S. Conference of Mayors, *A Status Report on Hunger and Homelessness in America's Cities: 1990* (Washington, D.C., 1990), p. 25.

39. Single men constitute more than 60 percent of the population in a number of cities including Minneapolis, Nashville, Phoenix, and San Diego; they make up less than 30 percent of the population in Los Angeles, Trenton, and Kansas City. Similarly, while the percentage of single women exceeds one-fifth in Denver, San Francisco, and Washington, D.C., they are less than 5 percent of the population in Charleston, Charlotte, and New Orleans. U.S. Conference of Mayors, *A Status Report on Hunger and Homeless in America's Cities: 1990*, p. 55.

40. U.S., Department of Housing and Urban Development, *The 1989 National Survey of Shelters for the Homeless* (Washington, D.C., 1989), p. 9.

41. U.S., Department of Housing and Urban Development, *The 1988 National Survey of Shelters for the Homeless*, (Washington, D.C., 1988) p. 9.

42. Compare the U.S. Conference of Mayors, *The Growth of Hunger and Homelessness in America's Cities in 1985*, p. 15 with the same organization's *A Status*

Report on Hunger and Homelessness in America's Cities: 1990 (Washington, D.C., 1990), p. 55. The one major exception to these numbers is Martha R. Burt and Barbara E. Cohen, *America's Homeless* (Washington, D.C.: The Urban Institute, 1989), which estimated the proportion of homeless families at 10 percent. See also Martha R. Burt and Barbara E. Cohen, "Differences Among Homeless Single Women, Women with Children, and Single Men," *Social Problems* 36 (5): 508–24 (December 1989).

43. Institute of Medicine, *Homelessness, Health, and Human Needs*, pp. 13–14. For a discussion of the psychological effects of homelessness on children, see Ellen Bassuk and Lenore Rubin, "Homeless Children: A Neglected Population," *American Journal of Orthopsychiatry* 57 (2): 279–86 (April 1987). And for two New York City studies of homeless children, see Janice Molnar, *Home is Where the Heart Is: The Crisis of Homeless Children and Families in New York City*, a report to Edna McConnell Clark Foundation (New York: Bank Street Street College of Education, 1988), and Citizens' Committee for Children, *Children in Storage: Families in New York City's Barracks-Style Shelters* (New York, 1988).

44. Cited in Richard First, Dee Roth, and Bobbie Darden Arewa, "Homelessness: Understanding the Dimensions of the Problem for Minorities," *Social Work* 33 (2): 120–24 (March–April 1988).

45. Burt and Cohen, *America's Homeless*, p. 45; U.S., Department of Housing and Urban Development, *The 1988 National Survey of Shelters for the Homeless*, p. 11.

46. See, for example, Myron Magnet, "The Homeless," *Fortune* 116 (12): 170–89 (23 November 1987); and David Whitman, "Who's Who Among the Homeless," *New Republic* 198 (23): 18–20 (6 June 1988).

47. See, for example, F. Stevens Redburn and Terry F. Buss, *Responding to America's Homeless* (New York: Praeger, 1986), p. 94; Emergency Services Network of Alameda County, *Homelessness in Alameda County* (Alameda County, 1988), p. 8; U.S. Conference of Mayors, *A Status Report on Hunger and Homelessness in America's Cities: 1990*, p. 55.

48. U.S. Conference of Mayors, *A Status Report on Hunger and Homelessness in America's Cities: 1990*, p. 55.

49. See, for example, E. Fuller Torrey, *Nowhere To Go: The Tragic Odyssey of the Homeless Mentally Ill* (New York: Harper and Row, 1988), p. 7; James Wright, "The Worthy and Unworthy Homeless," *Society* 25 (5): 64–69 (July/August 1988); U.S. Conference of Mayors, *A Status Report on Hunger in Homelessness in America's Cities: 1990*, p. 55. Institute of Medicine, *Homelessness, Health, and Human Needs*, p. 52. For local studies, there is the 33 percent found in New York by the Human Resources Administration in *Chronic and Situational Dependency* (New York, 1982); the 29 percent identified in Virginia by E. Goplerud, "Homeless in Fairfax County: Needs Assessment of Homeless Persons and Implications for Programs and Policies," George Mason University Department of Psychology, 1987; and the 36 percent diagnosed as schizophrenic in San Francisco by Robert Surber et al., "Medical and Psychiatric Needs of the Homeless—A Preliminary Response," *Social Work* 33 (2): 116–19 (March–April 1988). All this research illustrates what appears to be a growing consensus.

50. Some of the methodological problems are discussed in Ellen Bassuk, "The Homelessness Problem," *Scientific American* 251 (1): 40–45; Leona Bachrach, "Interpreting Research on the Homeless Mentally ill: Some Caveats," *Hos-*

pital and Community Psychiatry 35 (9): 914–17; and Carole Mowbray, "Homelessness in America: Myths and Realities," *American Journal of Orthopsychiatry* 55 (1): 4–8.

51. The incidence of mental illness in the general population is discussed in Leo Srole, Thomas Langner, Stanley Michael, Price Kirkpatrick, Marvin Opler, and Thomas Rennie, *Mental Health in the Metropolis* (New York: Harper Torchbooks, 1975); see also the review of studies in Darrel Regier et al., "Historical Context, Major Objectives and Study Design," in *Epidemiologic Field Methods in Psychiatry*, ed. William W. Eaton and Larry Kessler, (New York: Academic Press, 1985), pp. 3–19, esp. p. 9.

52. See Institute of Medicine, *Homelessness, Health, and Human Needs*, p. 7 and the Ohio Department of Mental Health, *Homelessness in Ohio: A Study of People in Need*, p. 33. The three New York studies, all authored by the Human Resources Administration, are *Chronic and Situational Dependency* (1982), *The Homeless in New York City Shelters* (1984), and *One-Day Study* (1984). Chicago's number comes out of Peter Rossi et al., *The Condition of the Homeless in Chicago*. For Memphis, see Barrett A. Lee, "Homelessness in Tennessee," in *Homelessness in the United States*, ed. Jamshid A. Momemi (Westwood, Conn.: Greenwood Press, 1989), pp. 181–203; and for Los Angeles, see Greenstein, *Report of the Countywide Task Force on the Homeless*.

53. See Institute of Medicine, *Homelessness, Health, and Human Needs*, p. 7 for comparative data on Chicago. The Los Angeles rate is found in Roper, *The Invisible Homeless: A New Human Ecology*, p. 58; for Ohio, see Ohio Department of Mental Health, *Homelessness in Ohio: A Study of People in Need*, p. 33.

54. Nels Anderson, "The Homeless in New York City," Welfare Council of New York City Research Bureau, unpublished manuscript, 1934, p. 180.

55. U.S. Conference of Mayors, *A Status Report on Hunger and Homelessness in America's Cities: 1990*, pp. 25, 55.

56. See U.S., Department of Housing and Urban Development, *The 1988 National Survey of Shelters for the Homeless*, p. 16; The Human Resources Administration, *The Homeless in New York City Shelters*; for Los Angeles, see Ropers, *The Invisible Homeless*, p. 46; for Chicago, see Rossi et al., *The Condition of the Homeless of Chicago*; and for Portland, see Multnomah County, Oregon Department of Human Services, *The Homeless Poor* (Multnomah County, 1984).

57. Sara Rimer, "After 8 Years, a Dip in Families in Shelters," *New York Times*, 28 February 1989. For Los Angeles, see The Shelter Partnership, *The Short-Term Housing System of Los Angeles County: Serving the Housing Needs of the Homeless* (Los Angeles, 1987).

58. U.S., Department of Housing and Urban Development, *The 1988 National Survey of Shelters for the Homeless*, p. 16.

59. Freeman and Hall, *Permanent Homelessness in America?*, p. 15.

60. New York City Office of the Comptroller, *Soldiers of Misfortune: Homeless Veterans in New York City* (Office of the Comptroller, 1982); for Los Angeles, see Rodger K. Farr and Paul Koegel, *A Study of Homelessness and Mental Illness in the Skid Row Area of Los Angeles* (Los Angeles: Los Angeles County Department of Mental Health, 1986).

61. M.J. Rosenow et al., *Listening to the Homeless: A Study of Mentally Ill Persons in Milwaukee* (Milwaukee: Milwaukee Human Services Triangle, 1985), pp. 29–30; Ohio Department of Mental Health, *Homelessness in Ohio: A Study of People in Need*, p. 33; and Russell Schutt, *Boston's Homeless: Their Backgrounds, Problems,*

and Needs (Boston: University of Massachusetts, 1985), p. 7. For an overview of the issue and a list of studies, see Majorie Robertson, "Homeless Veterans," in *The Homeless in Contemporary Society*, pp. 64–81.

62. James D. Wright, "The Worthy and the Unworthy Homeless," *Society* 25 (5): 64–69.

63. See Mary Robertson, "Homeless Veterans," p. 65.

64. Piliavin, Sosin, and Westerfelt, *Conditions Contributing to Long-Term Homelessness*, p. 22; Joel Blau and Barbara Kleiman, *Homeless Youth in the New York City Municipal Shelter System: The Project A.I.D. Final Report* (New York: Human Resources Administration, 1985), p. 15; and Richard Barth, "On Their Own: The Experiences of Youth After Foster Care," *Child and Adolescent Social Work* 7(5): 419–40 (October 1990).

65. Gioglio, "Homelessness in New Jersey: The Social Service Network and the People Served," in *Homelessness in the United States*, pp. 125.

66. Human Resources Administration, *The Homeless in the New York City Shelters*.

67. Ellen Bassuk and Lenore Rubin, "Homeless Children: A Neglected Population," *American Journal of Orthopsychiatry* 57(2): 279–86.

68. National Coalition for the Homeless, *American Nightmare: A Decade of Homelessness in the United States* (Washington, D.C.: 1989), pp. 9–18; Mireya Navarro, "Double Jeopardy: Life with AIDS and No Place to Live," *New York Times*, 14 May 1991.

Chapter 3

1. Francis Wayland, A Paper on Tramps Read at the Saratoga Meeting of the American Social Science Association Before the Conference of State Charities, New Haven, Hoggson & Robinson Printers, 6 September 1877.

2. See Agnes Eggli, "Criminal Element's 'Housekeeping' Turning Street into Cesspool," letter to the editor of the *Santa Barbara News-Press*, 25 February 1988.

3. Michael Katz, *Poverty and Policy in American History* (New York: Academic Press, 1983), p. 174.

4. Ibid. pp. 180–81.

5. Cited in Frank Leonard, "Helping the Unemployed in the Nineteenth Century: The Case of the American Tramp," *Social Service Review* 40(4): 429–34 (1982).

6. See Thomas Main, "The Homeless of New York," *The Public Interest*, no. 72 (Summer 1983), pp. 3–28 for the assertion that services create their own demand; William Tucker, "Where Do the Homeless Come From?," *National Review* 39 (19): 32–43 for an analysis of homelessness and rent control; and Roger M. Nooe and Maryanne Lynch, "Family Relationships and Homelessness: Educational Challenges" (Paper presented at the Annual Program Meeting of the Council on Social Work Education, Atlanta, Georgia, March 1988 for the discussion of birth order and family size).

7. F. Stevens Redburn and Terry Buss, *Responding to America's Homeless: Public Policy Alternatives* (New York: Praeger, 1986), p. 55.

8. Bennett Harrison and Barry Bluestone, *The Great U-Turn* (New York: Basic Books, 1988), pp. 8–9. For a more general overview of the effects of

international competition and the American decline, see Michael Moffitt, "Shocks, Deadlocks, and Scorched Earth," *World Policy Journal* 4(4): 553–82 (Fall 1987).

9. Barry Commoner, *The Poverty of Power* (New York: Alfred Knopf, 1976), p. 243.

10. For a discussion of the postwar capital-labor accord, see Samuel Bowles, David Gordon, and Thomas Weisskopf, *Beyond the Wasteland: A Democratic Alternative to Economic Decline* (New York: Anchor Press, Doubleday, 1983), pp. 84–91; for an analysis of the politics of the growth coalition, see Alan Wolfe, *America's Impasse* (Boston: South End Press, 1982).

11. Bowles, Gordon, and Weisskopf, *Beyond the Wasteland*, pp. 84–86.

12. Harrison and Bluestone, *The Great U-Turn*, p. 99, citing David Vogel, "The 'New' Social Regulation in Historical and Comparative Perspective," in *Regulation in Perspective*, ed. Thomas K. McGraw (Cambridge: Harvard University Press, 1981), p. 162.

13. Harrison and Bluestone, *The Great U-Turn*, pp. 99–100; see, also, for a more general treatment of this issue, James O' Connor, *The Fiscal Crisis of the State* (New York: St. Martin's Press, 1973), pp. 175–78.

14. Bowles, Gordon, and Weisskpof, *Beyond the Wasteland*, p. 39.

15. Ibid., pp. 39–40.

16. Harrison and Bluestone, *The Great U-Turn*, p. 7. See also, more generally, James O' Connor, *Accumulation Crisis* (New York: Basil Blackwell, 1984).

17. As chairman of the Federal Reserve Bank, Paul Volcker was especially adept at evasive descriptions of what was in store for the American economy. See William Greider, *Secrets of the Temple* (New York: Simon & Schuster, 1987). A typical call for a new social contract appear in the special issue of *Business Week* entitled "The Reindustrialization of America," 30 June 1980 at the height of pre-Reagan concern about the loss of American economic power.

18. William Greider, "The Education of David Stockman," *Atlantic Monthly* 248 (6): 46(December 1981).

19. Kevin Philips, *The Politics of Rich and Poor* (New York: Random House, 1990); Benjamin M. Friedman, *Day of Reckoning* (New York: Random House, 1988), pp. 128–29; Greider, *Secrets of the Temple*, p. 401; and Frank Ackerman, *Reagonomics* (Boston: South End Press, 1982), pp. 39–55. For the data on quintiles, see Thomas Ferguson and Joel Rogers, *Right Turn* (New York: Hill and Wang, 1986), p. 123.

20. Friedman, *Day of Reckoning*, p. 263; Greider, *Secrets of the Temple*, p. 401. The failure of some corporations to pay any taxes produced a public outcry that resulted in the cancellation of one of the law's most egregious provisions permitting firms to sell the tax credits they could not use because they did not owe any taxes. See Friedman, *Day of Reckoning*, p. 263.

21. The $570 billion estimate is cited in Greider, *Secrets of the Temple*, pp. 455–56.

22. Michael D. Reagan, *Regulation: The Politics of Policy* (Boston: Little, Brown, 1987), p. 105, cited in Harrison and Bluestone, *The Great U-Turn*, p. 100.

23. The decline in enforcement levels is contained in George C. Eads and Michael Fix, *Relief or Reform? Reagan's Regulatory Dilemma* (Washington, D.C.: The Urban Institute, 1984), p. 195; the $6.50 estimates comes from the U.S., Congress Office of Technology Assessment, *Preventing Illness and Injury in the*

Workplace (Washington, D.C.: General Printing Office, 1985), p. 236. Both are cited in Ferguson and Rogers, *Right Turn*, p. 134.

24. Ferguson and Rogers, *Right Turn*, p. 134.

25. See Jonathan Tasini, "Why Labor is At Odds with the N.L.R.B," *New York Times*, 30 October 1988; for further background, see Sam Rosenberg, "Restructuring the Labor Force: The Role of Government Policies," in The Union for Radical Political Economics, *The Imperiled Economy* (New York, 1988), p. 30.

26. Harrison and Bluestone, *The Great U-Turn*, p. 40.

27. Ibid., pp. 42–43, 45.

28. See David Ellwood, *Poor Support* (New York: Basic Books, 1988), pp. 110–13; Center on Budget and Policy Priorities, *Making Work Pay: A New Agenda for Poverty Policies* (Washington, D.C., 1989).

29. The standard work on deindustrialization is Bennett Harrison and Barry Bluestone, *The Deindustrialization of America* (New York: Basic Books, 1982).

30. See Rosenberg, "Restructuring the Labor Force," p. 27 for data on the percent of the workforce in the manufacturing sector. An especially helpful government document is U.S. Congress, Office of Technology Assessment, *Paying the Bill: Manufacturing & America's Trade Deficit* (Washington, D.C.: Government Printing Office, 1988), which notes that nearly three-quarters of the trade deficit originates in three product areas—motor vehicles, textiles and apparel, and electronic equipment. For the increase in debt for each family, and discussions of the effects of the budget deficit on trade, see Friedman, *Day of Reckoning*, pp. 6, 10–11. The prediction about the percent employed in the future workforce is contained in The Hudson Institute, *Workforce 2000: Work and Workers for the 21st Century* (Indianapolis, Ind., 1987), p. 58.

31. U.S. Congress, Office of Technology Assessment, *Technology and Structural Unemployment: Reemploying Displaced Adults* (Washington, D.C.: Government Printing Office, 1986), pp. 3, 7. A subsequent Department of Labor study of the 1983–88 period showed that 9.7 million people had lost their jobs, including 4.7 million who had held them for more than three years. While 71 percent had obtained another job by the end of the survey period—up from 60 percent in 1984—30 percent of the reemployed had to accept pay cuts of at least 20 percent. See the Associated Press, "As Economy Grew Since '83, Closings and Layoffs Took 9.7 Million Jobs," *New York Times*, 13 December 1988.

32. For discussions of the relationship between an industrial and service economies, see Saskia Sassen, *The Mobility of Labor and Capital* (Cambridge: Cambridge University Press, 1987); Rhon Baiman, "Structural Subemployment in the United States and the Full Employment Debate," in Union of Radical Political Economics, *The Imperiled Economy* (New York, 1988), p. 70; and U.S. Congress, Office of Technology Assessment, *Paying the Bill*, pp. 53–57.

33. Steve Lohr, "The Growth of the Global Office," *New York Times*, 10 October 1988.

34. Janice Simpson, "A Shallow Labor Pool Spurs Business to Act to Bolster Education," *Wall Street Journal*, 28 September 1987. See The Hudson Institute, *Workforce 2000*, pp. 97–101 for a discussion of the educational levels that will be required in new jobs.

35. Harrison and Bluestone, *The Great U-Turn*, p. 7.

36. Ibid., p. 125 for the assertion about a one-to-one correlation; also, "The Great American Job Machine: The Proliferation of Low Wage Employment in

the U.S. Economy," U.S. Congress, Joint Economic Committee, December, 1986; and their article "The Grim Truth About the Job Miracle, *New York Times*, 1 February 1987.

37. For discussions of this issue, see Gary Burtless, ed., *A Future of Lousy Jobs* (Washington, D.C.: The Brookings Institute, 1990); Marvin Kosters and Murray N. Ross, "The Distribution of Earnings and Employment Opportunities: A Reexamination of the Evidence," *Studies in Economic Policy* (Washington, D.C.: American Enterprise Institute, 1987); Robert Samuelson, "The American Job Machine," *Newsweek*, 23 February 1987, p. 57; Warren T. Brookes, "Low-Pay Jobs: The Big Lie," *Wall Street Journal*, 25 March, 1987; and Janet Norwood, "A Cyclical Rebound: The Job Machine Has Not Broken Down," *New York Times*, 22 February, 1987.

In general, critics of this thesis have argued that it merely captures the entry of the baby boom generation into the workforce, or that it compares the rate of job creation in good years with the rate of job creation of the 1981–82 recession. There have also been allegations that Harrison and Bluestone's choice of an income deflator, the Consumer Price Index (CPI-U), distorted the data.

In 1983, the Bureau of Labor Statistics replaced the CPI-U with the CPI-X1, because the CPI-U included appreciation of the asset value of a home and thereby confused the investment and consumption dimensions of homeownership. Several commentators have therefore urged that the issue be reexamined using either the CPI-X1 or the Bureau of Economic Analysis' index of Personal Consumption Expenditure (PCE), both of which show a lower rate of inflation. For example, from 1973 to 1987, the CPI grew 156 percent, while the CPI-X1 grew 139 percent. See Sheldon Danziger, Peter Gottschalk, and Eugene Smolensky, "American Income Inequality: How the Rich Have Fared, 1973–1987," *American Economic Association Papers and Proceedings* 79 (2): 310–14, esp. p. 311, footnote 4.

Inevitably, the questions clouding the choice of an income deflator are both technical and value-laden. The PCE indicator tracks individuals rather than families and includes the noncash benefits from some entitlement programs such as food stamps, Medicare, and Medicaid. It rises in step with the CPI until 1970, and then continues to rise at a slower pace even when the CPI has begun its steady decline. Most researchers still employ the CPI, but the PCE measure is available for those who wish to diminish the effects of inflation and broaden the definition of income.

38. Harrison and Bluestone, *The Great U-Turn*, pp. 5; 124–25; and p. 222, note 19, where the effect of using the PCE to recalculate their data is discussed. In the middle of debates during the 1988 presidential campaign about good jobs at good wages, the Democratic Staff of the Senate Budget Committee updated this information through 1987. They found that in the period from 1979 to 1987, slightly more than half of the year-round, full-time jobs created during the period paid wages of less than $11,611. Since this figure was even higher than the Harrison and Bluestone data, it was quickly attacked for its political partisanship. See the Associated Press, "Study of New Jobs Since '79 Says Half Pay Poverty Wage," *New York Times*, 26 September 1988.

39. Louis Uchitelle, "Not Getting Ahead? Better Get Used to It," *New York Times*, 16 December 1990.

40. John D. Kasarda, "Urban Industrial Transition and the Underclass," *Annals* 501: 33 (January 1989).

41. See William Julius Wilson, *The Truly Disadvantaged* (Chicago: University of Chicago Press, 1987); Lois J. D. Wacquant and William Julius Wilson, "The Cost of Racial and Class Exclusion in the Inner City," *Annals* 501: 8–25 (January 1989); and Kasarda, "Urban Industrial Transition and the Underclass," pp. 26–47. For some statistical data about the continuing increase in black poverty, see the Center on Budget and Policy Priorities, *Still Far From the Dream: Recent Developments in Black Income, Employment, and Poverty* (Washington, D.C., 1988).

42. The CBO study is summarized in Center for Budget and Policy Priorities, *Drifting Apart: New Findings in Growing Income Disparities Between the Rich, the Poor, and the Middle Class* (Washington, D.C., 1990), esp. pp. 3, 7. For other comparable data, see Katherine Bradbury, "The Changing Fortunes of U.S. Families," *New England Economic Review*, (July/August 1990), pp. 25–40, and Kevin Phillips, *The Politics of Rich and Poor* (New York: Random House, 1990).

43. Center for Budget and Policy Priorities, "Rich-Poor Income Gap Hits 40-Year High As Poverty Rate Stalls," (Washington, D.C., 1990), p. 2. For discussion of this issue, see Frank Levy, "The Middle Class: Is It Really Vanishing?," *The Brookings Review*, Summer 1987, p. 20; Michael W. Horrigan and Steven E. Haugen, "The Declining Middle-Class Thesis: A Sensitivity Analysis," *Monthly Labor Review* 111 (5): 3–11 (May 1988); Neal H. Rosenthal, "The Shrinking Middle Class: Myth or Reality? *Monthly Labor Review* 108(3): 3–10 (March 1985); and Patrick J. McMahon and John H. Tshetter, "The Declining Middle Class: A Further Analysis," *Monthly Labor Review* 109 (9): 22–27, (September 1986).

44. See U.S., Congress, Joint Economic Committee, *The Concentration of Wealth in the United States* (Washington, D.C.: Government Printing Office, 1986). The controversy about this study revolved around the fact that under pressure from the Reagan Treasury Department, the wealthiest individual in the sample—a Texas oilman worth an estimated $200 million—had been removed. In the revised version, the top 0.5 percent of households owned 26.9 percent of the nation's wealth, up, but not as sharply, from the 25.4 percent figure in 1965. See Phillips, *The Politics of Rich and Poor*, p. 11 and Appendix B. For a discussion of this controversy and arguments that the original study was correct, see "Scandal at the Fed?" *Dollars & Sense*, no. 125, April 1987, pp. 10–11, 22.

45. Danziger, Gottschalk, and Smolensky, "American Income Inequality: How the Rich Have Fared, 1973–87," p. 312.

46. Ibid.

47. Ohio Department of Mental Health, *Homelessness in Ohio: A Study of People in Need* (Columbus, Ohio, 1985), p. 36.

48. See the comparative chart of studies containing unemployment data in Richard H. Ropers, *The Invisible Homeless: A New Urban Ecology* (New York: Human Science's Press, 1988), pp. 36–37.

49. Even the authors of the Ohio study where 21 percent of the respondents mentioned unemployment acknowledge that altogether, about 50 percent of those interviewed cited economic factors. See Dee Roth and Gerald Bean, "New Findings From A Statewide Epidemiological Study," *Hospital and Community Psychiatry* 37(7): 712–19 (July 1986).

Chapter 4

1. Quoted in Karl de Schweinitz, *England's Road to Social Security* (New York: A. S. Barnes, 1943), p. 123.

2. See Gosta Esping-Andersen, *Politics Against Markets* (Princeton, N.J.: Princeton University Press, 1985) and *The Three Worlds of Welfare Capitalism* (Princeton, N. J.: Princeton University Press, 1990); Alfred J. Kahn and Sheila Kamerman, *Not for the Poor Alone: European Social Services* (Philadelphia: Temple University Press, 1975); and Arnold Heidenheimer, Hugh Heclo, and Carolyn Teich Adams, *Comparative Public Policy: The Politics of Social Choice in Europe and America* (New York: St Martin's Press, 1975).

3. Quoted in David Rosenbaum, "Reagan Thesis: Issue is Entitlement," *New York Times*, 24 March 1981.

4. Samuel Bowles and Herbert Gintis, "The Crisis of Liberal Democratic Capitalism," *Politics and Society* 11(1): 51–93.

5. Cited in Martin Tolchin, "Welfare Denied to Many of Poor Over Paperwork," *New York Times*, 29 October 1988; Texas Department of Human Services, Office of Strategic Management, Research and Development, *Income Assistance Service Delivery Study*, Phase I Report, November 1988.

6. New York City Human Resources Administration, Office of Policy and Economic Research, *Thirty Day Administrative Closing: How Often and To Whom?* (New York, 1987), pp. 4, 17. The sample in Table 2 is approximately one-tenth the total caseload. The 4,798 figure listed in the table should therefore be multiplied by ten.

7. See Frances Fox Piven and Richard Cloward, *Regulating the Poor* (New York: Vintage, 1971) for the original thesis that public assistance programs expand and contract in response to changing political and economic conditions. In *The New Class War* (New York: Pantheon Books, 1982), Piven and Cloward modify this thesis by arguing that the old cyclical pattern no longer applies: the welfare state will continue to expand, despite conservative cutbacks. Although I agree that the welfare state will continue to expand, I think *The New Class War* underestimated the degree to which the attack on public assistance programs was consistent with the "regulating the poor" tradition.

8. U.S., Congress, House, Committee on Ways and Means, *1991 Background Material and Data on Programs Within the Jurisdiction of the Committee on Ways and Means*, p. 618, Table 19.

9. Center on Social Welfare Policy and Law, *Beyond the Myths* (New York, 1985), p. 9; U.S., Committee on Ways and Means, *1991 Background Material*, pp. 622–623, Table 22; Mimi Abramovitz, *Regulating the Lives of Women* (Boston: South End Press, 1988), esp. pp. 313–42, which describes how social welfare policy, and AFDC in particular, have punished women who have deviated from the "family ethic."

10. National Coalition for the Homeless, *National Neglect/National Shame— America's Homeless: Outlook—Winter, 1986–1987* (Washington, D.C. 1986), p. 52; see also, U.S., General Accounting Office, *An Evaluation of the 1981 AFDC Changes: Final Report* (Washington, D.C. 1985), pp. 20–23.

11. Kim Hopper and Jill Hamberg, *The Making of America's Homeless: From Skid Row to the New Poor* (New York: Community Service Society, 1985).

12. U.S., General Accounting Office, *An Evaluation of the 1981 AFDC Changes:*

Final Report, cited in Center on Budget and Policy Priorities, *Smaller Slices of the Pie: The Growing Economic Vulnerability of Poor and Moderate Income Americans* (Washington, D.C. 1985), p. 22.

13. U.S., Committee on Ways and Means, *1991 Background Material* pp. 597–598, Table 7, and pp. 604–5, Table 10.

14. A fine analysis of one part of this history is Daniel T. Rodgers, *The Work Ethic in Industrial America, 1850–1920* (Chicago: University of Chicago Press, 1974).

15. For Boston, see City of Boston, *Dignity & Respect: Making Room for Boston's Homeless, Winter 1987/88* (Boston: Emergency Shelter Commission, 1987), p. 3; the treadmill is discussed in David M. Schneider, *The History of Public Welfare in New York State, 1607–1867* (Chicago: University of Chicago Press, 1938), 1: 153–54. For the 1840s, see Edward Spann, *The New Metropolis: New York City, 1840–1857* (New York: Columbia University Press, 1981), pp. 79–81; the labor camps, in David M. Schneider and Albert Deutsch, *The History of Public Welfare in New York State, 1867–1940* (Chicago: University of Chicago, 1941), 2:203. Lastly, for the rise of work tests, see Charles Hoch, "A Brief History of the Homeless Problem in the United States," in *The Homeless in Contemporary Society*, ed. Richard Bingham, Roy Green, and Sammis White (Beverly Hills, Calif.: Sage Publications, 1987), pp. 16–32.

16. For discussion of the conflict between the desire to impose work discipline and the pressure to reduce welfare costs, see Fred Block and John Noakes, "The Politics of the New-Style Workfare," *Socialist Review* 18(3): 31–58 (July–September 1988).

The literature on the Family Support Act is extensive. Some of the most helpful writing includes the Congressional Budget Office, *Work and Welfare: The Family Support Act of 1988* (Washington, D.C. 1989); the special issue on Welfare Reform and Poverty of *Focus* 11 (1) (Spring 1988) published by the Institute for Research on Poverty of the University of Wisconsin-Madison, and the summary of the act itself in *Focus* 11(4): 15–18 (Winter 1988–1989); Howard Karger and David Stoesz, "Welfare Reforms: Maximum Feasible Exaggeration," *Tikkun* 4(2): 23–25, 118–22 (March/April 1989); and Mimi Abramovitz, "Why Welfare Reform Is a Sham," *The Nation* 1: 238–41 (26 September 1988). The U.S., General Accounting Office, *Work and Welfare: Current AFDC Work Programs and Implications for Federal Policy* (Washington, D.C. 1987) contains essential background material, as does the summary of the workfare programs on which the legislation is based, Judith M. Gueron's *Reforming Welfare With Work* (New York: The Ford Foundation, 1987). Finally, for a historical review of work programs from the New Deal to Family Support Act, see Nancy Rose, "From the WPA to Workfare: It's Time for a Truly Progressive Government Work Program," *Journal for Progressive Human Services* 1 (2): 17–42 (1990).

17. Congressional Budget Office, *Work and Welfare: The Family Support Act of 1988*, p. 56; Ann Nichols-Casebolt and Marieka Klawitter, "Child Support Enforcement Reform: Can It Reduce the Welfare Dependency of Never-Married Mothers," *Journal of Sociology and Social Welfare* 17 (3): 23–54 (September 1990); and Becky Glass, "Child Support Enforcement: An Implementation Analysis," *Social Service Review* 64 (4): 542–58, esp. p. 555 (December 1990).

18. Gueron, *Reforming Welfare with Work*, pp. 24–27.

19. The first Moynihan quote appears in the *Congressional Record*, 133:120 (21 July 1987), p. S10403; the second is from a 2 July 1987 document circulated

by Moynihan's office. The *New York Times* discusses the bill in its editorial, "Give Welfare Consensus a Chance," 27 July 1987. The *Fortune* quote comes from Monci Jo Williams, "Is Workfare the Answer?" *Fortune* 114(9): 105–12 (27 October 1986). All are cited in Block and Noakes, "The Politics of the New-Style Workfare," p. 31.

20. Block and Noakes, "The Politics of the New-Style Workfare," p. 45.

21. These totals are annualized figures calculated from Chart 2 in Gueron, *Reforming Welfare with Work*, pp. 24–27.

22. See Karger and Stoecz; "Welfare Reform: Maximum Feasible Exaggeration," p. 25.

23. For a discussion of the U.S. labor needs, see The National Alliance of Business, *Employment Policies: Looking to the Year 2000* (Washington, D.C. 1986) and The Hudson Institute, *Workforce 2000: Work and Workers For The 21st Century* (Indianapolis, Ind., 1987).

24. National Alliance of Business, *Employment Policies: Looking Toward the Year 2000*, p. 8.

25. Abramovitz, *Regulating the Lives of Women*, pp. 370–71.

26. Howard Goldman and Antoinette Gattozzi, "Murder in the Cathedral Revisited: President Reagan and the Mentally Disabled," *Hospital and Community Psychiatry* 39 (5):507.

27. See Ibid., pp. 505–509; U.S., General Accounting Office, *Homelessness: A Complex Problem and the Federal Response* (Washington, D.C., 1985); Paul Applebaum, "Housing for the Mentally Ill: The Unexpected Outcome of a Class-Action Suit Against SSA," *Hospital and Community Psychiatry* 39 (5): 479–80.

28. U.S., Committee on Ways and Means, *1991 Background Material*, pp. 63 Table 10, and p. 752, Table 12.

29. U.S., General Accounting Office, *Homelessness: A Complex Problem and the Federal Response*, p. 23, citing U.S. Conference of Mayors, "Homelessness in America's Cities: Ten Case Studies," June 1984, pp. 6–7, 26, 30, 36.

30. Kim Hopper and Jill Hamberg, "The Making of America's Homeless: From Skid Row to New Poor, 1945–1984" in *Critical Perspectives on Housing*, ed. Rachel Bratt, Chester Hartman, and Ann Meyerson (Philadelphia: Temple University Press, 1986), p. 27. Mentally disabled people have an even higher representation in the SSI program, where they also absorbed a disproportionate share of the cuts. See Goldman and Gattozzi, "Murder in the Cathedral Revisited: President Reagan and the Mentally Disabled," p. 506.

31. Children's Defense Fund, *A Children's Defense Budget* (Washington, D.C. 1986), pp. 182–83, cited in The National Coalition for the Homeless, *National Neglect/National Shame—America's Homeless: Outlook—Winter, 1986–1987*, p. 53.

32. U.S., Committee on Ways and Means, *1991 Background Material*, p. 1120, Table 8.

33. U.S. Conference of Mayors, *A Status Report on Hunger and Homelessness in America's Cities: 1990* (Washington, D.C., 1990), p. 7.

34. Isaac Shapiro and Marion E. Nichols, *Unprotected: Unemployment Insurance and Jobless Workers in 1988* (Washington, D.C.: Center on Budget and Policy Priorities, 1989), pp. 1–2; David Ellwood, *Poor Support* (New York: Basic Books, Inc., 1988), p. 102; David E. Rosenbaum, "Unemployment Insurance Aiding Fewer Workers," *New York Times*, 2 December 1990.

35. Shapiro and Nichols, *Unprotected: Unemployment Insurance and Jobless Workers in 1988*, pp. 3–4.

36. Ibid., pp. 6–7.

37. Ibid., p. 4.

38. U.S., Committee on Ways and Means, *1991 Background Material*, pp. 483–484; Rebecca M. Blank and Alan S. Blinder, "Macroeconomics, Income Distribution, and Poverty," in *Fighting Poverty: What Works and What Doesn't*, ed. Sheldon Danziger and Daniel Weinberg, (Cambridge: Harvard University Press, 1986), pp. 181–208, esp. p. 192.

39. Shapiro and Nichols, *Unprotected: Unemployment Insurance and Jobless Workers in 1988*, p. 18; David E. Rosenbaum, "Unemployment Insurance," *New York Times*, 2 December 1990.

40. U.S., Committee on Ways and Means, 1991 *Background Material*, p. 487.

Chapter 5

1. U.S. Congress, House Committee on Ways and Means, *1991 Background Material and Data on Programs within the Jurisdiction of the Committee on Ways and Means*, p. 1444, Table 24, and U.S., Department of Commerce, *Statistical Abstract of the United States, 1989* (Washington, D.C.: Government Printing Office, 1989), p. 45, Table 58.

2. For recent data on Britain, see Steve Schifferes, "The Dilemmas of British Housing Policy," in *Critical Perspectives on Housing*, ed. Rachel Bratt, Chester Hartman, and Ann Meyerson (Philadelphia: Temple University Press, 1986), p. 514; for France, see Kenneth T. Jackson, *Crabgrass Frontier* (New York: Oxford University Press, 1985), p. 224; and for Sweden, see Mats Forsberg, *The Evolution of Social Welfare Policy in Sweden* (Sweden: The Swedish Institute, 1984), p. 39.

3. John Gilderbloom and Richard Applebaum, *Rethinking Rental Housing* (Philadelphia: Temple University Press, 1988), p. 37.

4. Jackson, *Crabgrass Frontier*, p. 7.

5. Apgar and Brown, *The State of the Nation's Housing, 1988*, p. 12; Associated Press, "Census Study Finds Drop in Homeownership," *New York Times*, 16 June 1991.

6. Ibid.

7. Peter Marcuse, "The Myth of the Benevolent State," in *Critical Perspectives on Housing*, p. 261.

8. See Michael Stone, "Housing and the Dynamics of U.S. Capitalism," in *Critical Perspectives on Housing*, pp. 41–67.

9. Ibid., p. 50.

10. Ibid. and Ann Meyerson, "Deregulation and the Restructuring of the Housing Finance System," in *Critical Perspectives on Housing*, p. 71; and Edwin Amenta and Theda S. Skocpol, "Redefining the New Deal: World War II and the Development of Social Provision in the United States," in *The Politics of Social Policy in the United States*, ed. Margaret Weir, Ann Shola Orloff, and Theda Skocpol (Princeton, N.J.: Princeton University Press, 1988), p. 85; and U.S., Congressional Budget Office, *The Housing Finance System and Federal Policy: Recent Changes and Options for the Future* (Washington, D.C., 1983).

11. Jackson, *Crabgrass Frontier*, p. 238; Barry Checkoway, "Large Builders, Federal Housing Programs, and Postwar Suburbanization," in *Critical Perspectives on Housing*, p. 125.

12. See Alan Wolfe, *America's Impasse: The Rise and Fall of the Politics of Growth*

(Boston: South End Press, 1981), pp. 84–88, 95–100, and Citizens Commission on Civil Rights, "The Federal Government and Equal Housing Opportunity: A Continuing Failure," in *Critical Perspectives on Housing*, p. 300.

13. See "Adding Up the Tax Breaks," *Dollars & Sense*, no. 140, October 1988, p. 23; U.S., Congressional Budget Office, *Tax Expenditures: Current Issues and Five Year Budget Projects for Fiscal Years 1984–1988* (Washington, D.C., 1983); U.S., Joint Committee on Taxation, *Estimates of Federal Tax Expenditures for Fiscal Years 1989–1993* (Washington, D.C.: Government Printing Office, 1988).

14. Ibid., p. 12; Low Income Housing Information Service, *The 1990 Low Income Housing Budget* (Washington, D.C., 1989).

15. Robert Kuttner, "Bad Housekeeping," *New Republic*, 25 April 1988, p. 25; The National Low Income Housing Coalition, *Homelessness and the Low Income Housing Crisis* (Washington, D.C., 1987), p. 5.

16. Kenneth Jackson writes of this triangle as it involves the process of suburbanization, but the concept may also be applied more broadly—see *Crabgrass Frontier*, p. 216.

17. Roy Lubove, *The Progressives and the Slums* (Pittsburgh: University of Pittsburgh Press, 1962), p. 104.

18. See Ibid., p. 9; Edward Spann, *The New Metropolis* (New York: Columbia University Press, 1981), pp. 142–45; and Michael Katz, *In the Shadow of the Poorhouse* (New York: Basic Books, 1986), pp. 171–73.

19. Katz, *In the Shadow of the Poorhouse*, pp. 171–74; Jackson, *Crabgrass Frontier*, pp. 219–21; James Patterson, *America's Struggle Against Poverty* (Cambridge: Harvard University Press, 1981), p. 33.

20. Rachel Bratt, "Public Housing: The Controversy and Contribution," in *Critical Perspectives on Housing*, pp. 336–37, and Jackson, *Crabgrass Frontier*, pp. 224–25.

21. John Ehrenreich, *The Altruistic Imagination: A History of Social Work and Social Policy in the United States* (Ithaca, N.Y.: Cornell University Press, 1985), p. 144; Wolfe, *America's Impasse*, pp. 84–85; Jackson, *Crabgrass Frontier*, p. 227.

22. Helene Slessarev, "Racial Tension and Institutional Support: Social Programs during a Period of Retrenchment," in *The Politics of Social Policy in the United States*, pp. 362–73; Kuttner, "Bad Housekeeping," pp. 23–24.

23. Kuttner, "Bad Housekeeping," p. 24.

24. U.S., Congressional Budget Office, *Federal Subsidies for Public Housing: Issues and Options* (Washington, D.C., 1983), pp. 15–16.

25. Clay, *At Risk of Loss*, p. 15.

26. *Report of the President's Commission on Housing* (Washington, D.C.: Government Printing Office, 1982); U.S., General Accounting Office, *Evaluation of Alternatives for Financing Low and Moderate Income Rental Housing* (Washington, D.C., 1980), p. 113; and Urban Systems Engineering and Research, Inc., *The Costs of HUD Multifamily Housing Programs* (Washington, D.C.: Government Printing Office, 1982), all cited in Bratt, "Public Housing: The Controversy and Contribution," pp. 350–53.

27. National Housing Task Force, *A Decent Place to Live* (Washington, D.C., 1988), p. 6.

28. For a more positive view, see Peter Salins, "Toward a Permanent Housing Problem," *The Public Interest*, no. 85, Fall 1986, pp. 22–33.

29. See, for example, Anthony Downs, *Rental Housing in the 1980s* (Washington, D.C.: Brookings Institute, 1983).

30. See Kenneth Baar, "Guidelines for Drafting Rent Control Laws: Lessons of a Decade," *Rutgers Law Review* 35 (4): 721–85 (1983), and Kenneth Baar, "Facts and Fallacies in the Rental Housing Market," *Western City*, September 1986, pp. 47–86, both as cited in Gilderbloom and Applebaum, *Rethinking Rental Housing*, p. 127.

31. Gilderbloom and Applebaum, *Rethinking Rental Housing*, pp. 128–29.

32. See William Tucker, "Where Do the Homeless Come From?," Manhattan Institute for Policy Research Associates Memo, no. 5, 20 November 1987; "Where Do the Homeless Come From?" *National Review* 39 (18): 32–43 (25 September 1987); and *New York Times*, 14 November 1987. Tucker's book, *The Excluded Americans: Homelessness and Housing Policy* (Chicago: Regnery Gateway, 1990), presents a full treatment of his data.

33. See Tucker, "Where Do the Homeless Come From?," *National Review*, p. 41.

34. See the insightful critique by Richard Appelbaum et al., "Scapegoating Rent Control: Masking the Causes of Homelessness," Economic Policy Institute Briefing Paper, October 1989; as well as John Atlas and Peter Dreier, "The Phony Case Against Rent Control," *Progressive* 53 (4):26–31 (April 1989).

35. See Appelbaum et al., "Scapegoating Rent Control: Masking the Causes of Homelessness," pp. 9–10.

36. *Report of the President's Commission on Housing* as cited in Chester Hartman, "Housing Policies Under the Reagan Administration," in *Critical Perspectives on Housing*, p. 363.

37. Paul Leonard, Cushing N. Dolbeare, and Edward B. Lazere, *A Place To Call Home: The Crisis in Housing for the Poor* (Washington, D.C.: Center on Budget and Policy Priorities, 1989), p. 28; "Reagan Condemns Public Housing," *Dollars and Sense*, no. 86, April 1983, pp. 12–15.

38. See, for example, *William* Tucker, "Where Do the Homeless Come From?" *National Review*, p. 32; Robert C. Ellickson, "The Homelessness Muddle," *The Public Interest*, no. 99, Spring 1990, pp. 45–60.

39. Leonard, Dolbeare, and Lazere, *A Place to Call Home: The Crisis in Housing for the Poor*, p. 29.

40. National Housing Task Force, *A Decent Place to Live*, p. 6.

41. Anthony DePalma, "Are Rent Vouchers a Boon or a Bust?" *New York Times*, 1 November 1987, and Michael Winerip, "In New York, H.U.D. Vouchers Pay for Already Cheap Housing," *New York Times*, 31 December 1989. The latter article explains that because vouchers are so hard to use in New York City, they have been given to some very poor families who are already subsidized. As a result, these families have had to pay little or no rent.

42. L. J. Davis, "Chronicle of A Debacle Foretold: How Deregulation Begat the S & L Scandal," *Harper's* 281 (1684): 50–66 (September 1990); Ann Meyerson, "Deregulation and the Restructuring of the Housing Finance System," in *Critical Perspectives on Housing*, pp. 68–98, esp. pp 70–74.

43. See Gilderbloom and Applebaum, *Rethinking Rental Housing*, pp. 80–82; National Housing Task Force, *A Decent Place to Live*, pp. 39–43; Clay, *At Risk of Loss: The Endangered Future of Low-Income Rental Housing Resources*, pp. 23–27

44. National Coalition for the Homeless, "Kemp Announces Reforms HUD Reforms in the Face of Scandal," *Safety Network* 8(11): 2 (November 1989).

45. Bob Eleff, "Proposed Housing Plan Commits Few Resources," *In These Times*, 2–8 May 1990, p. 7; Center for Budget and Policy Priorities, *The Bush*

Administration Budget: Rhetoric and Reality (Washington, D.C., 1990), and *One Step Forward: The Deficit Reduction Package of 1990* (Washington, D.C. 1990), p. 35; Low Income Housing Information Service, *Roundup*, no. 137, November 1990.

46. William Apgar, *The Declining Supply of Low Income Housing* (Cambridge,: Joint Center for Housing Studies of the Massachusetts Institute of Technology and Harvard, 1987), p. 2.

47. Leonard, Dolbeare, and Lazere, *A Place to Call Home*, p. 16.

48. Center on Budget and Policy Priorities, *Holes in the Safety Net: Poverty Programs and Policies in the States* (Washington, D.C., 1988), p. 31.

49. Leonard, Dolbeare, and Lazere, *A Place to Call Home*, p. 27.

50. Apgar, *The Declining Supply of Low Income Housing*, p. 9.

51. Gilderbloom and Applebaum, *Rethinking Rental Housing*, p. 48.

52. Apgar, *The Declining Supply of Low-Income Housing*, p. 15.

53. Teresa Riordan, "Housekeeping at HUD," *Common Cause Magazine*, March/April 1987, p. 27.

54. The national total comes from the U.S., Congress, House Committee on Government Operations, *The Federal Response to the Homeless Crisis, Third Report*, 18 April 1985, p. 3, as cited in S. Anna Kondratas, *A Strategy for Helping America's Homeless*, Heritage Foundation Backgrounder, no. 431, p. 8. The Phoenix number appears in Todd Bensman, "Reaching Out to Help the Homeless," *Scottsdale Progress Saturday Magazine*, 26 March 1988; the other data is cited in "Help for the Homeless," *Newsweek*, 11 April 1988. For a good summary of this issue, see Philip Kasinitz, "Gentrification and Homelessness: The Single Room Occupant and the Inner City Revival," in *Housing the Homeless*, ed. Jon Erickson and Charles Wilhelm, (Rutgers, N.J.: Center for Urban Policy Research, 1986), pp. 241–52.

55. Thomas Lueck, "Federally Subsidized Housing At Risk," *New York Times*, 1 April 1990.

56. See Leonard, Dolbeare, and Lazere, *A Place to Call Home*, pp. 38–39. This issue is also discussed, albeit with slightly different numbers, in National Housing Task Force, *A Decent Place to Live*, p. 33; and Clay, *At Risk of Loss: The Endangered Future of Low-Income Rental Housing*, pp. 7–13. The $7.7 billion figure is cited in the summary of HUD Appropriations and the 1991 Budget Agreement by the Low Income Housing Information Service, *Roundup*, no. 137, November 1990.

57. Clay, *At Risk of Loss: The Endangered Future of Low-Income Rental Housing Resources.*

Chapter 6

1. See S. Anna Kondratas, *A Strategy for Helping America's Homeless* (Washington, D.C.: The Heritage Foundation, 1985), reprinted in Jon Erickson and Charles Wilhelm, eds., *Housing the Homeless* (New Brunswick, N.J.: Center for Urban Policy Research, 1986), pp. 144–49; Myron Magnet, "The Homeless," *Fortune* 116 (12): 170–89 (23 November 1987); Myron Magnet, "Homelessness: Craziness, Dope and Danger," *New York Times*, 26 January 1990; and Joseph Perkins, "New Institutions for the Homeless," *Wall Street Journal*, 26 February 1985.

2. For the Philadelphia data, see A. Anthony Arce, Marilyn Tadlock, Michael J. Vergare, and Stuart Shapiro, "A Psychiatric Profile of Street People Admitted to an Emergency Shelter," *Hospital and Community Psychiatry* 34 (9):

812–16 (September 1983); for Boston, see Ellen Bassuk, "The Homelessness Problem," *Scientific American* 251 (1): 40–45 (July 1984); and, for New York, see Frank R. Lipton, Albert Sabatini, and Steven E. Katz, "Down and Out in the City: The Homeless Mentally Ill," *Hospital and Community Psychiatry* 34 (9): 817–21.

3. American Psychiatric Association, *Desk Reference to the Diagnostic and Statistical Manual, III-R* (Washington, D.C., 1987), p. 115.

4. See, for example, William Breakey et al., "Health and Mental Health Problems of Homeless Men and Women in Baltimore," *Journal of the American Medical Association* 262 (10): 1352–357; Leona Bachrach, "The Homeless Mentally Ill and Mental Health Services: An Analytic Review of the Literature," Alcohol, Drug Abuse, and Mental Health Administration, U.S., Department of Health and Human Services, 1984, and "Interpreting Research on the Homeless Mentally Ill: Some Caveats," *Hospital and Community Psychiatry* 35 (9): 914–16; Irene Shifren Levine and James Stockdill, "Mentally Ill and Homeless: A National Problem," in *Treating the Homeless: Urban Psychiatry's Challenge*, ed. Billy E. Jones, (Washington, D.C.: American Psychiatric Press, 1986), pp. 1–16; and Carol Mowbray, "Homelessness in America: Myths and Realities," *American Journal of Orthopsychiatry* 55 (1): 4–8.

5. David Snow, Susan Baker, Leon Anderson, and Michael Martin, "The Myth of Pervasive Mental Illness Among the Homeless," *Social Problems* 33 (5): 407–23; quote from pp. 412–13.

6. Paul Koegel, *Ethnographic Perspectives on Homeless and Homeless Mentally Ill Women*, Proceedings of a Two-Day Workshop Sponsored by the Division of Education and Service System Liaison, National Institute of Mental Health, 30–31 October 1986

7. See Howard Goldman, Neal Adams, and Carl Taube, "Deinstitutionalization: The Data Demythologized," *Hospital and Community Psychiatry* 34 (2): 129–34, 220.

8. The periods described are not the same as those listed in Howard Goldman and Joseph Morrisey, "The Alchemy of Mental Health Policy: Homelessness and the Fourth Cycle of Reform," *American Journal of Public Health* 75 (7): 727–30, though the article does influence my overall treatment of this history.

9. David Rothman, *The Discovery of the Asylum* (Boston: Little, Brown, 1971), esp. pp. 114–15.

10. See ibid., pp. 237–64, and Michael Katz, *In the Shadow of the Poorhouse* (New York: Basic Books, 1986), p. 101.

11. See Gerald Grob, *Mental Illness and American Society, 1875–1940* (Princeton, N.J.: Princeton University Press, 1983).

12. E. Fuller Torrey, *Nowhere To Go: The Tragic Odyssey of the Homeless Mentally Ill* (New York: Harper and Row, 1988), pp. 39–50.

13. Ibid., pp. 39, 51.

14. For this history of the introduction of psychotropic medicine into New York State, see Daniel P. Moynihan's recollections in his senatorial newsletter, *Letter to New York*, 10 March 1989, and in "Promise to the Mentally Ill Has Not Been Kept," letter to *New York Times*, 22 May 1989.

15. Tim Golden, "Ill, Possibly Violent, and No Place to Go," *New York Times*, 2 April 1990; Kevin Sack, "Crossroads in Mental Health: Red Ink and Unused Wards," *New York Times*, 19 February 1991.

16. For a discussion of the marketing of chlorpromazine, see Ann Braden

Johnson, *Out of Bedlam* (New York: Basic Books, 1990), pp. 38–52, and Judith P. Swazey, *Chlorpromazine in Psychiatry: A Study in Therapeutic Innovation* (Cambridge, Mass.: MIT Press, 1974).

17. Johnson, *Out of Bedlam*, p. 47; Stephen M. Rose, "Deciphering Deinstitutionalization: Complexities in Policy and Program Analysis," Milbank Memorial Fund Quarterly *Health and Society* 57 (4): 429–60, esp. p. 443; David Cohen, "Good Intentions Are Not Enough," *Social Service Review* 63 (4): 660–64 (December 1989).

18. Torrey, *Nowhere to Go*, pp. 145–46.

19. H. Richard Lamb, "Deinstitutionalization and the Homeless Mentally Ill," *Hospital and Community Psychiatry* 35 (9): 899–907.

20. Majorie Hope and James Young, "From Backwards to Back Alleys: Deinstitutionalization," *Urban and Social Change Review* 17 (2): 7–11 (1984); Torrey, *Nowhere to Go*, p. 224.

21. Torrey, *Nowhere to Go*, pp. 151–52.

22. See Jerome Goldsmith, *Final Report of the Governor's Select Commission on the Future of the State-Local Mental Health System* (Albany, N.Y., 1984), p. 5, and Kathyrn Moss, "Institutional Reform Through Litigation," *Social Service Review* 58 (3): 421–33.

23. Torrey, *Nowhere to Go*, p. 155. For a discussion of the political difficulties associated with closing one rural mental hospital, see Sack, "Crossroads in Mental Health: Red Ink and Unused Wards."

24. See Bert Pepper and Hilary Ryglewicz, "The Role of the State Hospital: A New Mandate for a New Era," *Psychiatric Quarterly* 57 (3 & 4): 230–51; Leona Bachrach, "Young Adult Chronic Patients: An Analytic Review of the Literature," *Hospital and Community Psychiatry* 33 (3): 189–97 (March 1982); H. Richard Lamb, "Young Adult Chronic Patients: The New Drifters," *Hospital and Community Psychiatry* 33: 465–68 (June, 1982).

25. Quoted in Goldsmith, *Final Report of the Governor's Select Commission on the Future of the State-Local Mental Health System*, pp. 5–6; see also Alan D. Miller, "Deinstitutionalization in Retrospect," *Psychiatric Quarterly* 57 (3 & 4): 160–71 (Fall/Winter 1985).

26. Goldsmith, *Final Report of the Governor's Select Commission on the Future of the State-Local Mental Health System*, p. 6.

27. For Ohio, see the Bureau of Statistics, Ohio Department of Mental Health, *Annual Report Fiscal Year 1982*, p. 26, cited in Dan Salerno, Kim Hopper, and Ellen Baxter, *Hardship in the Heartland: Homelessness in Eight U.S. Cities* (New York: Community Service Society, 1984), p. 93; for Massachusetts, see Raymond Flynn, *Dignity & Respect: Making Room for Boston's Homeless*, (Boston: City of Boston, 1987/88), p. v; for the other states, see Torrey, *Nowhere to Go*, pp. 139–40.

28. Howard Goldman, Neal Adams, and Carl Taube, "Deinstitutionalization: The Data Demythologized," *Hospital and Community Psychiatry* 34 (2): 129–34 (February 1983).

29. Ibid., p. 133.

30. Howard Goldman, A. Gattozzi, and Carle Taube, "Defining and Counting the Chronically Mentally Ill," *Hospital and Community Psychiatry* 32: 21–27, and Howard Goldman, *Long-term Care for the Chronically Mentally Ill* (Washington, D.C.: Urban Institute Working Paper, 1981), cited in Goldman and Morrisey, "The Alchemy of Mental Health Policy and the Fourth Cycle of Reform," p. 728.

31. Goldman, Adams, and Taube, "Deinstitutionalization: The Data Demythologized," p. 130; Pepper and Ryglewicz, "The Role of the State Hospital: A New Mandate for a New Era," p. 236.

32. National Institute of Mental Health; Alcohol, Drug Abuse, and Mental Health Administration; and the U.S., Department of Health and Human Services, *Deinstitutionalization Policy and Homelessness: A Report to Congress*, 1990.

33. Snow et al., "The Myth of Pervasive Mental Illness Among the Homeless," p. 420.

34. Steven Segal, Jim Baumol, and Elsie Johnson, "Mental Disorder and Social Margin in a Young Vagrant Population," *Social Problems* 24 (3): 387–401 (1977); Ohio Department of Mental Health, *Homelessness in Ohio: A Study of People in Need* (Columbus, Ohio, 1985), p. 113.

35. See the chart in Institute of Medicine, *Homelessness, Health, and Human Needs* (Washington, D.C.: National Academy Press, 1988), p. 52.

36. For an analysis from this perspective, see Donald Lindhorst, "A Redefinition of the Problem of Homelessness Among Persons with a Chronic Mental Illness," *Journal of Sociology and Social Welfare* 17 (4): 43–56 (December 1990).

37. William Fisher, Glenn Pierce, and Paul Applebaum, "How Flexible Are Our Civil Commitment Statutes?" *Hospital and Community Psychiatry* 39 (7): 711–12 (July 1988); Ron Sullivan, "Ferry Slashing Report Assails Hospital for Freeing Suspect," *New York Times*, 12 July 1986, and "State Faults Ferry Suspect's Release," *New York Times*, 19 July 1986; Jeanie Kasindorf, "The Real Life Story of Billy Boggs," *New York Magazine*, 2 May 1988, pp. 36–44; "Joyce Brown Released From Bellevue," *New York Civil Liberties Union* 36 (2): 1 (March 1988).

38. Daniel Goleman, "States Move to Ease Law Committing Mentally Ill," *New York Times*, 9 December 1986.

39. Katz, *In the Shadow of the Poorhouse*, pp. 99–103; Rothman, *The Discovery of the Asylum*, pp. 283–87.

40. Goleman, "States Move to Ease Law Committing Mentally Ill."

41. American Psychiatric Association, *Task Force on the Homeless Mentally Ill* (Washington, D.C., 1984), pp. 5–14.

Chapter 7

1. For the information about efforts to organize the homeless, see the Right to Housing Report, 1 (1): update A, (September 1986), cited in Peter Marcuse, "Neutralizing Homelessness," *Socialist Review* 88 (1): 69–96, 80–81; Sara Rimer, "Homeless Organize to Fight for Themselves," *New York Times*, 26 January 1989; and Kim Hopper, "Advocacy for the Homeless in the 1980s," in *Homelessness in America*, ed. Carol Caton, (New York: Oxford University Press, 1990), pp. 160–73.

2. Katharine Bishop, "Tent Cities Becoming the Front Lines," *New York Times*, 11 September 1989; Richard H. Ropers, *The Invisible Homeless: A New Urban Ecology* (New York: Human Sciences Press, 1988), pp. 199–208; Sarah Ferguson, "Tent City Blues," *Mother Jones* September/October 1990, pp. 29–30; David Wagner and Marcia Cohen, *Preliminary Report on Tent City Research Project* (Portland, Maine, 1990).

3. The Conference Board, *Community Affairs: 1987–1990*, no. 9, December 1987, cited in Interagency Council on the Homeless, *A Nation Concerned: A Report*

to the President and the Congress On the Response to Homelessness in America (Washington, D.C., 1988), p. 2–27.

4. For a more positive view of Hands Across America, see Lynn Stolarski, "Right to Shelter: History of the Mobilization of the Homeless as a Model of Voluntary Action," *Journal of Voluntary Action Research* 17 (1): 36–43 (1988).

5. See, for example, Anthony Oberschall, *Social Conflict and Social Movements* (Englewood Cliffs, N.J.: Prentice-Hall, 1973); Charles Tilly, *From Mobilization to Revolution* (Reading, Mass.: Addison-Wesley, 1978); William Gamson, *The Strategy of Social Protest* (Homewood, Ill.: Dorsey, 1975); John McCarthy and Mayer Zald, "Resource Mobilization and Social Movements: A Partial Theory," *American Journal of Sociology* 82 (6): 1212–241; and a collection of their essays, *Social Movements in an Organizational Society* (New Brunswick, N.J.: Transaction Books, 1987). For an insightful analysis of these essays that raises some important questions about their work, see the book review by Stanley Wenocur in *Social Service Review* 63 (2): 324–27 (June 1989). Lastly, for an entirely different perspective that is critical of McCarthy and Zald, see Daniel A. Foss and Ralph Larkin, *Beyond Revolution: A New Theory of Social Movement* (New York: Bergin & Garvey, 1986).

6. McCarthy and Zald, "Resource Mobilization and Social Movements: A Partial Theory," p. 1222.

7. Sara Nelson, "The Homeless Avant-Garde," *7 Days* 2 (40): 29–34 (18 October 1989).

8. "Statewide Homeless Coalitions Spreading," *Safety Network*, December 1990/January 1991; p. 4. Coalitions were also forming in six other states—Alabama, Michigan, New Mexico, Oklahoma, Wisconsin, and Wyoming.

9. See Heron Marquez Estrada, "Homeless Advocate Sees Self as 'Mom'," *Santa Barbara News-Press*, 25 December 1989.

10. Todd Bensman, "Reaching Out A Helping Hand to the Homeless," *Scottsdale Progress/Saturday Magazine*, 26 March 1988; Carol Sowers and Jacquee G. Petchel, "National Leader Quits Valley Homeless Panel Over Police Screening," *Arizona Republic*, 25 March 1987.

11. See Steven Brill, "Attorney for the Defenseless," *Esquire* 102 (6): 245–48 (December 1984); and Christine Robitscher Ladd, "A Right to Shelter for the Homeless in New York State," *New York University Law Review* 61: 272–99, esp. p. 295.

12. *Callahan et al.* v. *Carey et al*, No. 42582/79, Supreme Court of the State of New York, p. 3

13. "Nor do state and city officials offer one iota of proof that the Men's Shelter on the Bowery or its satellite 'hotels' are sufficient to house all of the destitute and homeless alcoholics, addicts, mentally impaired derelicts, flotsam and jetsam, and others during the winter months" (*Callahan* et al. v. *Carey* et al. *New York Law Journal*, 11 December 1979, p. 11, col. 4, cited in Robert Hayes, "Litigating on Behalf of Shelter for the Poor," *Harvard Civil Rights-Civil Liberties Law Review* 22: 79–93, 81).

14. Coalition of the Homeless, *Safety Network*, January 1985; Joe Calderone, "City: Cut Showers, Toilets," *New York Newsday*, 8 November 1985.

15. Suzanne Daley, "Record Number Given Housing in City Shelters," *New York Times*, 27 January 1987.

16. In "Litigating on Behalf of Shelter for the Poor," 22:79, Robert Hayes writes of outgrowing his conception that the litigator appeals to philosopher-

kings. More generally, a good summary of the problems legal advocates face is contained in Kim Hopper and L. Stuart Cox, "Litigation in Advocacy for the Homeless: The Case of New York City," in *Housing the Homeless*, ed. Jon Erickson and Charles Wilhelm (Rutgers, N.J.: Center for Urban Policy, 1986), pp. 303–14.

17. There is, of course, a vigorous debate about the whole concept of rights. Some of the most useful literature includes Paul Brest, "The Fundamental Rights Controversy: The Essential Contradictions of Normative Constitutional Scholarship," *Yale Law Journal* 90: 1063–109; John Rawls, *A Theory of Justice* (New York: Oxford University Press, 1971); Bruce Ackerman, *Social Justice in the Liberal State* (New Haven, Conn.: Yale University Press, 1980); Ronald Dworkin, *Taking Rights Seriously* (London: Duckworth, 1977); Samuel Bowles and Herbert Gintis, *Democracy and Capitalism: Property, Community, and the Contradictions of Modern Social Thought* (New York: Basic Books, 1987); and Jerome Waldron, ed., *Nonsense About Stilts: Bentham, Burke and Marx on the Rights of Man* (New York: Methuen, 1987).

18. Donald Horowitz, *The Courts and Social Policy* (Washington, D.C.: The Brooking Institution, 1977), p. 298.

19. Ibid., p. 18.

20. There is a considerable literature on the concept of "relative autonomy." Its most famous European expression is probably Nicos Poulantzas, *State, Power, and Socialism* (London: New Left Books, 1978), but in the United States, the concept has been most highly developed by Theda Skocpol and Fred Block. For some of Skocpol's work, see her book, edited with Margaret Weir and Ann Shola Orloff, *The Politics of Social Policy in the United States* (Princeton, N.J.: Princeton University Press, 1988); or another jointly edited volume, with Peter Evans and Dietrich Rueschemeger, *Bringing the State Back In* (New York: Cambridge University Press, 1985). Fred Block's essays are collected in *Revising State Theory* (Philadelphia: Temple University Press, 1987). For an example of the theory's specific application to the law, see Thomas Kleven, "The Relative Autonomy of the United States Supreme Court," *Yale Journal of Law and Liberation* 1(1): 43–66 (Fall 1989).

21. *Lindsey v. Normet*, 405 U.S. 56, is cited on p. 944, footnote 23 in Geoffrey Mort, "Establishing a Right to Shelter for the Homeless," *Brooklyn Law Review* 50:939–94; *Lavine v. Milne*, 424 U.S. 577 is cited on p. 60, footnote 242 in Peter Edelman, "The Next Century of Our Constitution: Rethinking Our Duty to the Poor," *Hastings Law Journal* 39 (1): 1–61; *Rosado v. Wyman*, 397 U.S. 397, is discussed on p. 273 in Michael Sosin, "Legal Rights and Welfare Change," in *Fighting Poverty*, ed. Sheldon Danziger and Daniel H. Weinberger (Cambridge: Harvard University Press, 1986), p.260–86; and *Dandridge v. Williams*, 397 U.S. 471 is analyzed in both Edelman, "The Next Century," p. 38 and on p. 270 in Rand E. Rosenblatt, "Legal Entitlement and Welfare Benefits," in *The Politics of the Law: A Progressive Critique*, ed. David Kairys (New York: Pantheon Books, 1982), pp. 262–78.

22. Legal advocates sued the New York City Metropolitan Transit Authority when the agency sought to outlaw begging in the subways. While victorious in federal district court, their claim to commercial free speech was overturned on appeal, a decision affirmed by the refusal of the U.S. Supreme Court to hear the case. Miami and Seattle have similar ordinances. See Linda Greenhouse,

"Ban Is Left Intact on Subway Begging," *New York Times*, 27 November 1990, and Ronald Smothers, "Atlanta Mayor Calls for Crackdown on Begging," *New York Times* 13 June 1991.

Right to vote cases have usually been successful. They include Santa Barbara, Calif. (*Collier* v. *Menzel*, 221 Calif. Rptr 110; 176 Calif. App. 3d 24); Connecticut (by letter of the secretary of state to Shirley Bergert, Neighborhood Legal Services, Hartford, Connecticut, 28 July 1986); The District of Columbia (*In Re Applications for Voter Registration of Willie Jenkins et al. Before the D.C. Board of Elections and Ethics*; the board reversed itself and granted the right to vote to homeless people who designate a shelter as their mailing address); Illinois (*Board of Election Commissioners* v. *Chicago/Gary Area Union of the Homeless*, No. 86–29, Ill. Cir. 26 September 1986); New York (*Pitts* v. *Black*, S.D. N.Y. 10 October 1984); and Pennsylvania (*Committee for Dignity and Fairness for the Homeless* v. *Tartaglinoe*, No. 84–3447, E. D. Pa. order and decree 14 September 1986).

Suits about sleeping in public have met with mixed results. Legal advocates won in Louisiana (*Thompson* v. *City of New Orleans*, No. 85–5475, E.D. La. 12 May 1986), but they lost in California (*Davenport* v. *People of the State of California*, No. 85–6171, Cal. Super. Ct. 1985), Georgia (*State of Georgia* v. *Davis*), and Oregon (*United States* v. *Martin*, No. 88–848-MA, Oregon Distr. Ct. filed 28 July 1988). Ironically, in both the Georgia and Oregon cases, homeless people were ordered to leave vacant low-income housing buildings on the grounds that they had occupied them illegally and were trespassing.

23. The National Housing Law Project, 1950 Addison Street, Berkeley, California 94704 publishes an annotated list of homelessness litigation that employs different categories, but summarizes the cases well.

24. *Martin* v. *Milwaukee County*, No. 656–770, Wisconsin Cir. Ct., 9 January 1985); *Turner* v. *City of New Orleans*, No. 878281, La Distr. Ct., dismissed 26 April 1989.

25. *Eisenheim* v. *Board of Supervisors of Los Angeles County*, No. C 479453, Cal. Super. Ct., 1984. The history and background of the Los Angeles cases are described in Gregory Goldin, "Gimme Shelter," *California Lawyer* 7 (5): 1–5 (May 1987); Alexander Stille, "Seeking Shelter in the Law," *National Law Journal*, 10 February 1987, pp. 1–4; and Gary Blasi, "Litigation on Behalf of the Homeless: Systematic Approaches," *Journal of Urban and Contemporary Law* 31: 137–42.

26. *Ross* v. *Board of Supervisors*, No. C 501603, filed Cal. Ct. App., 11 June 1984; *Paris* v. *Board of Supervisors*, No. C523361, Cal. Super. Ct., filed 20 November 1984. Stille, "Seeking Shelter in the Law," p. 2 offers a good description of the background to these cases.

27. *Bannister* v. *Board of Supervisors of Los Angeles County*, No. 535833; see Blasi, "Litigation on Behalf of the Homeless," p. 142.

28. For *Jiggetts* v. *Grinker*, see Kevin Sack, "New York Court Sets a Standard for Housing Aid," *New York Times*, 4 April 1990, and "NY Court Rules AFDC Housing Allowance Must Be Adequate," *Safety Network* 9 (5): 1–2 May 1990. If the court orders New York to pay 100 percent of the rents currently being paid by the state's 1.3 million welfare recipients, it would cost the state somewhere between $90 and $140 million. The amount would be twice as large if New York must pay "fair market" rents. See Kevin Sack, "Welfare Suit Could Hurt Cuomo Budget," *New York Times*, 7 February 1991.

At the same time, in *Poverty Resistance Center* v. *Hart*, the California Supreme

Court reached a similar decision; see the California Homeless Coalition, "Victory in Court," *Connections*, July 1990.

29. *Massachusetts Coalition for the Homeless* v. *Dukakis*, 400 Mass. 806.

30. Barbara Sard, "The Role of the Courts In Welfare Reform," *Clearinghouse Review* 22 (4): 367–88 (August–September 1988).

31. *Hansen* v. *McMahon* 193 Cal. App. 3d 283, 238 Cal. Rptr. 232 (Cal. App. 2d Distr., 1987); *In the Matter of Derek W. Burns*, 519 A. 2d 638 (Delaware, 1986); *In the Matter of G. et al.* (District of Columbia Super. Ct. filed 12 April 1982); *In re Annette W.*, No. 87–17975, Ill. Cir. Ct. 26 August 1988); *In the Interest of S.A.D.*, 555 A. 2d 123 (Penn. Super. Ct., 1989); and *Consentino* v. *Perales* 138 2d 212; 524 N.Y.S. 2d 121 (NY Supr. Ct., 1987) *appeal pending* N.Y. App. Div., 1989).

32. James K. Langdon and Mark A. Kass, "Homelessness in America: Looking for the Right to Shelter," *Columbia Journal of Law and Social Problems*, pp. 307, 332–33, and appendix with a detailed analysis of each state constitution. By contrast, Hayes, "Litigating on Behalf of Shelter for the Poor," p. 80, says that only two states, New York and Montana, have constitutions that impose a clear obligation to help the poor.

33. *Graham* v. *Schoemehl*, No. 854–00035 Consent Decree, Mo. Cir. Ct.; *Maticka* v. *Atlantic City* 524 A. 2d 416 (N.J. Super. Ct., App. Div., 1987); *Algor* v. *County of Ocean*, No. Am–388–85T5 (N.J. Super. Ct., 23 December 1985); *Lubetkin* v. *Hartford*, Conn. Super. Ct. filed 4 February 1984. For an analysis of why the Northeast shows a greater openness to reform, see Martin Shefter, "Regional Receptivity to Reform," *Political Science Quarterly* 98 (3): 459–83 (Fall 1983).

34. *Hodge* v. *Ginsberg*, 303 S.E. 2d 245 (West Virginia, 1983).

35. *Eldredge* v. *Koch* 118 Misc. 2d 163, 459 N.Y.S. 2d 960 (N.Y. Supr. Ct.); reversed in part, 98 A.D. 2d 675, 469 N.Y.S. 2d 744 (1st Department, 1983).

36. *McCain* v. *Koch* 70 N.Y. 2d 109, 510 N.E. 62, 517 N.Y.S. 2d 918 (1987), reversed in part, 117 A.D. 198, 502 N.Y.S. 2d 720, N.Y, App. Div., (1st Department, 1986).

37. *Tucker* v. *Toia*, 43 N.Y. 2d 1 (1977), p. 7, as cited in Christine Robitscher Ladd, "A Right to Shelter in New York State," *New York University Law Review* 61: 272–99, at p. 276, upon which this discussion draws.

38. *Bernstein* v. *Toia* 43 N.Y. 2d 437, 373 N.E. 2d 238, 402 N.Y.S. 2d 342 (1977); *RAM* v. *Blum*, 1032d 237, 425 N.Y.S. 735; 77 A.D. 2d 278, 432 N.Y.S. 2d 892 (1980). See the discussion in Ladd, "A Right to Shelter in New York State," pp. 275–81, and Edelman, "The Next Century of Our Constitution: Rethinking Our Duty to the Poor," pp. 59–60.

39. For example, Hayes, "Litigating on Behalf of Shelter for the Poor," pp. 88–89, and Sard, "The Role of the Courts in Welfare Reform," p. 67.

Chapter 8

1. For a classic statement of this position, see Paul E. Peterson, *City Limits* (Chicago: University of Chicago Press, 1981).

2. For some examples of urban sociology in this vein, see Manuel Castells, *The Urban Question* (Cambridge, Mass: MIT Press, 1981); Mark Gottdiener, *The Social Production of Urban Space* (Austin: University of Texas Press, 1985); John R. Logan and Harvey Molotch, *Urban Fortunes: The Political Economy of Place*

(Berkeley: University of California Press, 1987); and Michael Smith, *The City and Social Theory* (New York: St. Martin's Press, 1979).

3. Ted Robert Gurr and Desmond King, *The State and the City* (Chicago: University of Chicago Press, 1987). This book grants too much autonomy to the state, but it is very useful in developing a theory of comparative municipal responses.

4. Ibid., p. 90.

5. Michael deCourcy Hinds with Erik Eckholm, "80's Leaves States and Cities in Need," *New York Times*, 30 December 1990.

6. Although much has since been written about homelessness in the United States, the record of these hearings still make moving reading. See U.S., Congress, House, Subcommittee on Housing and Community Development of the Committee on Banking, Finance, and Urban Affairs, *Hearing on Homelessness in America*, 15 December 1982.

7. See Lee Walker, *Homelessness in the States* (Lexington, Ky.: Council of State Governments, 1989), p. 11; F. Stevens Redburn and Terry F. Buss, *Responding to America's Homeless* (New York: Praeger Publishing, 1986), p. 115; Majorie Hope and James Young, *The Faces of Homelessness* (Lexington, Mass.: Lexington Books, 1986), p. 143.

8. Interagency Council on the Homeless, *A Nation Concerned* (Washington, D.C., 1988), p. 3–9. By 1990, a total of fifteen Department of Defense facilities had been allocated for the homeless. See the U.S., General Accounting Office, *Homelessness: Action Needed to Make Surplus Property Program More Effective* (Washington, D.C., October 1990), p. 43.

9. Walker, *Homelessness in the States*, p. 11; Hope and Young, *The Faces of Homelessness*, p. 143.

10. Walker, *Homelessness in the States*, p. 12; Jason DeParle, "Bush Homeless Plan: 'Godsend' or False Hope?" *New York Times*, 12 February 1990. For an analysis of the effects of the McKinney Act in ten states, see the National Coalition for the Homeless, *Unfinished Business: The Stewart B. McKinney Homeless Assistance Act After Two Years* (Washington, D.C., 1989).

11. See the U.S., General Accounting Office, *Homelessness: Access to McKinney Act Programs Improved but Better Oversight Needed* (Washington, D.C., December 1990), p. 2 plus the chart on 1991–92 fiscal year expenditures in *Safety Network*, March 1991, p. 3.

12. Walker, *Homelessness in the States*, p. 14; U.S., General Accounting Office, *Homelessness: HUD's and FEMA's Progress in Implementing the McKinney Act*, May 1989, p. 17; U.S., General Accounting Office, *Homelessness: McKinney Act Programs and Funding for Fiscal Year 1989* (Washington, D.C., 1990).

13. DeParle, "Bush Homeless Plan: 'Godsend' or False Hope?" 12 February 1990. In October 1989, HUD waived the requirement for environmental reviews of housing projects that were only receiving operational funds. See U.S., General Accounting Office, *Homelessness: Access to McKinney Act Programs Improved but Better Oversight Needed*, p. 3.

14. U.S., General Accounting Office, *Homelessness: Additional Information on the Interagency Council on the Homeless* (Washington, D.C., 1989), p. 2.

15. The data comes from a 1988 survey conducted by the Council on State Governments. Governors in thirty-eight states, or 76 percent, responded. For the complete survey, see Walker, *Homelessness in the States*.

16. Ibid., p. 20 and p. 31, Table 2.

17. Ibid., pp. 32–35.

18. Interagency Council on the Homeless, *A Nation Concerned*, pp. 2–4–2–7.

19. This method of classification is adopted from the U.S., General Accounting Office, *Homelessness: A Complex Problem and the Federal Response* (Washington, D.C., 1985), pp. 43–44. Citing HUD's 1984 study, the General Accounting Office found that 20 percent of cities directly operated shelters; 60 percent were involved in some form of voucher or contracting out; and by implication, another 20 percent did nothing. The latter percentage has undoubtedly diminished, but the system of classification remains sound.

20. National Coalition for the Homeless, *American Nightmare: A Decade of Homelessness in the United States* (Washington, D.C., 1989), pp. 78–79.

21. Doug A. Timmer and J. David Knottnerus, "Homelessness in Florida," in *Homelessness in the United States*, ed. Jamshid Momeni (New York: Greenwood Press, 1989), p. 54.

22. Miami Coalition for Care to the Homeless, *A Report on the Homeless*, Summer 1987, pp. 19–20; "Miami Fined for Violating Homeless Rights," *New York Times*, 20 March 1991.

23. Interagency Council on the Homeless, *A Nation Concerned*, pp. 2–16; U.S., Department of Housing and Urban Development, *Homeless Assistance Policy and Practice in the Nation's Five Largest Cities* (Washington, D.C., 1989), p. 28.

24. Feagin, *Free Enterprise City*, p. 261; City of Houston, *Comprehensive Homeless Assistance Plan*, pp. 5–7; Andrade, *Living in the Gray Zone*, p. 69; U.S., Department of Housing and Urban Development, *Homeless Assistance Policy*, pp. 19, 23, 34.

25. For an analysis of the evolution of Houston's political economy, see Joe R. Feagin, *Free Enterprise City* (New Brunswick, N.J.: Rutgers University Press, 1988), and Gurr and King, *The State and the City*, p. 196.

26. *Statistical Abstract of the United States, 1989*, p. 396; Sally Andrade, *Living in the Gray Zone: Health Care Needs of Homeless People* (San Antonio, Tex.: Texas Department of Human Services, 1988), p. 27; City of Houston, *Comprehensive Homeless Assistance Plan*, September 1987.

27. Calculated from the U.S., Department of Commerce, Bureau of the Census, *City Government Finances in 1985–6* (Washington, D.C.: Government Printing Office, 1988), p. 57.

28. U.S., Department of Housing and Urban Development, *Homeless Assistance Policy* pp. 8, 23.

29. Ibid., pp. 35–37.

30. Dan Salerno, Kim Hopper, and Ellen Baxter, *Hardship in the Heartland* (New York: Community Service Society, 1984), p. 77; U.S., Department of Housing and Urban Development, *Homeless Assistance Policy*, p. 27; the 40,000 estimate comes from Michael Marubio of the Chicago Coalition for the Homeless and is cited in National Coalition for the Homeless, *American Nightmare*, p. 33.

31. Michael Sosin, Paul Colson, and Susan Grossman, *Homelessness in Chicago* (Chicago: Chicago Community Trust, 1988), pp. 236–37; U.S., Department of Housing and Urban Development, *Homeless Assistance Policy*, p. 48; Stewart B. McKinney Comprehensive Homeless Assistance Plan for the City of Chicago, September 1987.

32. National Coalition for the Homeless, *America's Nightmare*, p. 38; Salerno et al., *Hardship in the Heartland*, p. 79; Charles Hoch and Robert A. Slayton, *New Homeless and Old* (Philadelphia: Temple University Press, 1989), pp. 183–85.

33. National Coalition for the Homeless, *America's Nightmare*, p. 133; U.S. Conference of Mayors, *A Status Report on Hunger and Homelessness in America's Cities: 1990* (Washington, D.C., 1990), p. 54.

34. National Coalition for the Homeless, *American Nightmare*, p. 135; Interview with Lisa Gualtieri, Public Advocates, Inc., 19 July 1988; San Francisco Board of Supervisors Memorandum "City's 1987–88 Cost of Services to the Homeless, 1 March 1988; Jane Gross, "San Francisco Treating Ex-Squatters as Guests," *New York Times*, 19 July 1990.

35. National Coalition for the Homeless, *America's Nightmare*, pp. 135–39.

36. Interview with Randall Shaw, Tenderloin Housing Clinic, 20 July 1988. For Feinstein's business ties, see Thomas Ferguson and Joel Rodgers, *Right Turn: The Decline of the Democrats and the Future of American Politics* (New York: Hill and Wang, 1986), p. 183. One of Feinstein's biggest supporters, developer Walter Shorenstein, was heavily involved in the real estate industry; so was Feinstein's husband. Not surprisingly, the real estate community was one of the major forces behind Feinstein's 1984 campaign for the vice-presidential nomination on the Mondale ticket.

37. See Karen Koenig and Sara Colm, "Times Interview: Bob Prentice, Homeless Coordinator," and Josh Brandon, "Homeless Meet with City to Push for Longer Hotel Stays," in *Tenderloin Times* 12 (5): 1, 8–9 (June/July 1988); Dianne Feinstein to the Social Service Commission, 21 July 1987.

38. National Coalition for the Homeless, *America's Nightmare*, pp. 139–40; Jane Gross, "San Francisco Treating Ex-Squatters as Guests," 19 July 1990; Telephone Interview with Florence Stagner, San Francisco Mayor's Office, 6 November 1990; National Law Center on Homelessness and Poverty, *In Just Times* 2 (1): 2(January 1991).

39. Michael McCabe and Nanette Asimov, "Bay Area Grapples with 'New Homeless,'" *San Francisco Chronicle*, 20 November 1989; Jane Gross, "San Francisco Treating Ex-Squatters as Guests," 19 July 1990.

40. See U.S., Department of Housing and Urban Development, *Homeless Assistance Policy*, pp. 29, 52.

41. See Mayor Tom Bradley, *Housing the Future*, 1988 Blue Ribbon Panel on Affordable Housing, City of Los Angeles Office of the Mayor; Kathleen Sharp, "Market for Resale Houses Is Cooling Off," *New York Times*, 11 March 1990; California Assembly, *Over the Brink: Homeless Families in Los Angeles* (Sacramento, Calif.: Office of Research), p. 11; California State Legislature, Senate Office Research, *Housing Alert: Estimates of the Low-Income Rental Units Subject to Termination of Rent and/or Mortgage Subsidies, 1988–2008* (Sacramento, Calif.: Joint Publications, 1987), p. iii.

42. U.S., Department of Housing and Urban Development, *Homeless Assistance Policy*, p. 36.

43. Shelter Partnership, *The Short-Term Housing System of Los Angeles County: Serving the Housing Needs of the Homeless* (Los Angeles, 1987); Interview with Toni Reinis, California Homeless Coalition, 27 July 1988.

44. National Coalition for the Homeless, California Homeless Coalition, Commission of Conscience, and Los Angeles Homeless Health Care Project, *Less than Zero: Backlash Against Homeless People and the Programs That Serve Them* (Los Angeles, 1987).

45. Allan David Heskin, "Los Angeles: Innovative Local Approaches," in *The*

Homeless in Contemporary Society, ed. Richard Bingham, Roy E. Green, and Sammis B. White (Newbury Park, Calif.: Sage Publications, 1987), pp. 170–83.

46. National Coalition for the Homeless, *American Nightmare*, p. 127.

47. Interagency Task Force on the Homeless, *A Nation Concerned*, pp. 2–21; Julia S. Kunz, "Homelessness in Missouri: Populations, Problems, and Policy," in *Homelessness in the United States*, p. 94.

48. Alice Johnson, Larry Kreuger, and John Stretch offer a complete chronology and analysis of *Graham* v. *Schoemehl* in "A Court-Ordered Consent Decree for the Homeless: Process, Conflict and Control," *Journal of Sociology and Social Welfare* 16 (3): 29–42.

49. Ibid., pp. 37–38; U.S., Department of Housing and Urban Development, *Homeless Assistance Policy*, p. 42.

50. National Coalition for the Homeless, *American Nightmare*, p. 129.

51. "For Seattle's Homeless, Home Rule and Self-Pride," *New York Times*, 20 December 1990; Fritz Brooks, "Winter 1991 Equals Shelter Controversy," *Sea-Town Crier*, 1 April 1991.

52. Interviews with Sylvia McGee and Martha Dilts, 12 July 1988.

53. Ibid.; King County Housing and Community Development Division, *Homelessness Revisited: 1986 Seattle-King County Emergency Shelter Study Update* (Housing and Community Development Division, 1986), p. 42.

54. Gerald F. Blake and Martin L. Abbott, "Homelessness in the Pacific Northwest," in *Homelessness in the United States*, pp. 165–80. Ronald Smothers, "Atlanta Mayor Calls for Crackdown on Begging," *New York Times* 13 June 1991, describes the outcome of the Seattle lawsuit.

55. U.S., Department of Housing and Urban Development, *Homeless Assistance Policy*, pp. 28, 42.

56. Ibid., p. 38 and Michael deCourcy Hinds, "50% Cutback in Funds for Homeless in Philadelphia Is Fiercely Protested," *New York Times*, 15 September 1989.

57. U.S. Conference of Mayors, *Local Responses to the Needs of Homeless Mentally Ill Persons* (Washington, D.C., 1987), pp. 53–59. I have also drawn on the New York City Council's memorandum of 11 March 1988 drafted by Robert Altman, counsel to the Subcommittee on the Homeless, describing the project's operation.

58. Cited in U.S. Conference of Mayors, *Local Responses to the Needs of Homeless Mentally Ill Persons*, p. 59.

59. deCourcy Hinds, "50% Cutback in Funds for Homeless In Philadelphia Is Fiercely Protested."

60. Gurr and King, *The State and the City*, p. 109; U.S., Department of Commerce, Bureau of the Census, *City Government Finances in 1985–6*, p. 34.

61. Flynn, *Commitment and Compassion: Boston's Comprehensive Policy for the Homeless, 1988–1989*.

62. Gurr and King, *The State and the City*, p. 198.

Chapter 9

1. U.S., Department of Housing and Urban Development, *Homeless Assistance Policy and Practice in the Nation's Five Largest Cities* (Washington, D.C., 1989).

2. William Grinker to Councilman Abraham Gerges, chair of the Council

Subcommittee on the Homeless, in response to a draft of the subcommittee's final report, 15 December 1986. Also, for a similar passage, see Mayor's Advisory Task Force on the Homeless, *Toward A Comprehensive Policy on Homelessness*, 1987, p. 34.

3. The figure is from a 1989 *New York Times*/CBS poll. See Josh Barbanel, "Poll Shows New Yorkers Fault City Efforts for the Homeless," New York Times, 29 June 1989.

4. The figure is the upper range of a 35,000 to 90,000 estimate derived from the city's 1987 Comprehensive Homeless Assistance Plan (CHAP). CHAPs are required by the McKinney Act. In 1989, the Coalition for the Homeless used an estimate of from 70,000 to 90,000 people. See The National Coalition for the Homeless, *American Nightmare* (Washington, D.C., 1989), p. 105.

5. Martin Shefter, *Political Crisis/Fiscal Crisis: The Collapse and Revival of New York City* (New York: Basic Books, 1987).

6. William K. Tabb, *The Long Default* (New York: Monthly Review Press, 1982).

7. Shefter, *Political Crisis/Fiscal Crisis*, p. 176.

8. Tom Robbins and Annette Fuentes, "Tax Breaks By Check-Off," *City Limits*, October 1984, pp. 10–12; Glenn von Nostitz, "New Tax Program Is the Same Old Giveway," *City Limits*, April 1986, pp. 33–34; Committee on Economic Development and Select Committee on Revenue Enhancement of the New York City Council, "Oversight Hearing on the Industrial and Commercial Incentive Program and on the Departure of Various Corporations from New York City," Briefing paper, May 4, 1987.

9. Thomas Lueck, "Chase, With 235 Million Incentive Package, Picks Brooklyn," *New York Times*, 10 November 1988; Thomas Lueck, "Chase Deal Reflects Era of Subsidies," *New York Times*, 11 November 1988.

10. See Carol Felstein and Sydelle Knepper, *Housing Need and Production in New York City* (New York: Pratt Institute for Community and Environmental Development, 1985), p. 16; and the Coalition for the Homeless, *Single Room Occupancy Hotels: Standing in the Way of the Gentry* (New York: 1985). The New York City study is *Chronic and Situational Dependency* (1982).

New York modified the J-51 program in 1988, making it more difficult for higher price rental buildings to get benefits. Benefits granted in 1988 will still cost $120 million over the next twenty years. See Alan Oser, "Abatements Broaden for Co-Ops and Condos," *New York Times*, 9 October 1988, and Ariel Golowa, "Changes in J-51 Tax Incentive Abatement," *Real Estate Weekly*, 22 August 1988.

11. Thomas J. Lueck, "Pervasive Problems Threaten New York's Economic Base," *New York Times*, 26 June 1988; Walter Stafford, *Closed Labor Markets: The Underrepresentation of Blacks, Hispanics, and Women in New York City's Core Industries and Jobs* (New York: Community Service Society, 1985).

12. Thomas J. Lueck, "45% of New Yorkers Are Outside the Labor Force," *New York Times*, 3 August 1988; Terry J. Rosenberg, *Poverty in New York City: 1980–85* (New York: Community Service Society, 1987).

13. Michael A. Stegman, *Housing and Vacancy Report: New York City, 1987* (New York: Housing Preservation and Development, 1987), p. 106.

14. Richard Levine, "New York City's Economic Growth Fails to Curb Rise of 'New Poverty,' " *New York Times*, 28 February 1989.

15. Stegman, *Housing and Vacancy Report: New York City, 1987*, pp. 43, 47.

16. Ibid., p. 6, Table 2.5, and p. 15.

17. Coalition for the Homeless, *Single Room Occupancy Hotels*, p. 14.

18. Alan Finder, "Supreme Court Won't Review S.R.O. Ruling," *New York Times*, 11 November 1989.

19. Martha R. Burt and Barbara E. Cohen, *America's Homeless* (Washington, D.C.: The Urban Institute, 1989), pp. 74–75. Although the data refer to both families and single adults, the authors say that these groups bear more resemblance to each other than they do to their counterparts elsewhere.

20. See John Darnton, "Alone and Homeless, 'Shutouts' of Society Sleep in Doorways," *New York Times*, 26 October 1971. Pranay Gupte, "The Derelict Population is Declining, But The Whole City Is Its Flophouse," *New York Times*, 23 November 1973, is one of the first news account to mention the effects of deinstitutionalization. For an early demographic study, see The Human Resources Administration, Bureau of Program Planning, Monitoring, and Evaluation, *An Investigation of the Shelter Care Center for Men Operations and Clientele* (New York, 1976). Finally, John Hess, "Vagrants and Panhandlers Appearing in New Haunts," *New York Times*, 16 August 1976, describes how the population was proliferating.

21. For an example of this official history, see The Human Resources Administration, *New York City Plan for Homeless Adults* (New York, 1984).

22. Quoted in Robert Hayes, "Reforming Current City Policies," *Citizen Budget Commission Quarterly* 2 (2): 1–4 (1982).

23. Kim Hopper and L. Stuart Cox, "Litigation in Advocacy for the Homeless: The Case of New York City," *Development: Seeds of Change* (2): 57–62(1982); Coalition for the Homeless, *Cruel Brinkmanship: Planning for the Homeless* (New York, 1982), p. 7.

24. Final Judgment by Consent, *Callahan* v. *Carey*, No. 42582/79, p. 3.

25. U.S., Department of Housing and Urban Development, *Homeless Assistance Policy*, Appendix A-1; Edward Koch, *Efforts of the City of New York to Assist the Homeless* (New York: City of New York, 1983), p. 6.

26. Human Resources Administration, *New York City For Homeless Adults*, p. 3; Ronald Sullivan, "Coalition Seeks to Compel Closing of Armory Shelters," *New York Times*, 2 May 1990.

27. The Fort Washington Armory housed 1,400 men in the winter of 1984–85; see the Coalition for the Homeless, *Safety Network*, January 1985. For the discarded city proposals, see Joyce Purnick, "Plan to Put Homeless in Trailers Sets Off Debate," *New York Times*, 30 May 1985; Michael Goodwin, "Koch Considers Using Ships As Shelters for the Homeless," *New York Times*, 28 April 1984; Michael Goodwin, "City Offers Apartment-Sharing Plan for the Homeless," *New York Times*, 27 June 1984; and Clara Hemphill, "City May Build Shelters for Homeless on Islands," *New York Newsday*, 7 April 1989.

28. Quoted in Deidre Carmody, "The City Sees No Solutions for the Homeless," *New York Times*, 10 October 1984.

29. William Grinker, *Five Year Plan for Housing and Assisting Homeless Single Adults* (New York, 1988), pp. 58–62.

30. Richard Beattie, *Outline for Action: New Directions for HRA* (New York: City of New York Commission on Human Service Reorganization, 1985), pp. 65–66; for the others, see Carol Bellamy, "Homeless Should Be Rehoused," *New York Times*, 18 May 1984; Abraham Gerges, *Report of the Select Committee on the Homeless* (Council of the City of New York, 1987); and Coalition for the Homeless,

Safety Network, October 1985, which quotes Governor Cuomo as saying that their lawsuit about shelter size had "validity."

31. The twenty-six dollar a night cost comes from Human Resources Administration, *New York City Plan for Homeless Adults*, pp. 5–6; the national figures are cited in the 1984 HUD study, pp. 42–43. Some typical examples of the Koch administration seeking to explain away the St. Franciscan Residences include a memorandum from HRA Commissioner James Krauskopf to Edward Koch, "The St. Franciscan Residence," 15 January 1982; Deputy Mayor Stanley Brezenoff's memorandum to Edward Koch, City Supports for Housing Programs for the Homeless, 22 June 1984; and the Human Resources Administration's *New York City Plan for Homeless Adults*, pp. 56–58.

32. Deputy Mayor Stanley Brezenoff's memorandum to Edward Koch, "City Supports for Housing Programs for the Homeless," 22 June 1984. Despite these criticisms, when real estate developer Harry Macklowe paid the city a $2 million fine for his illegal January 1985 demolition of the Times Square SRO, the city gave the money to the Franciscan friars to purchase their third building. See David Bird, "3 Franciscans Housing the Homeless Find Spending $2 Million a Challenge," *New York Times*, 6 July 1985.

33. Kim Hopper, Ellen Baxter, Stuart Cox, and Lawrence Klein, *One Year Later* (New York: Community Service Society, 1982), p. 36.

34. Crystal Nix, "Guards Held in 2 Shelter Killings," *New York Times*, 31 October 1986; Josh Barbanel, "Reacting to Homelessness," *New York Times*, 17 December 1988.

35. Office of the Inspector General, Human Resources Administration *A Study of the HRA Adult Shelter Program* (New York: 1986), p. 32. This study was particularly harsh on the performance of HRA security guards, two of whom were charged with murdering two residents soon after its publication. The security guards were paid little more than minimum wage and received scant training. For these reasons, they often reported, rather than stopped, physical confrontations. While HRA has taken steps in recent years to improve the quality of its security, including abandoning its policy of awarding contracts to the lowest bidder, few would claim that the shelters have gotten much safer.

36. Hopper et al., *One Year Later*, p. 39.

37. Bella English, "Harlem Battling the Homeless," *New York Daily News*, 22 November 1982.

38. Bill Breen, "City Lied About Shelter Plans," *Park Slope Paper*, 3–9 May 1986; B. J. Kowalski, "Homeless Women To Be Housed in Armory Shelter," *Prospect Press*, 14–27 August 1986.

39. For some ideas about how to deal with neighborhood concerns, see Rose Aniello and Tillie Shuster, "Community Relations Strategies," in *Housing the Homeless*, ed. Jon Erickson and Charles Wilhelm, (New Brunswick, N.J.: Center for Urban Policy Research, 1986), pp. 376–89.

40. See Sara Rimer, "Koch Offers 500 Million Plan To Replace Armory Shelters," *New York Times*, 17 May 1989, and Ronald Sullivan, "Coalition Seeks to Compel Closing of Armory Shelters," *New York Times*, 2 May 1990.

41. The office, the Bureau of Management Systems, Planning, Research, and Evaluation, was responsible for *Chronic and Situational Dependency* (1982), *New Arrivals* (1983), *The Homeless in New York City Shelters* (1984), and *One Day Study* (1984), among other studies. All demonstrated that significant demographic changes had occurred within the homeless population.

42. Coalition for the Homeless, *Safety Network* 4 (6): 1, (September 1985).

43. See Crystal Nix, "City Proposes Separate Housing of the Homeless with Special Needs," *New York Times*, 30 May 1986. For a full description of the updated plan which increased the total number of beds to 6,311, see Grinker, *Five Year Plan for Housing and Assisting Homeless Single Adults*, pp. 46–50, and Robert Altman, Counsel to New York City Council Subcommittee on the Homeless, Memorandum for the Hearing on the Five Year Plan, 14 March 1988. Lastly, the fiscal year 1987 cutbacks are described in the *New York Times*, 1 July 1986.

44. See the Human Resources Administration, *Chronic and Situational Dependency: Long-Term Care in a Shelter for Men* (New York, 1982), and Thomas Main, "The Homeless of New York," *Public Interest*, no. 72, Summer 1983, pp. 3–28. For an earlier study, see the Human Resources Administration, *An Investigation of the Shelter Care Center for Men Operations and Clientele*.

45. Human Resources Administration, *Harlem Shelter Work Experience Program* (New York, July 1983), p. 1.

46. Human Resources Administration, *Monthly Shelter Report*, July 1986. By 1990, this figure had declined to approximately 1,500 people. See the Human Resources Administration, *Monthly Shelter Report*, March 1990, p. 16.

47. Coalition for the Homeless, *Safety Network*, April 1984.

48. New York State Department of Social Services, *Homelessness in New York State*, October 1984, p. 48; U.S., Department of Housing and Urban Development, *A Report to the Secretary on Homelessness and Emergency Shelters* (Washington, D.C., 1984), p. 38.

49. For a discussion of this process of "shelterization," see Jeffrey Grunberg and Paula Eagle, ""Shelterization: How the Homeless Adapt to Shelter Living," *Hospital and Community Psychiatry* 41 (5): 521–25 (May 1990).

50. Human Resources Administration, *An Evaluation of the Work Experience Program At Three Shelters* (New York, 1986), p. 54.

51. See the summary of SEHP in the HRA newspaper by Marjorie Valleau, "Jobs and Housing Program Helps Shelter Clients," *Us* 5 (8):1. The salary estimate comes from an analysis of SEHP's first 212 placements, whose average was $4.87 an hour. See the Human Resources Administration, *Determinants of Success in the Shelter Employment Project* (New York, 1986), p. 6. By 1989, New York City had incorporated SEHP into an Independent Living Division. This division placed a total of 647 men and women in fiscal year 1989. See the Human Resources Administration, *Monthly Shelter Report*, March 1990, p. 19.

52. Eugene Becker et al. to Luis Marcos, vice-president for Mental Hygiene Services of the New York City Health and Hospitals Corporation, 24 February 1988.

53. Kevin Sack, "Crossroads in Mental Health: Red Ink and Unused Wards," *New York Times*, 19 February 1991; Josh Barbanel, "Mentally Ill Homeless: Policy at Issue," *New York Times*, 15 November 1985; Ron Sullivan, "Judge Orders Homeless Aid in New York," *New York Times*, 28 February 1991.

54. New York City Health and Hospitals Corporation, *Crisis in Mental Health: Issues Affecting HHC Psychiatric Inpatient and Emergency Room Services* (New York, 1989), pp. 1–8.

55. New York State Commission on the Quality of Care for the Mentally Disabled, *Psychiatric Emergency Room Overcrowding: A Case Study*, 1989, p. 5.

56. Grinker, *Five-Year Plan for Housing and Assisting Homeless Single Adults*, p. 19.

57. Robert Altman memorandum to the New York City Select Committee

on the Homeless, "Help for the Homeless in Transport Stations," 25 February 1988.

58. Neal Cohen, Jane Putnam, and Anne Sullivan, "The Mentally Ill Homeless: Isolation and Adaption," *Hospital and Community Psychiatry* 35 (9): 922.

59. See, for example, Jeanie Kasindorf, "The Real Life Story of Billy Boggs," *New York Magazine*, 2 May 1988, pp. 36–44; Francine Cournos, "Involuntary Medication and the Case of Joyce Brown," *Hospital and Community Psychiatry* 40 (7): 736–40; Thomas Main, "What We Know About the Homeless," *Commentary* 85 (5): 26–31; and Josh Barbanel, "Joyce Brown's Ascent from Anonymity," *New York Times*, 15 February 1988.

60. Josh Barbanel, "Psychiatric Care for Ill Homeless May Be Lengthy," *New York Times*, 7 December 1987.

61. Josh Barbanel, "Hospitalizing the Homeless: Planning is Lagging in New York," *New York Times*, 11 April 1988; and "New York Planning Transfers of Mental Patients to Shelter," *New York Times*, 25 February 1989.

Chapter 10

1. Edward Koch, *Toward a Comprehensive Policy on Homelessness* (New York: The Mayor's Advisory Task Force on the Homeless, 1987), p. 53.

2. Center on Budget and Policy Priorities, *Holes in the Safety Nets* (Washington, D.C., 1988), p. 7; Koch, *Toward a Comprehensive Policy on Homelessness*, pp. 52–53.

3. Michael A. Stegman, *Housing and Vacancy Report, 1987* (New York: Department of Housing Preservation and Development, 1987).

4. Alan Finder, "Doubling Up by Tenants Costing New York Millions," *New York Times*, 1 October 1988.

5. Stegman, *Housing and Vacancy Report, 1987*, pp. 138–42; for some typical studies about the relationship of doubling up and homelessness in New York City, see the Human Resources Administration, *A One-Day Snapshot of Homeless Families at the Forbell Street Shelter and the Martinique Hotel* (New York: Office of Program Evaluation, 1986); Human Resources Administration, *Characteristics and Housing Histories of Families Seeking Shelter From HRA* (New York: Office of Program Evaluation, 1986); and Health Research Program, Graduate School of Public Administration, New York University, *A Study of Homeless Families in New York City: Risk Assessment Models and Strategies for Prevention* (New York: The Robert F. Wagner Graduate School of Public Service, 1989).

6. Stegman, *Housing and Vacancy Report, 1987*, p. 31; Carol Felstein and Michael Stegman, *Toward the 21st Century: Housing in New York City* (New York: Commission on the Year 2000, 1987), p. 102.

7. Stegman, *Housing and Vacancy Report, 1987*, p. 55; Frederick K. Mehlman to *New York Times*, "Ad on New York City Co-ops Understates Warehousing Figures," 1 April 1988; Alan Finder, "Apartments Left Vacant as Shelters Fill," *New York Times*, 16 March 1988; and Sarah Ferguson, "Who has the Key?," *Village Voice*, 25 April 1989.

8. William Grinker, *Five Year Plan for Housing and Assisting Homeless Families* (New York: The Human Resources Administration, 1988), p. 10; New York State Coalition for the Homeless, *Losing Ground* (New York, 1990), pp. 5–7;

Thomas Morgan, "Again, Grim Shelters House a Rising Number of Families," *New York Times*, 19 June, 1991.

9. Health Research Program, Graduate School of Public Administration, New York University, *A Study of Homeless Families in New York City: Risk Assessment Models and Strategies for Prevention*, September, 1989.

10. James Dumpson and David Dinkins, *A Shelter Is Not A Home*, report of the Manhattan Borough President's Task Force on Housing for Homeless Families (New York: Office of the Manhattan Borough President, 1987), p. 13; Jonathan Kozol, *Rachel and Her Children* (New York: Crown Publishers, 1988).

11. Diana Gordon, *City Limits: Barriers to Change in Urban Government* (New York: Charterhouse, 1973), pp. 255–93.

12. William Bastone, "Who Owns the Welfare Hotels?" *Village Voice*, 1 April 1986.

13. Ibid.

14. Council of the City of New York, Select Committee on the Homeless, *Report on the Homeless Crisis*, pp. 82–83. In its *Holland Hotel Task Force Final Report* of 18 March 1986, the New York City Department of General Services had estimated the rate at 47 percent ($3,023, 105 on revenues of $6,360,212). The Select Committee, however, recalculated the hotel's revenues at $1,571,000 and obtained the lower figure.

15. See Kozol, *Rachel and Her Children*; U.S., General Accounting Office, *Welfare Hotels: Uses, Costs, and Alternatives* (Washington, D.C., 1989); Community Service Society, *Alternatives to the Welfare Hotel* (New York, 1987); Dumpson and Dinkins, *A Shelter Is Not A Home*; and Janice Molnar, *Home is Where the Heart Is: The Crisis of Homeless Children and Families in New York City* (New York: Bank Street College of Education, 1988).

16. The data comes from a memorandum from Kenneth Murphy, deputy commissioner, Crisis Intervention Services of the Human Resources Administration, "Homeless Family Census," 18 May 1988.

17. Plaintiffs' brief for *McCain* v. *Koch*, New York County Clerk's Index No. 41023/83, p. 9.

18. Cited in Advocates for Children, *Learning in Limbo: The Educational Deprivation of Homeless Children* (Long Island City, New York, 1989), pp. 35–37.

19. Jill Blair, Testimony on Homelessness and the Educational System, City Council Committee on the General Welfare, 21 October 1988.

20. See Advocates for Children, *Learning in Limbo*, p. 9.

21. Report of the Legal Services Division, the New York City Council Committee on the General Welfare, 22 October 1987; U.S., General Accounting Office, *Welfare Hotels: Uses, Costs, and Alternatives*, pp. 4–5.

22. John Tierney, "Using Housing Projects for Welfare Angers Tenants," *New York Times*, 28 June 1990; Thomas Morgan, "New York To Resume Putting the Homeless into Welfare Hotels," *New York Times*, 19 September 1990; Thomas Morgan, "Views Divided Over a New Plan on the Homeless," *New York Times*, 23 November 1990; Thomas Morgan, "Again, Grim Shelters House a Rising Number of Families, *New York Times*, 19 June 1991.

23. Grinker, *Five Year Plan For Housing and Assisting Homeless Families*, pp. 31–35.

24. Robert Altman, Memorandum for the Oversight Hearing on the Board of Estimate Shelter Plan Compromise, Select Committee on the Homeless of the New York City Council, 29 October 1987.

25. For a description of the design and construction of the first family shelter (the Powers Avenue complex, near 141st Street in the South Bronx), see Alan S. Oser, "The New Shelters for Homeless Families," *New York Times*, 8 April 1990.

26. Dumpson and Dinkins, *A Shelter is Not A Home*, p. 96.

27. Todd Purnum, "Council Bill Would Limit Mass Shelters," *New York Times*, 8 May 1990.

28. Alan S. Oser, "Putting a Dinkins Imprint on a Koch Plan," *New York Times*, 8 July 1990.

29. See Doug Henwood, "Subsidizing the Rich," *Village Voice*, 30 August 1988; Philip Weitzman, "Calculations and Controversy: What's The City's Median Income?" *City Limits* 14 (3): 18–19 (March 1989); Bonnie Brower, *Missing the Mark: Subsidizing Housing for the Privileged, Displacing the Poor* (New York: The Association for Neighborhood and Housing Development and Housing Justice Campaign, 1989), p. 49.

30. Brower, *Missing the Mark*, p. 32. After five years of problems including a lawsuit by the community, deteriorating municipal finances, and the absence of a profit for developers, the Dinkins administration cancelled the 1,000 apartment Tibbetts Garden complex, which was to have been the first phase of this plan. See Alan Finder, "New York Giving Up 5-Year Drive to Build Middle-Income Units," *New York Times*, 18 December 1990.

31. See Brower, *Missing the Mark*, p. 72, where the $19,000 figure is set at the 42nd percentile.

32. Ibid., pp. 41–42.

33. Ibid., p. 97 and Appendix A, p. 141.

34. Ibid., pp. 118–19; Carmen Jose Vergara, "Rebuilding Drug City," *Village Voice*, 27 March 1990.

35. Ronald Lawson and Mark Naison, *The Tenant Movement in New York City, 1904–1984* (New Brunswick, N.J.: Rutgers University Press, 1986), pp. 239–40; Brower, *Missing the Mark*, p. 23.

36. Anthony de Palma, "New York Plays Reluctant Landlord," *New York Times*, 14 December 1986.

37. Brower, *Missing the Mark*, pp. 24–32; Lawson and Naison, *The Tenant Movement in New York City, 1904–1984*, pp. 240–42.

38. Henwood, "Subsidizing the Rich."

39. Alan Finder, "Renovators Running Out of Abandoned Buildings," *New York Times*, 16 April 1990; Don Terry, "Dinkins Adds a 'Human Face' to Housing Program," *New York Times*, 17 May 1990; Oser, "Putting a Dinkins Imprint on a Koch Plan."

40. Felstein and Stegman, *Toward the 21st Century: Housing in New York City*.

41. Sam Roberts, "Dinkins Gaining Support Among Business Executives," *New York Times*, 26 September 1989.

Chapter 11

1. *Statistical Abstract of the United States, 1989*, p. 380, Tables 626 and 627.

2. The term *reluctant welfare state* comes from Harold Wilensky and Charles Lebeaux, *Industrial Society and Social Welfare* (New York: Free Press, 1965). For the best comparison of different welfare states, see Gosta Esping-Andersen, *The*

Three Worlds of Welfare Capitalism (Princeton, N.J.: Princeton University Press, 1990).

3. Some readers will note that this paragraph blends several different interpretations of the role of social policy. These interpretations include "regulating the poor" from the book of the same name by Frances Fox Piven and Richard Cloward (New York: Vintage, 1971); the conflict between "accumulation and legitimation," first elaborated by James O'Connor in *The Fiscal Crisis of the State* (New York: St. Martin's Press, 1973); and the maintenance of the nonworking population, from Ian Gough, *The Political Economy of the Welfare State* (New York: Macmillan, 1979). For a review of these and other explanations, see Joel Blau, "Theories of the Welfare State," *Social Service Review* 63 (1): 26–38 (March 1989).

4. Robert Pear, "White House Spurns Expansion of Nation's Anti-Poverty Efforts," *New York Times*, 6 July 1990.

5. See, for example, U.S., Congress, Office of Technology Assessment, *Making Things Better: Competing in Manufacturing* (Washington, D.C.: Government Printing Office, 1990); Bennett Harrison and Barry Bluestone, *The Great U-Turn* (New York: Basic Books, 1988); Robert Reich, *The Next American Frontier* (New York: Penguin Books, 1983).

6. Some efforts have been made to reconceptualize social welfare spending as an investment in human capital. The General Accounting Office, for example, estimated that in fiscal year 1988, $534 billion of social welfare spending should be so classified. This analysis has not yet been employed to justify an expansion of social programs. See U.S., General Accounting Office, *Budget Issues: Human Resource Programs Warranting Considerations as Human Capital* (Washington, D.C., 1990).

Chapter 12

1. Although the percentages would undoubtedly vary with the specifics of the program, there is broad support for national health care. Republicans favor it by a 53–39 majority, Democrats, by an even larger 74–21 percent. See *New York Times*/CBS poll, in *New York Times*, 4 November 1990.

2. Peter Gabel, "Dukakis' Defeat and the Transformative Possibilities of Legal Culture," *Tikkun* 4(2): 13–16, 106–14 is very helpful on this point.

3. See Helen Ginsburg, *Full Employment and Public Policy: The United States and Sweden* (Lexington, Mass.: Lexington Books, D. C. Heath and Company, 1983).

4. See Vincent J. Burke and Lee Burke, *Nixon's Good Deed: Welfare Reform* (New York: Columbia University Press, 1974); James T. Paterson, *America's Struggle Against Poverty, 1900–1980* (Cambridge: Harvard University Press, 1981), pp. 190–96; and Gilbert Steiner, *The State of Welfare* (Washington, D.C.: The Brookings Institution, 1971).

5. In recent years, William J. Wilson has been the prime U.S. exponent of universal principles of social welfare. His fullest treatment of the case for universalism is *The Truly Disadvantaged* (Chicago: University of Chicago Press, 1987). For a contrary, and more typically American view, see Chapter 5, pp. 86–97, "On Universal and Income-Tested Social Programs," of Nathan Glazer, *The Limits of Social Policy* (Cambridge: Harvard University Press, 1988).

6. For comparison, see Peter Edelman, "The Next Century of Our Consti-

tution: Rethinking Our Duty to the Poor," *Hastings Law Journal* 39 (1): 1–61, who recommends setting the standard at 60 percent; U.S. Committee on Ways and Means, *1991 Background Material*, p. 595.

7. The Center for Budget and Policy Priorities, *One Step Forward* (Washington, D.C., 1990), p. 16. For a similar recommendation, see David Ellwood, *Poor Support* (New York: Basic Books, 1988), and Christopher Jencks and Kathryn Edin, "The Real Welfare Problem," *The American Prospect* 1 (1): 31–50.

8. Issac Shapiro and Robert Greenstein, *Fulfilling Work's Promise* (Washington, D.C.: Center on Budget and Policies Priorities, 1990), p. xvi.

9. These paragraphs briefly summarize a highly developed proposal originating from the Institute for Policy Studies. See *A Progressive Housing Program for America* (Washington, D.C., 1987). For another short synopsis, see Robert Kuttner, "Bad Housekeeping," *New Republic*, 25 April 1988.

10. See Paul Kennedy, *The Rise and Fall of the Great Powers* (New York: Random House, 1987) for a discussion of this pattern as it has manifested itself in various modern empires, including Spain, France, and Great Britain.

11. John Miller and James Goodno, "Much Ado About Nothing," *Dollars and Sense*, no. 162, December 1990, pp. 16–17.

12. The $225 billion estimate comes from Doug Henwood in *Left Business Observer*, no. 41, October 1990 p. 2; Katharine Bradbury, "Changing Fortunes of American Families in the 1980s," *New England Economic Review*, July/August 1990, p. 26 is the source of the data about the richest quintile. It should be noted that in a 1990 poll, 87 percent favored a tax increase for those making more than $100,000. See *New York Times*/CBS poll in *New York Times*, 9 October 1990.

Index

Advocacy, 96–98
Age of adult homeless, 25
Agnos, Art (Mayor), 121–22
Aid to Families with Dependent Children
  court decisions, 102–5
  deflation in value, 52
  reductions, 49, 52–56
  stigma, 52
  Unemployed Parent program, 53
Aid to the Disabled, 82
AIDS, 30
Alcohol abuse, 26–27
Algor v. *County of Ocean*, 105
Association to Improve the Condition of
  the Poor, 64–65

Banks, Steve, 98, 104
Bannister v. *Board of Supervisors of Los An-*
  geles County, 104
Barracks shelters, 162–63
Bellevue Hospital, 153–54
Beneficiary constituencies, 95–96
Bensonhurst Homeless Residence in
  Brooklyn, 113
Bernstein v. *Toia*, 107
Blacks. *See* Race factors
Blasi, Gary, 103
Bluestone, Barry, 44
Boston programs, 129–31
Bowery District, 25
Brooklyn Men's Shelter, 145
Brown, Joyce, 153
Bucchieri, Joseph, 113–14
Budget deficit effects, 49
Burlington, Vermont, 4

Burnside Community council, 96
Bush administration
  antipoverty initiative rejection, 178
  funding, 113–14
  housing policy, 70–73
Business community
  New York City, 168–69
  public sector relationship, 179
  Reagan years, 39–41
  and response to homeless, 132, 178–79
  short-term profit emphasis, 178

Callahan v. *Carey*, 99–100, 106, 140–41
Capital-labor accord, 37
Capitalism, 9–10
Capture-recapture techniques, 24
Census-based studies, 22–23
Census Bureau estimate, 1990, 23–24
Center City Project, 128–29
Central Arizona Shelter Services, 97
Chackes, Kenneth, 98
Chappell, Jean, 93
Charity. *See* Private charity
Charity Organization Societies, 5, 13
Chase Manhattan Bank, 136
Chicago, 120–21
  homeless numbers, 23
  policy toward homeless, 120–21
Child-rearing, 55
Child support payments, 53–54
Children. *See* Homeless children
Chlorpromazine, 81
Chronic and Situational Dependency, 148
Chronic mental patients, 82
Churning, 51

229